Sketches from the Life of Paul

Ellen G. White

Sketches from the Life of Paul

Copyright © 2019 Indo-European Publishing

The present edition is a reproduction of previous publication of this classic work. Minor typographical errors may have been corrected without note, however, for an authentic reading experience the spelling, punctuation, and capitalization have been retained from the original text.

ISBN: 978-1-64439-119-8

CONTENTS

Saul the Persecutor

From among the most bitter and relentless persecutors of the church of Christ, arose the ablest defender and most successful herald of the gospel. With the apostolic brotherhood of the chosen twelve, who had companied with Christ from his baptism even to his ascension, was numbered one who had never seen the Lord while he dwelt among men, and who had heard his name uttered only in unbelief and contempt. But beneath the blindness and bigotry of the zealot and the Pharisee, Infinite Wisdom discerned a heart loyal to truth and duty. And the voice from Heaven made itself heard above the clamours of pride and prejudice. In the promulgation of the gospel, Divine Providence would unite with the zeal and devotion of the Galilean peasants, the fiery vigour and intellectual power of a rabbi of Jerusalem. To lead the battle against pagan philosophy and Jewish formalism, was chosen one who had himself witnessed the debasing power of heathen worship, and endured the spiritual bondage of Pharisaic exaction.

Saul of Tarsus was a Jew, not only by descent, but by the stronger ties of lifelong training, patriotic devotion, and religious faith. Though a Roman citizen, born in a Gentile city, he was educated in Jerusalem by the most eminent of the rabbis, and diligently instructed in all the laws and traditions of the Fathers. Thus he shared, to the fullest extent, the hopes and aspirations, the lofty pride and unyielding prejudice, of his nation. He declares himself to have been "a Hebrew of the Hebrews; as touching the law, a Pharisee; concerning zeal, persecuting the church; touching the righteousness which is in the law, blameless." He was regarded by the Jewish leaders as a young man of great promise, and high hopes were cherished concerning him as an able and zealous defender of the ancient faith.

In common with his nation, Saul had cherished the hope of a Messiah who should reign as a temporal prince, to break from the neck of Israel the Roman yoke, and exalt her to the throne of universal empire. He had no personal knowledge of Jesus of Nazareth or of his mission, but he readily imbibed the scorn and hatred of the rabbis toward one who was so far from fulfilling their ambitious hopes; and after the death of Christ, he eagerly joined with priests and rulers in the persecution of his followers as a proscribed and hated sect.

The Jewish leaders had supposed that the work of Christ would end with him; that when his voice was no longer heard, the excitement would die out, and the people would return to the doctrines and traditions of men. But instead of this, they witnessed the marvellous scenes of the day of Pentecost. The disciples, endowed with a power and energy hitherto unknown, preached Christ to the vast multitude that from all parts of the world assembled at the feast. Signs and wonders confirmed their words; and in the very stronghold of Judaism, thousands openly declared their faith in Jesus of Nazareth, the crucified malefactor, as the promised Messiah.

And but a short time after the events of Pentecost, a mighty miracle, wrought by the apostles, filled all Jerusalem with excitement. A cripple who had been lame from his birth was healed by Peter and John in the presence of the people, within the very precincts of the temple. This astonishing cure was performed in the name of Jesus, the apostles declaring that he had ascended to the heavens, and thence imparted power to his followers; and they fearlessly charged upon the Jews the crime of his rejection and murder. Great numbers of the people received the doctrines preached by the apostles. Many of the most determined opponents could but believe, though they refused to acknowledge, that Jesus had risen from the dead. They did not, however, repent of their terrible crime in putting him to death. When the power from Heaven came upon the apostles in so remarkable a manner, fear held the priests and elders from violence; but their bitterness and malice were unchanged. Five thousand had already openly declared their faith in Christ; and both Pharisees and Sadducees decided among themselves that if those new teachers were suffered to go on unchecked, their own influence would be in greater danger than when Jesus was upon earth. If one or two discourses from the apostles could produce results so marvellous, the world would soon believe on Christ, and the influence of priests and rulers would be lost. They therefore seized upon the apostles, and thrust them into prison, expecting to intimidate and silence them. But the disciple who in cowardice had once denied his Lord, now boldly declared the power of a risen Saviour. In vain the rulers commanded to speak no more in that name. Their threats were powerless, and at last, being restrained from violence by fear of the people, they set the apostles at liberty.

Subsequent events served but to augment their fears and their hatred. The power with which the apostles still proclaimed the gospel, the wonders wrought by them in the name of Jesus, the converts daily added to the church, the union and harmony that pervaded the body of believers, the swift and terrible manifestation of divine judgment in the case of Ananias and Sapphira,—all were marked by the Jewish leaders, and urged them on to still more determined efforts to crush the powerful heresy. Again the apostles were arrested and imprisoned, and the Sanhedrim was called to try their case. A large number of learned men in addition to the council was summoned, and they conferred together as to what should be done with these disturbers of the peace.

But the angel of the Lord by night opened the prison doors, and brought forth his servants, bidding them again proclaim in the temple the words of life. Great was the amazement of priests and rulers when, being assembled at dawn to pass sentence upon the prisoners, they received the report that the prison doors were securely bolted and the guard stationed before them, but that the apostles themselves had been mysteriously delivered, and were already preaching in the temple.

Once more summoning them before the council, the high priest angrily reminded them of the warning they had received, and charged them with endeavouring to bring upon the Jews the blood of Christ. They were not as willing to bear the blame of slaying Jesus as when they swelled the cry with the debased mob, "His blood be on us and on our children!"

Peter and his brethren repeated their former assertion, that they must obey God rather than men. And then the accused became the accusers, and as they were moved by the Spirit of God, they solemnly charged the murder of Christ upon the priests and rulers who composed the council. These dignitaries were now so enraged that they decided without further trial, to take the law into their own hands, and put the prisoners to death. They would have executed their murderous designs at once but for the calm and judicious counsel of Gamaliel, who warned them to beware of proceeding to violent measures before the character of the movement they opposed should be fully developed, lest haply they should be found fighting against God. The learning and high position of this eminent rabbi gave weight to his words. The priests could not deny the reasonableness of his views. They very reluctantly released their prisoners, after beating them with rods, and charging them again and again to preach no more in the name of Jesus or their lives would pay the penalty of their boldness.

But punishments and threats were alike unheeded. The apostles "departed from the presence of the council, rejoicing that they were counted worthy to suffer shame for His name. And daily in the temple and in every house they ceased not to teach and preach Jesus Christ." Despite all opposition, "the number of the disciples was multiplied."

And now occurred a series of events, which, though seeming to bring only defeat and loss to the cause of Christ, were to result in its triumph, giving to the world one of the noblest examples of Christian faith, and winning from the ranks of its opposers their most active and successful champion. Most of the early believers were cut off from family and friends by the zealous bigotry of the Jews. Many of the converts had been thrown out of business and exiled from their homes, because they had espoused the cause of Christ. It was necessary to provide this large number, congregated at Jerusalem, with homes and sustenance. Those having money and possessions cheerfully sacrificed them to meet the existing emergency. Their means were laid at the feet of the apostles, who made distribution to every man according as he had need.

Among the believers were not only those who were Jews by birth and spoke the Hebrew tongue, but also residents of other countries, who used the Greek language. Between these two classes there had long existed distrust, and even antagonism; and though their hearts were now softened and united by Christian love, yet the old jealousies were easily rekindled. Thus it came to pass that as disciples were multiplied, "there arose a murmuring of the Grecians against the Hebrews." The cause of complaint was an alleged neglect of the Greek widows in the distribution of the fund set apart for the poor. Such inequality would have been contrary to the spirit of the gospel, and prompt measures were taken to remove all occasion for dissatisfaction. Summoning a meeting of the believers, the apostles stated that the time had come when they should be relieved from the task of apportioning to the poor, and from similar burdens, so that they could be left free to preach Christ. "Wherefore, brethren," said they, "look ye out among you seven men of honest report, full of the Holy Ghost and wisdom, whom we may appoint over this business. But we will give ourselves continually to prayer, and to the ministry of the word." This advice was followed, and the seven chosen men were solemnly set apart for their duties by prayer and the laying on of hands.

The appointment of the seven was greatly blessed of God. The church advanced in numbers and strength, "and a great company of the priests were obedient to the faith." This success was due both to the greater freedom secured to the apostles, and to the zeal and power manifested by the seven deacons. The fact that these brethren had been ordained for a special work, did not exclude them from teaching the faith. On the contrary, they were fully qualified to instruct in the truth, and they engaged in the work with great earnestness and success.

The foremost of the seven was Stephen, who, "full of faith and power, did great wonders and miracles among the people." Though a Jew by birth, he spoke the Greek language, and was familiar with the customs and manners of the Greeks. He therefore found opportunity to proclaim the gospel in the synagogues of the Greek Jews. Learned rabbis and doctors of the law engaged in public discussion with him, confidently expecting an easy victory. But "they were not able to resist the wisdom and the spirit by which he spake." Not only did he speak by the power of the Holy Ghost, but it was plain that he was a student of the prophecies, and learned in all matters of the law. He ably defended the truths which he advocated, and utterly defeated his opponents.

The priests and rulers who witnessed the wonderful manifestation of the power that attended the ministration of Stephen, were filled with bitter hatred. Instead of yielding to the weight of evidence he presented, they determined to silence his voice by putting him to death. They had on several occasions bribed the Roman authorities to pass over without comment instances where the Jews had taken the law into their own hands, and tried, condemned, and executed prisoners according to their national custom. The enemies of Stephen did not doubt that they could pursue such a course without danger to themselves. They determined to risk the consequences at all events, and they therefore seized Stephen and brought him before the Sanhedrim council for trial.

Learned Jews from the surrounding countries were summoned for the purpose of refuting the arguments of the accused. Saul was also present, and took a leading part against Stephen. He brought the weight of eloquence and the logic of the rabbis to bear upon the case, to convince the people that Stephen was preaching delusive and dangerous doctrines. But he met in Stephen one as highly educated as himself, and one who had a full understanding of the purpose of God in the spreading of the gospel to other nations.

The priests and rulers prevailed nothing against the clear, calm wisdom of Stephen, though they were vehement in their opposition. They determined to make an example of him, and, while they thus satisfied their revengeful hatred, prevent others, through fear, from adopting his belief. False witnesses were hired to testify that they had heard him speak blasphemous words against the temple and the law. Said they, "For we have heard him say, that this Jesus of Nazareth shall destroy this place, and shall change the customs which Moses delivered us."

As Stephen stood face to face with his judges, to answer to the crime of blasphemy, a holy radiance shone upon his countenance. "And all that sat in the council, looking steadfastly on him, saw his face as it had been the face of an angel." Those who exalted Moses might have seen in the face of the prisoner the same holy light which radiated the face of that ancient prophet. Many who beheld the lighted countenance of Stephen trembled and veiled their faces; but stubborn unbelief and prejudice never faltered.

Stephen was questioned as to the truth of the charges against him, and took up his defence in a clear, thrilling voice that rang through the council hall. He proceeded to rehearse the history of the chosen people of God, in words that held the assembly spell-bound. He showed a thorough knowledge of the Jewish economy, and the spiritual interpretation of it now made manifest through Christ. He made plain his own loyalty to God and to the Jewish faith, while he showed that the law in which they trusted for salvation had not been able to preserve Israel from idolatry. He connected Jesus Christ with all the Jewish history. He referred to the building of the temple by Solomon, and to the words of both Solomon and Isaiah: "Howbeit the Most High dwelleth not in temples made with hands." "Heaven is my throne, and earth is my footstool. What house will ye build me? saith the Lord; or what is the place of my rest? Hath not my hand made all these things?" The place of God's highest worship was in Heaven.

When Stephen had reached this point, there was a tumult among the people. The prisoner read his fate in the countenances before him. He perceived the resistance that met his words, which were spoken at the dictation of the Holy Ghost. He knew that he was giving his last testimony. When he connected Jesus Christ with the prophecies, and spoke of the temple as he did, the priest, affecting to be horror-stricken, rent his robe. This act was to Stephen a signal that his voice would soon be silenced forever. Although he was just in the midst of his sermon, he abruptly concluded it by suddenly breaking away from the chain of history, and, turning upon his infuriated judges, said, "Ye stiff-necked and uncircumcised in heart and ears, ye do always resist the Holy Ghost; as your fathers did, so do ye. Which of the prophets have not your fathers persecuted? and they have slain them which showed before of the coming of the Just One; of whom ye have been now the betrayers and murderers; who have received the law by the disposition of angels, and have not kept it."

At this the priests and rulers were beside themselves with anger. They were more like wild beasts of prey than like human beings. They rushed upon Stephen, gnashing their teeth. But he was not intimidated; he had expected this. His face was calm, and shone with an angelic light. The infuriated priests and the excited mob had no terrors for him. The scene about him faded from his vision; the gates of Heaven were ajar, and Stephen, looking in, saw the glory of the courts of God, and Christ, as if just risen from his throne, standing ready to sustain his servant, who was about to suffer martyrdom for his name. When Stephen proclaimed the glorious scene opened before him, it was more than his persecutors could endure. They stopped their ears, that they might not hear his words, and uttering loud cries ran furiously upon him with one accord. "And they stoned Stephen, calling upon God, and saying, Lord Jesus, receive my spirit. And he kneeled down, and cried with a loud voice, Lord, lay not this sin to their charge. And when he had said this, he fell asleep." The witnesses who had accused him were required to cast the first stones. These persons laid down their clothes at the feet of Saul, who had taken an active part in the disputation, and had consented to the prisoner's death.

The martyrdom of Stephen made a deep impression upon all who witnessed it. It was a sore trial to the church, but resulted in the conversion of Saul. The faith, constancy, and glorification of the martyr could not be effaced from his memory. The signet of God upon his face, his words, that reached to the very soul of those who heard them, remained in the memory of the beholders, and testified to the truth of that which he had proclaimed.

There had been no legal sentence passed upon Stephen; but the Roman authorities were bribed by large sums of money to make no investigation of the case. Saul seemed to be imbued with a frenzied zeal at the scene of Stephen's trial and death. He seemed to be angered at his own secret convictions that Stephen was honoured of God at the very period when he was dishonoured of men. He continued to persecute the church of God, hunting them down, seizing them in their houses, and delivering them up to the priests and rulers for imprisonment and death. His zeal in carrying forward the persecution was a terror to the Christians in Jerusalem. The Roman authorities made no special effort to stay the cruel work, and secretly aided the Jews in order to conciliate them, and to secure their favour.

Saul was greatly esteemed by the Jews for his zeal in persecuting the believers. After the death of Stephen, he was elected a member of the Sanhedrim council, in consideration of the part he had acted on that occasion. This learned and zealous rabbi was a mighty instrument in the hand of Satan to carry out his rebellion against the Son of God; but he was soon to be employed to build up the church he was now tearing down. A Mightier than Satan had selected Saul to take the place of the martyred Stephen, to preach and suffer for his name, and to spread far and wide the glad tidings of salvation through his blood.

Conversion of Saul

The mind of Saul was greatly stirred by the triumphant death of Stephen. He was shaken in his prejudice; but the opinions and arguments of the priests and rulers finally convinced him that Stephen was a blasphemer; that Jesus Christ whom he preached was an impostor, and that those ministering in holy offices must be right. Being a man of decided mind and strong purpose, he became very bitter in his opposition to Christianity, after having once entirely settled in his mind that the views of the priests and scribes were right. His zeal led him to voluntarily engage in persecuting the believers. He caused holy men to be dragged before the councils, and to be imprisoned or condemned to death without evidence of any offense, save their faith in Jesus. Of a similar character, though in a different direction, was the zeal of James and John, when they would have called down fire from heaven to consume those who slighted and scorned their Master. (LP 21.1)

Saul was about to journey to Damascus upon his own business; but he was determined to accomplish a double purpose, by searching out, as he went, all the believers in Christ. For this purpose he obtained letters from the high priest to read in the synagogues, which authorized him to seize all those who were suspected of being believers in Jesus, and to send them by messengers to Jerusalem, there to be tried and punished. He set out upon his way, full of the strength and vigour of manhood and the fire of a mistaken zeal. (LP 21.2)

As the weary travellers neared Damascus, the eyes of Saul rested with pleasure upon the fertile land, the beautiful gardens, the fruitful orchards, and the cool streams that ran murmuring amid the fresh green shrubbery. It was very refreshing to look upon such a scene after a long, wearisome journey over a desolate waste. While Saul, with his companions, was gazing and admiring, suddenly a light above the brightness of the sun shone round about him, "and he fell to the earth, and heard a voice saying unto him, Saul, Saul, why persecutest thou me? And he said, who art thou, Lord? And the Lord said, I am Jesus whom thou persecutest; it is hard for thee to kick against the pricks." (LP 22.1)

The scene was one of the greatest confusion. The companions of Saul were stricken with terror, and almost blinded by the intensity of the light. They heard the voice, but saw no one, and to them all was unintelligible and mysterious. But Saul, lying prostrate upon the ground, understood the words that were spoken, and saw clearly before him the Son of God. One look upon that glorious Being, imprinted his image forever upon the soul of the stricken Jew. The words struck home to his heart with appalling force. A flood of light poured in upon the darkened chambers of his mind, revealing his ignorance and error. He saw that while imagining himself to be zealously serving God in persecuting the followers of Christ, he had in reality been doing the work of Satan. (LP 22.2)

He saw his folly in resting his faith upon the assurances of the priests and rulers, whose sacred office had given them great influence over his mind, and caused him to believe that the story of the resurrection was an artful fabrication of the disciples of Jesus. Now that Christ was revealed to Saul, the sermon of Stephen was brought forcibly to his mind. Those words which the priests had pronounced blasphemy, now appeared to him as truth. In that time of wonderful illumination, his mind acted with remarkable rapidity. He traced down through prophetic history, and saw that the rejection of Jesus by the Jews, his crucifixion, resurrection, and ascension had been foretold by the prophets, and proved him to be the promised Messiah. He remembered the words of Stephen: "I see the heavens opened, and the Son of man standing on the right hand of God," and he knew that the dying saint had looked upon the kingdom of glory. (LP 22.3)

What a revelation was all this to the persecutor of the believers! Light, clear but terrible, had broken in upon his soul. Christ was revealed to him as having come to earth in fulfilment of his mission, being rejected, abused, condemned, and crucified by those whom he came to save, and as having risen from the dead, and ascended into the heavens. In that terrible moment he remembered that the holy Stephen had been sacrificed by his consent; and that through his instrumentality many worthy saints had met their death by cruel persecution. (LP 23.1)

"And he, trembling and astonished, said, Lord, what wilt thou have me to do? And the Lord said unto him, Arise and go into the city, and it shall be told thee what thou must do." No doubt entered the mind of Saul that this was Jesus of Nazareth who spoke to him, and that he was indeed the long-looked-for Messiah, the Consolation and Redeemer of Israel. And now this Jesus, who had, while teaching upon earth, spoken in parables to his hearers, using familiar objects to illustrate his meaning, likened the work of Saul, in persecuting the followers of Christ, to kicking against the pricks. Those forcible words illustrated the fact that it would be impossible for any man to stay the onward progress of the truth of Christ. It would march on to triumph and victory, while every effort to stay it would result in injury to the opposer. The persecutor, in the end, would suffer a thousand-fold more than those whom he had persecuted. Sooner or later his own heart would condemn him; he would find that he had, indeed, been kicking against the pricks. (LP 23.2)

The Saviour had spoken to Saul through Stephen, whose clear reasoning from the Scriptures could not be controverted. The learned Jew had seen the face of the martyr reflecting the light of Christ's glory, and looking like the face of an angel. He had witnessed his forbearance toward his enemies, and his forgiveness of them. He had further witnessed the fortitude and cheerful resignation of other believers in Jesus while tormented and afflicted, some of whom had yielded up their lives with rejoicing for their faith's sake. (LP 24.1)

All this testimony had appealed loudly to Saul, and thrust conviction upon his mind; but his education and prejudices, his respect for priests and rulers, and his pride of popularity, braced him to rebel against the voice of conscience and the grace of God. He had struggled entire nights against conviction, and had always ended the matter by avowing his belief that Jesus was not the Messiah, that he was an impostor, and that his followers were deluded fanatics. (LP 24.2)

Now Christ had spoken to Saul with his own voice: "Saul, Saul, why persecutest thou me?" And the question, "Who art thou, Lord?" was answered by the same voice, "I am Jesus, whom thou persecutest." Here Christ identifies himself with his suffering people. Saul, in persecuting the followers of Jesus, had struck directly against the Lord of Heaven. Jesus declares that in afflicting his brethren upon earth, Saul had struck against their Head and Representative in Heaven. In falsely accusing and testifying against them, he had falsely accused and testified against the Saviour of the world. Here it is plainly seen that Christ suffers in the person of his saints. (LP 25.1)

When the effulgent glory was withdrawn, and Saul arose from the earth, he found himself totally deprived of sight. The brightness of Christ's glory had been too intense for his mortal sight, and when it was removed, the blackness of night settled upon his vision. He believed that his blindness was the punishment of God for his cruel persecution of the followers of Jesus. He groped about in terrible darkness, and his companions, in fear and amazement, led him by the hand into Damascus. (LP 25.2)

How different from what he had anticipated was his entrance into that city! In proud satisfaction he had neared Damascus, expecting on his arrival to be greeted with ostentation and applause because of the honour conferred upon him by the high priest, and the great zeal and penetration he had manifested in searching out the believers, to carry them as captives to Jerusalem, there to be condemned, and punished without mercy. He had determined that his journey should be crowned with success; and his courageous and persevering spirit quailed at no difficulties or dangers in the pursuance of his object. He had determined that no Christian should escape his vigilance; he would inquire of men, women, and children concerning their faith, and that of those with whom they were connected; he would enter houses, with power to seize their inmates, and to send them as prisoners to Jerusalem. (LP 25.3)

But how changed was the scene from that which he had anticipated! Instead of wielding power and receiving honour, he was himself virtually a prisoner, being deprived of sight, and dependent upon the guidance of his companions. Helpless, and tortured by remorse, he felt himself to be under sentence of death, and knew not what further disposition the Lord would make of him. (LP 26.1)

He was taken to the house of the disciple Judas, and there he remained, in solitude, studying upon the strange revelation that had broken up all his plans, and changed the entire current of his life. He passed three days in perfect blindness, occupying that terrible time with reflection, repentance, and earnest prayer, neither eating nor drinking during that entire period. With bitterness he remembered Stephen, and the evidence he had given of being sustained by a power higher than that of earth. He thought with horror of his own guilt in allowing himself to be controlled by the malice and prejudice of the priests and rulers, closing his eyes and ears against the most striking evidence, and relentlessly urging on the persecution of the believers in Christ. (LP 26.2)

He was in lonely seclusion; he had no communication with the church; for they had been warned of the purpose of his journey to Damascus by the believers in Jerusalem; and they believed that he was acting a part the better to carry out his design of persecuting them. He had no desire to appeal to the unconverted Jews; for he knew they would not listen to or heed his statements. He seemed to be utterly shut out from human sympathy; and he reflected, and prayed with a thoroughly broken and repentant spirit. (LP 27.1)

Those three days were like three years to the blind and conscience-smitten Jew. He was no novice in the Scriptures, and in his darkness and solitude he recalled the passages which referred to the Messiah, and traced down the prophecies, with a memory sharpened by the conviction that had taken possession of his mind. He became astonished at his former blindness of understanding, and at the blindness of the Jews in general, in rejecting Jesus as the promised Messiah. All now seemed plain to him, and he knew that it was prejudice and unbelief which had clouded his perceptions, and prevented him from discerning in Jesus of Nazareth the Messiah of prophecy. (LP 27.2)

This wonderful conversion of Saul demonstrates in a startling manner the miraculous power of Christ in convicting the mind and heart of man. Saul had verily believed that to have faith in Jesus was virtually to repudiate the law of God and the service of sacrificial offerings. He had believed that Jesus had himself disregarded the law, and had taught his disciples that it was now of no effect. He believed it to be his duty to strive with his utmost power to exterminate the alarming doctrine that Jesus was the Prince of life; and with conscientious zeal he had become a persevering persecutor of the church of Christ. (LP 27.3)

But Jesus, whose name of all others he most hated and despised, had revealed himself to Saul, for the purpose of arresting him in his mad career, and of making, from this most unpromising subject, an instrument by which to bear the gospel to the Gentiles. Saul was overwhelmed by this revelation, and perceived that in opposing Jesus of Nazareth, he had arrayed himself against the Redeemer of the world. Overcome by a sense of his guilt, he cried out, "Lord, what wilt thou have me to do?" Jesus did not then and there inform him of the work he had assigned him, but sent him for instruction to the very disciples whom he had so bitterly persecuted. (LP 28.1)

The marvellous light that illuminated the darkness of Saul was the work of the Lord; but there was also a work that was to be done for him by the disciples of Christ. The answer to Saul's question is, "Arise, and go into the city, and it shall be told thee what thou must do." Jesus sends the inquiring Jew to his church, to obtain from them a knowledge of his duty. Christ performed the work of revelation and conviction; and now the penitent was in a condition to learn of those whom God had ordained to teach his truth. Thus Jesus gave sanction to the authority of his organized church, and placed Saul in connection with his representatives on earth. The light of heavenly illumination deprived Saul of sight; but Jesus, the great Healer, did not at once restore it. All blessings flow from Christ, but he had now established a church as his representative on earth, and to it belonged the work of directing the repentant sinner in the way of life. The very men whom Saul had purposed to destroy were to be his instructors in the religion he had despised and persecuted. (LP 28.2)

The faith of Saul was severely tested during the three days of fasting and prayer at the house of Judas, in Damascus. He was totally blind, and in utter darkness of mind as to what was required of him. He had been directed to go to Damascus, where it would be told him what he was to do. In his uncertainty and distress he cried earnestly to God. "And there was a certain disciple at Damascus, named Ananias; and to him said the Lord in a vision, Ananias. And he said, Behold, I am here, Lord. And the Lord said unto him, Arise, and go into the street which is called Straight, and inquire in the house of Judas for one called Saul, of Tarsus; for, behold, he prayeth, and hath seen in a vision a man named

Ananias coming in, and putting his hand on him, that he might receive his sight." (LP 29.1)

Ananias could hardly credit the words of the angel messenger, for Saul's bitter persecution of the saints at Jerusalem had spread far and near. He presumed to expostulate; said he, "Lord, I have heard by many of this man, how much evil he hath done to thy saints at Jerusalem. And here he hath authority from the chief priests to bind all that call on thy name." But the command to Ananias was imperative: "Go thy way, for he is a chosen vessel unto me, to bear my name before the Gentiles, and kings, and the children of Israel." (LP 29.2)

The disciple, obedient to the direction of the angel, sought out the man who had but recently breathed out threatenings against all who believed in the name of Jesus. He addressed him: "Brother Saul, the Lord, even Jesus, that appeared unto thee in the way as thou camest, hath sent me, that thou mightest receive thy sight and be filled with the Holy Ghost; and immediately there fell from his eyes as it had been scales, and he received sight forthwith, and arose and was baptized." (LP 30.1)

Christ here gives an example of his manner of working for the salvation of men. He might have done all this work directly for Saul; but this was not in accordance with his plan. His blessings were to come through the agencies which he had ordained. Saul had something to do in confession to those whose destruction he had meditated; and God had a responsible work for the men to do whom he had authorized to act in his stead. (LP 30.2)

Saul becomes a learner of the disciples. In the light of the law he sees himself a sinner. He sees that Jesus, whom in his ignorance he had considered an impostor, is the author and foundation of the religion of God's people from the days of Adam, and the finisher of the faith now so clear to his enlightened vision; the vindicator of the truth and the fulfiller of the prophecies. He had regarded Jesus as making of no effect the law of God; but when his spiritual vision was touched by the finger of God, he learned that Christ was the originator of the entire Jewish system of sacrifices; that he came into the world for the express purpose of vindicating his Father's law; and that in his death the typical law had met its antitype. By the light of the moral law, which he had believed himself to be zealously keeping, Saul saw himself a sinner of sinners. He repented, that is, died to sin, became obedient to the law of God, exercised faith in Jesus Christ as his Saviour, was baptized, and preached Jesus as earnestly and zealously as he had once denounced him. (LP 30.3)

The Redeemer of the world does not sanction experience and exercise in religious matters independent of his organized and acknowledged church. Many have an idea that they are responsible to

Christ alone for their light and experience, independent of his recognized followers on earth. But in the history of the conversion of Saul, important principles are given us, which we should ever bear in mind. He was brought directly into the presence of Christ. He was one whom Christ intended for a most important work, one who was to be "a chosen vessel" unto him; yet he did not personally impart to him the lessons of truth. He arrested his course and convicted him; but when asked by him, "What wilt thou have me to do?" the Saviour placed him in connection with his church, and let them direct him what to do. (LP 31.1)

Jesus is the friend of sinners; his heart is touched by their woe; he has all power, both in Heaven and upon earth; but he respects the means which he has ordained for the enlightenment and salvation of men; he directs sinners to the church, which he has made a channel of light to the world. (LP 31.2)

Saul was a learned teacher in Israel; but, while in the midst of his blind error and prejudice, Christ reveals himself to him, and then places him in communication with his church, which is the light of the world. In this case Ananias represents Christ, and also represents Christ's ministers upon earth, who are appointed to act in his stead. In Christ's stead, Ananias touches the eyes of Saul that they may receive sight. In Christ's stead, he places his hands upon him, and, praying in Christ's name, Saul receives the Holy Ghost. All is done in the name and by the authority of Christ; but the church is the channel of communication. (LP 32.1)

Paul Enters Upon His Ministry

Paul was baptized by Ananias in the river of Damascus. He was then strengthened by food, and immediately began to preach Jesus to the believers in the city, the very ones whom he had set out from Jerusalem with the purpose of destroying. He also taught in the synagogues that Jesus who had been put to death was indeed the Son of God. His arguments from prophecy were so conclusive, and his efforts were so attended by the power of God, that the opposing Jews were confounded and unable to answer him. Paul's rabbinical and Pharisaic education was now to be used to good account in preaching the gospel, and in sustaining the cause he had once used every effort to destroy. (LP 32.2)

The Jews were thoroughly surprised and confounded by the conversion of Paul. They were aware of his position at Jerusalem, and knew what was his principal errand to Damascus, and that he was armed with a commission from the high priest, that authorized him to take the believers in Jesus, and to send them as prisoners to Jerusalem; yet now they beheld him preaching the gospel of Jesus, strengthening those who were already its disciples, and continually making new converts to the faith he had once so zealously opposed. Paul demonstrated to all who heard him that his change of faith was not from impulse nor fanaticism, but was brought about by overwhelming evidence. (LP 33.1)

As he laboured in the synagogues, his faith grew stronger; his zeal in maintaining that Jesus was the Son of God increased, in the face of the fierce opposition of the Jews. He could not remain long in Damascus, for after the Jews had recovered from their surprise at his wonderful conversion and subsequent labours, they turned resolutely from the overwhelming evidence thus brought to bear in favour of the doctrine of Christ. Their astonishment at the conversion of Paul was changed into an intense hatred of him, like unto that which they had manifested against Jesus. (LP 33.2)

Paul's life was in peril, and he received a commission from God to leave Damascus for a time. He went into Arabia; and there, in comparative solitude, he had ample opportunity for communion with God, and for contemplation. He wished to be alone with God, to search his own heart, to deepen his repentance, and to prepare himself by prayer and study to engage in a work which appeared to him too great and too important for him to undertake. He was an apostle, not chosen of men, but chosen of God, and his work was plainly stated to be among the Gentiles. (LP 33.3)

While in Arabia he did not communicate with the apostles; he sought God earnestly with all his heart, determining not to rest till he knew for a certainty that his repentance was accepted, and his great sin pardoned. He would not give up the conflict until he had the assurance that Jesus would be with him in his coming ministry. He was ever to carry about with him in the body the marks of Christ's glory, in his eyes, which had been blinded by the heavenly light, and he desired also to bear with him constantly the assurance of Christ's sustaining grace. Paul came in close connection with Heaven, and Jesus communed with him, and established him in his faith, bestowing upon him his wisdom and grace. (LP 34.1)

Paul now returned to Damascus, and preached boldly in the name of Jesus. The Jews could not withstand the wisdom of his arguments, and they therefore counselled together to silence his voice by force—the only argument left to a sinking cause. They decided to assassinate him. The apostle was made acquainted with their purpose. The gates of the city were vigilantly guarded, day and night, to cut off his escape. The anxiety of the disciples drew them to God in prayer; there was little sleeping among them, as they were busy in devising ways and means for the escape of the chosen apostle. Finally they conceived a plan by which he was let down from a window, and lowered over the wall in a basket at night. In this humiliating manner Paul made his escape from Damascus. (LP 34.2)

He now proceeded to Jerusalem, wishing to become acquainted with the apostles there, and especially with Peter. He was very anxious to meet the Galilean fishermen who had lived, and prayed, and conversed with Christ upon earth. It was with a yearning heart that he desired to meet the chief of apostles. As Paul entered Jerusalem, he regarded with changed views the city and the temple. He now knew that the retributive judgment of God was hanging over them. (LP 35.1)

The grief and anger of the Jews because of the conversion of Paul knew no bounds. But he was firm as a rock, and flattered himself that when he related his wonderful experience to his friends, they would change their faith as he had done, and believe on Jesus. He had been strictly conscientious in his opposition to Christ and his followers, and when he was arrested and convicted of his sin, he immediately forsook his evil ways, and professed the faith of Jesus. He now fully believed that when his friends and former associates heard the circumstances of his marvellous conversion, and saw how changed he was from the proud Pharisee who persecuted and delivered unto death those who believed in Jesus as the Son of God, they would also become convicted of their error, and join the ranks of the believers. (LP 35.2)

He attempted to join himself to his brethren, the disciples; but great was his grief and disappointment when he found that they would not receive him as one of their number. They remembered his former persecutions, and suspected him of acting a part to deceive and destroy them. True, they had heard of his wonderful conversion, but as he had immediately retired into Arabia, and they had heard nothing definite of him farther, they had not credited the rumour of his great change. (LP 35.3)

Barnabas, who had liberally contributed of his means to sustain the cause of Christ, and to relieve the necessities of the poor, had been acquainted with Paul when he opposed the believers. He now came forward and renewed that acquaintance, heard the testimony of Paul in regard to his miraculous conversion, and his experience from that time. He fully believed and received Paul, took him by the hand, and led him into the presence of the apostles. He related his experience which he had just heard,— that Jesus had personally appeared to Paul while on his way to Damascus; that he had talked with him; that Paul had recovered his sight in answer to the prayers of Ananias, and had afterward maintained in the synagogues of the city, that Jesus was the Son of God. (LP 36.1)

The apostles no longer hesitated; they could not withstand God. Peter and James, who at that time were the only apostles in Jerusalem, gave the right hand of fellowship to the once fierce persecutor of their faith; and he was now as much beloved and respected as he had formerly been feared and avoided. Here the two grand characters of the new faith met—Peter, one of the chosen companions of Christ while he was upon earth, and Paul, a Pharisee, who, since the ascension of Jesus, had met him face to face, and had talked with him, and had also seen him in vision, and the nature of his work in Heaven. (LP 36.2)

This first interview was of great consequence to both these apostles, but it was of short duration, for Paul was eager to get about his Master's business. Soon the voice which had so earnestly disputed with Stephen, was heard in the same synagogue fearlessly proclaiming that Jesus was the Son of God—advocating the same cause that Stephen had died to vindicate. He related his own wonderful experience, and with a heart filled with yearning for his brethren and former associates, presented the evidences from prophecy, as Stephen had done, that Jesus, who had been crucified, was the Son of God. (LP 36.3)

But Paul had miscalculated the spirit of his Jewish brethren. The same fury that had burst forth upon Stephen was visited upon himself. He saw that he must separate from his brethren, and sorrow filled his heart. He would willingly have yielded up his life, if by that means they might have been brought to a knowledge of the truth. The Jews began to lay plans to take his life, and the disciples urged him to leave Jerusalem; but he lingered, unwilling to leave the place, and anxious to labour a little longer for his Jewish brethren. He had taken so active a part in the martyrdom of Stephen that he was deeply anxious to wipe out the stain by boldly vindicating the truth which had cost Stephen his life. It looked to him like cowardice to flee from Jerusalem. (LP 37.1)

While Paul, braving all the consequences of such a step, was praying earnestly to God in the temple, the Saviour appeared to him in vision, saying, "Make haste, and get thee quickly out of Jerusalem; for they will not receive thy testimony concerning me." Paul even then hesitated to leave Jerusalem without convincing the obstinate Jews of the truth of his faith; he thought that, even if his life should be sacrificed for the truth, it would not more than settle the fearful account which he held against himself for the death of Stephen. He answered, "Lord, they know that I imprisoned and beat in every synagogue them that believed on thee. And when the blood of thy martyr Stephen was shed, I also was standing by, and consenting unto his death, and kept the raiment of them that slew him." But the reply was more decided than before: "Depart; for I will send thee far hence unto the Gentiles." (LP 37.2)

When the brethren learned of the vision of Paul, and the care which God had over him, their anxiety on his behalf increased. They hastened his secret escape from Jerusalem, for fear of his assassination by the Jews. The departure of Paul suspended for a time the violent opposition of the Jews, and the church had a period of rest, in which many were added to the number of believers. (LP 38.1)

Christ had commanded his disciples to go and teach all nations; but the previous teachings which they had received from the Jews made it difficult for them to fully comprehend the words of their Master, and therefore they were slow to act upon them. They called themselves the children of Abraham, and regarded themselves as the heirs of divine promise. It was not until several years after the Lord's ascension that their minds were sufficiently expanded to clearly understand the intent of Christ's words, that they were to labour for the conversion of the Gentiles as well as of the Jews. Their minds were particularly called out to this part of the work by the Gentiles themselves, many of whom embraced the doctrine of Christ. Soon after the death of Stephen, and the consequent scattering of the believers throughout Palestine, Samaria was greatly stirred. The Samaritans received the believers kindly, and manifested a willingness to hear concerning Jesus, who, in his first public labours, had preached to them with great power. (LP 38.2)

The animosity existing between the Jews and Samaritans decreased, and it could no longer be said that they had no dealing with each other. Philip left Jerusalem, and preached a risen Redeemer in Samaria. Many believed and received Christian baptism. Philip's preaching was marked with so great success, and so many were gathered into the fold of Christ, that he finally sent to Jerusalem for help. The disciples now perceived the meaning of Christ, when he said, "Ye shall be witnesses unto me, both in Jerusalem, and in all Judea, and in Samaria, and unto the uttermost part of the earth." (LP 39.1)

Following these events, the conversion of the Ethiopian eunuch under the preaching of Philip, the vision of Peter at Joppa, and the outpouring of the Holy Spirit upon Cornelius and his household, served to convince the apostles and leading brethren at Jerusalem, that God had granted to the Gentiles repentance unto life. Thus was the way preparing for Paul to enter upon his mission. (LP 39.2)

Ordination of Paul and Barnabas

The apostles and disciples who left Jerusalem during the fierce persecution that raged there after the martyrdom of Stephen, preached Christ in the cities round about, confining their labours to the Hebrew and Greek Jews. "And the hand of the Lord was with them; and a great number believed, and turned unto the Lord." When the believers in Jerusalem heard the good tidings, they rejoiced; and Barnabas, "a good man, and full of the Holy Ghost and of faith," was sent to Antioch, the metropolis of Syria, to help the church there. He laboured there with great success. As the work increased, he solicited and obtained the help of Paul; and the two disciples laboured together in that city for a year, teaching the people, and adding to the numbers of the church of Christ. (LP 40.1)

Antioch had a large population both of Jews and Gentiles; it was a great resort for lovers of ease and pleasure, because of the healthfulness of its situation, its beautiful scenery, and the wealth, culture, and refinement that centred there. Its extensive commerce made it a place of great importance, where people of all nationalities were found. It was therefore a city of luxury and vice. The retribution of God finally came upon Antioch, because of the wickedness of its inhabitants. (LP 40.2)

It was here that the disciples were first called Christians. This name was given them because Christ was the main theme of their preaching, teaching, and conversation. They were continually recounting the incidents of his life, during the time in which his disciples were blessed with his personal company. They dwelt untiringly upon his teachings, his miracles of healing the sick, casting out devils, and raising the dead to life. With quivering lips and tearful eyes they spoke of his agony in the garden, his betrayal, trial, and execution, the forbearance and humility with which he endured the contumely and torture imposed upon him by his enemies, and the Godlike pity with which he prayed for those who persecuted him. His resurrection and ascension, and his work in Heaven as a Mediator for fallen man, were joyful topics with them. The heathen might well call them Christians, since they preached of Christ, and addressed their prayers to God through him. (LP 40.3)

In the populous city of Antioch, Paul found an excellent field of labour, where his great learning, wisdom, and zeal, combined, exerted a powerful influence over the inhabitants and frequenters of that city of culture. (LP 41.1)

Meanwhile the work of the apostles was centred at Jerusalem, where Jews of all tongues and countries came to worship at the temple during the stated festivals. At such times the apostles preached Christ with unflinching courage, though they knew that in so doing their lives were in constant jeopardy. Many converts to the faith were made, and these, dispersing to their homes in different parts of the country, scattered the seeds of truth throughout all nations, and among all classes of society. (LP 41.2)

Peter, James, and John felt confident that God had appointed them to preach Christ among their own countrymen at home. But Paul had received his commission from God, while praying in the temple, and his broad missionary field had been distinctly presented before him. To prepare him for his extensive and important work, God had brought him into close connection with himself, and had opened before his enraptured vision a glimpse of the beauty and glory of Heaven. (LP 41.3)

God communicated with the devout prophets and teachers in the church at Antioch. "As they ministered to the Lord, and fasted, the Holy Ghost said, Separate me Barnabas and Saul for the work whereunto I have called them." These apostles were therefore dedicated to God in a most solemn manner by fasting and prayer and the laying on of hands; and they were sent forth to their field of labour among the Gentiles. (LP 42.1)

Both Paul and Barnabas had been labouring as ministers of Christ, and God had abundantly blessed their efforts; but neither of them had previously been formally ordained to the gospel ministry by prayer and the laying on of hands. They were now authorized by the church, not only to teach the truth, but to baptize, and to organize churches, being invested with full ecclesiastical authority. This was an important era for the church. Though the middle wall of partition between Jew and Gentile had been broken down by the death of Christ, letting the Gentiles into the full privileges of the gospel, still the veil had not yet been torn from the eyes of many of the believing Jews, and they could not clearly discern to the end of that which was abolished by the Son of God. The work was now to be prosecuted with vigour among the Gentiles, and was to result in strengthening the church by a great ingathering of souls. (LP 42.2)

The apostles, in this their special work, were to be exposed to suspicion, prejudice, and jealousy. As a natural consequence of their departure from the exclusiveness of the Jews, their doctrine and views would be subject to the charge of heresy; and their credentials as ministers of the gospel would be questioned by many zealous, believing Jews. God foresaw all these difficulties which his servants would undergo, and, in his wise providence, caused them to be invested with unquestionable authority from the established church of God, that their work should be above challenge. (LP 43.1)

The brethren in Jerusalem and in Antioch were made thoroughly acquainted with all the particulars of this divine appointment, and the specific work of teaching the Gentiles, which the Lord had given to these apostles. Their ordination was an open recognition of their divine mission, as messengers specially chosen by the Holy Ghost for a special work. Paul witnesses in his Epistle to the Romans, that he considered this sacred appointment as a new and important epoch in his life; he names himself, "a servant of Jesus Christ, called to be an apostle, separated unto the gospel of God." (LP 43.2)

The ordination by the laying on of hands, was, at a later date, greatly abused; unwarrantable importance was attached to the act as though a power came at once upon those who received such ordination, which immediately qualified them for any and all ministerial work, as though virtue lay in the act of laying on of hands. We have, in the history of these two apostles, only a simple record of the laying on of hands, and its bearing upon their work. Both Paul and Barnabas had already received their commission from God himself; and the ceremony of the laying on of hands added no new grace or virtual qualification. It was merely setting the seal of the church upon the work of God—an acknowledged form of designation to an appointed office. (LP 43.3)

This form was a significant one to the Jews. When a Jewish father blessed his children, he laid his hands reverently upon their heads. When an animal was devoted to sacrifice, the hand of the one invested with priestly authority was laid upon the head of the victim. Therefore, when the ministers of Antioch laid their hands upon the apostles, they, by that action, asked God to bestow his blessing upon them, in their devotion to the specific work which God had chosen them to do. (LP 44.1)

The apostles started out upon their mission, taking with them Mark. They went into Seleucia, and from thence sailed to Cyprus. At Salamis they preached in the synagogues of the Jews. "And when they had gone through the isle unto Paphos, they found a certain sorcerer, a false prophet, a Jew, whose name was Bar-jesus; which was with the deputy of the country, Sergius Paulus, a prudent man; who called for Barnabas and Saul, and desired to hear the word of God. But Elymas the sorcerer (for so is his name by interpretation) withstood them, seeking to turn away the deputy from the faith." (LP 44.2)

The deputy being a man of repute and influence, the sorcerer Elymas, who was under the control of Satan, sought by false reports and various specious deceptions to turn him against the apostles and destroy their influence over him. As the magicians in Pharaoh's court withstood Moses and Aaron, so did this sorcerer withstand the apostles. When the deputy sent for the apostles, that he might be instructed in the truth, Satan was on hand with his servant, seeking to thwart the purpose of God, and prevent this influential man from embracing the faith of Christ. This agent of Satan greatly hindered the work of the apostles. Thus does the fallen foe ever work in a special manner to prevent persons of influence, who could be of great service to the cause, from embracing the truth of God. (LP 44.3)

But Paul, in the power of the Holy Ghost, rebuked the wicked deceiver. He "set his eyes on him, and said, O full of all subtlety and all mischief, thou child of the devil, thou enemy of all righteousness, wilt thou not cease to pervert the right ways of the Lord? And now, behold, the hand of the Lord is upon thee, and thou shalt be blind, not seeing the sun for a season. And immediately there fell on him a mist and a darkness; and he went about seeking some to lead him by the hand. Then the deputy, when he saw what was done, believed, being astonished at the doctrine of the Lord." (LP 45.1)

The sorcerer had closed his eyes to the evidences of truth, and the light of the gospel, therefore the Lord, in his righteous anger, caused his natural eyes to be closed, shutting out from him the light of day. This blindness was not permanent, but only for a season, to warn him to repent, and to seek pardon of God whom he had so offended. The confusion into which this man was brought, with all his boasted power, made of none effect all his subtle arts against the doctrine of Christ. The fact of his being obliged to grope about in blindness, proved to all beholders that the miracles which the apostles had performed, and which Elymas had denounced as being produced by sleight of hand, were in truth wrought by the power of God. The deputy was convinced of the truth of the doctrine taught by the apostles, and embraced the gospel of Christ. (LP 45.2)

Elymas was not a man of education, yet he was peculiarly fitted to do the work of Satan. Those who preach the truth of God will be obliged to meet the wily foe in many different forms. Sometimes it is in the person of learned, and often in the person of ignorant, men, whom Satan had educated to be his successful instruments in deceiving souls and in working iniquity. It is the duty of the minister of Christ to stand faithfully at his post, in the fear of God and in the power of his strength. Thus he may put to confusion the hosts of Satan, and triumph in the name of the Lord. (LP 46.1)

Paul and his company now continued their journey, going into Perga, in Pamphylia. Their way was toilsome, they encountered hardships and privations, and were beset by dangers on every side, which intimidated Mark, who was unused to hardships. As still greater difficulties were apprehended, he became disheartened, and refused to go farther, just at the time when his services were most needed. He

23

accordingly returned to Jerusalem, and to the peace and comfort of his home. (LP 46.2)

Mark did not apostatize from the faith of Christianity; but, like many young ministers, he shrank from hardships, and preferred the comfort and safety of home to the travels, labours, and dangers of the missionary field. This desertion caused Paul to judge him unfavourably and severely for a long time. He distrusted his steadiness of character, and his devotion to the cause of Christ. The mother of Mark was a convert to the Christian religion, and her home was an asylum for the disciples. There they were always sure of a welcome, and a season of rest, in which they could rally from the effect of the fierce persecutions that everywhere assailed them in their labours. (LP 46.3)

It was during one of these visits of the apostles to his mother's that Mark proposed to Paul and Barnabas that he should accompany them on their missionary tour. He had witnessed the wonderful power attending their ministry; he had felt the favour of God in his own heart; he had seen the faith of his mother tested and tried without wavering; he had witnessed the miracles performed by the apostles, and which set the seal of God upon their work; he had himself preached the Christian faith, and had longed to devote himself entirely to the work. He had, as the companion of the apostles, rejoiced in the success of their mission; but fear and discouragement overwhelmed him in the face of privation, persecution, and danger; and he sought the attractions of home at a time when his services were most needful to the apostles. (LP 47.1)

At a future period there was a sharp contention between Paul and Barnabas concerning Mark, who was still anxious to devote himself to the work of the ministry. This contention caused Paul and Barnabas to separate, the latter following out his convictions, and taking Mark with him in his work. Paul could not, at that time, excuse in any degree the weakness of Mark in deserting them and the work upon which they had entered, for the ease and quiet of home; and he urged that one with so little stamina was unfit for the gospel ministry, which required patience, self-denial, bravery, and faith, with a willingness to sacrifice even life if need be. (LP 47.2)

Barnabas, on the other hand, was inclined to excuse Mark, who was his nephew, because of his inexperience. He felt anxious that he should not abandon the ministry, for he saw in him qualifications for a useful labourer in the cause of Christ. Paul was afterward reconciled to Mark, and received him as a fellow-labourer. He also recommended him to the Colossians as one who was a "fellow-worker unto the kingdom of God," and a personal comfort to him, Paul. Again, not long prior to his own death, he spoke of Mark as profitable to him in the ministry. (LP 48.1)

After the departure of Mark, Paul and Barnabas visited Antioch in Pisidia, and on the Sabbath went into the synagogue, and sat down; "and after the reading of the law and the prophets, the rulers of the synagogue sent unto them, saying, Ye men and brethren, if ye have any word of exhortation for the people, say on." Being thus invited to speak, "Paul stood up, and beckoning with his hand said, Men of Israel, and ye that fear God, give audience." He then proceeded to give a history of the manner in which the Lord had dealt with the Jews from the time of their deliverance from Egyptian bondage, and how a Saviour had been promised of the seed of David. He then preached Jesus as the Saviour of men, the Messiah of prophecy. (LP 48.2)

When he had finished, and the Jews had left the synagogue, the Gentiles still lingered, and entreated that the same words might be spoken unto them the next Sabbath day. The apostles created a great interest in the place, among both Jews and Gentiles. They encouraged the believers and converts to stand fast in their faith, and to continue in the grace of God. The interest to hear the words of the apostles was so great that the whole city came together on the next Sabbath day. But now, as in the days of Christ, when the Jewish priests and rulers saw the multitudes that had assembled to hear the new doctrine, they were moved by envy and jealousy, and contradicted the words of the apostles with blasphemy. Their old bigotry and prejudice were also aroused, when they perceived great numbers of Gentiles mingling with the Jews in the congregation. They could not endure that the Gentiles should enjoy religious privileges on an equality with themselves, but clung tenaciously to the idea that the blessing of God was reserved exclusively for them. This had ever been the great sin of the Jews, which Christ, on several occasions, had rebuked. (LP 48.3)

They listened, on one Sabbath day, with intense interest to the teachings of Paul and Barnabas, who preached Jesus as the promised Messiah; and upon the next Sabbath day, because of the multitude of Gentiles who assembled also to hear them, they were excited to a frenzy of indignation, the words of the apostles were distorted in their minds, and they were unfitted to weigh the evidence presented by them. When they learned that the Messiah preached by the apostles was to be a light to the Gentiles, as well as the glory of his people Israel, they were beside themselves with rage, and used the most insulting language to the apostles. (LP 49.1)

The Gentiles, on the other hand, rejoiced exceedingly that Christ recognized them as the children of God, and with grateful hearts they listened to the word preached. The apostles now clearly discerned their duty, and the work which God would have them do. They turned without hesitation to the Gentiles, preaching Christ to them, and leaving the Jews to their bigotry, blindness of mind, and hardness of heart. The mind of Paul had been well prepared to make this decision, by the circumstances attending his conversion, his vision in the temple at Jerusalem, his appointment by God to preach to the Gentiles, and the success which had already crowned his efforts among them. (LP 50.1)

When Paul and Barnabas turned from the Jews who derided them, they addressed them boldly, saying, "It was necessary that the word of God should first have been spoken to you; but seeing ye put it from you, and judge yourselves unworthy of everlasting life, lo, we turn to the Gentiles. For so hath the Lord commanded us, saying, I have set thee to be a light of the Gentiles, that thou shouldest be for salvation unto the ends of the earth." (LP 50.2)

This gathering in of the Gentiles to the church of God had been traced by the pen of inspiration, but had been but faintly understood. Hosea had said, "Yet the number of the children of Israel shall be as the sand of the sea, which cannot be measured nor numbered, and it shall come to pass, that in the place where it was said unto them, Ye are not my people, there it shall be said unto them, Ye are the sons of the living God." And again, "I will sow her unto me in the earth; and I will have mercy upon her that had not obtained mercy; and I will say to them which were not my people, Thou art my people; and they shall say, Thou art my God." (LP 50.3)

During the life of Christ on earth he had sought to lead the Jews out of their exclusiveness. The conversion of the centurion, and of the Syrophenician woman, were instances of his direct work outside of the acknowledged people of Israel. The time had now come for active and continued work among the Gentiles, of whom whole communities received the gospel gladly, and glorified God for the light of an intelligent faith. The unbelief and malice of the Jews did not turn aside the purpose of God; for a new Israel was grafted into the old olive-tree. The synagogues were closed against the apostles; but private houses were thrown open for their use, and public buildings of the Gentiles were also used in which to preach the word of God. (LP 51.1)

The Jews, however, were not satisfied with closing their synagogues against the apostles, but desired to banish them from that region. To effect this purpose, they sought to prejudice certain devout and honourable women, who had great influence with the government, and also men of influence. This they accomplished by subtle arts, and false reports. These persons of good repute complained to the authorities against the apostles, and they were accordingly expelled from that district. (LP 51.2)

On this occasion the apostles followed the instruction of Christ: "Whosoever shall not receive you, nor hear you, when ye depart thence, shake off the dust under your feet for a testimony against them. Verily I say unto you, It shall be more tolerable for Sodom and Gomorrah in the day of Judgment, than for that city." The apostles were not discouraged by this expulsion; they remembered the words of their Master: "Blessed are ye when men shall revile you, and persecute you, and shall say all manner of evil against you falsely, for my sake. Rejoice, and be exceeding glad; for great is your reward in Heaven; for so persecuted they the prophets which were before you." (LP 51.3)

Preaching Among the Heathen

The apostles next visited Iconium. This place was a great resort for pleasure-seekers, and persons who had no particular object in life. The population was composed of Romans, Greeks, and Jews. The apostles here, as at Antioch, first commenced their labours in the synagogues for their own people, the Jews. They met with marked success; numbers of both Jews and Greeks accepted the gospel of Christ. But here, as in former places where the apostles had laboured, the unbelieving Jews commenced an unreasonable opposition to those who accepted the true faith, and, as far as lay in their power, influenced the Gentiles against them. (LP 52.1)

The apostles, however, were not easily turned from their work, for many were daily embracing the doctrine of Christ. They went on faithfully in the face of opposition, envy, and prejudice. Miracles were daily wrought by the disciples through the power of God; and all whose minds were open to evidence were affected by the convincing power of these things. (LP 52.2)

This increasing popularity of the doctrine of Christ stirred the unbelieving Jews to fresh opposition. They were filled with envy and hatred, and determined to stop the labours of the apostles at once. They went to the authorities, and represented their work in the most false and exaggerated light, leading the officers to fear that the entire city was in danger of being incited to insurrection. They stated that great numbers were attaching themselves to the apostles, and suggested that it was for secret and dangerous designs. (LP 53.1)

In consequence of these charges, the disciples were repeatedly brought before the authorities; but in every case they so ably defended themselves before the people, that, although the magistrates were prejudiced against them by the false statements they had heard, they dared not condemn them. They could but acknowledge that the teachings of the apostles were calculated to make men virtuous, law-abiding citizens. (LP 53.2)

The unprejudiced Jews and Greeks took the position that the morals and good order of the city would be improved if the apostles were allowed to remain and work there. Upon the occasions when the apostles were brought before the authorities, their defence was so clear and sensible, and the statement which they gave of their doctrine was so calm and comprehensive, that a considerable influence was exerted in their favour. The doctrine they preached gained great publicity, and was brought before a much larger number of unprejudiced hearers than ever before in that place. (LP 53.3)

The Jews perceived that their efforts to thwart the work of the apostles were unavailing, and only resulted in adding greater numbers to the new faith. The rage of the Jews was worked up to such a pitch on this account that they determined to compass their ends in some manner. They stirred up the worst passions of the ignorant, noisy mob, creating a tumult which they attributed to the efforts of the apostles. They then prepared to make a false charge of telling force, and to gain the help of the magistrates in carrying out their purpose. They determined that the apostles should have no opportunity to vindicate themselves; but that mob power should interfere, and put a stop to their labours by stoning them to death. (LP 54.1)

Friends of the apostles, although unbelievers, warned them of the designs of the malicious Jews, and urged them not to expose themselves uselessly to their fury, but to escape for their lives. They accordingly departed from Iconium in secret, and left the faithful and opposing parties to battle for themselves, trusting God to give victory to the doctrine of Christ. But they by no means took a final leave of Iconium; they purposed to return, after the excitement then raging had abated, and complete the work they had begun. (LP 54.2)

Those who observe and teach the binding claims of God's law, frequently receive, in a degree, similar treatment to that of the apostles at Iconium. They often meet a bitter opposition from ministers and people who persistently refuse the light of God, who, by misrepresentation and falsehood, close every door by which the messenger of truth might have access to the people. (LP 54.3)

The apostles next went to Lystra and Derbe, cities of Lycaonia. These were inhabited by a heathen, superstitious people; but among them were souls that would hear and accept the doctrine of Christ. The apostles chose to labour in those cities because they would not there meet Jewish prejudice and persecution. They now came in contact with an entirely new element,— heathen superstition and idolatry. (LP 55.1)

The apostles, in their work, met all grades of people, and all kinds of faith and religion. They were brought in opposition to Jewish bigotry and intolerance, sorcery, blasphemy, unjust magistrates who loved to exercise their power, false shepherds, superstition, and idolatry. While persecution and opposition met them on every hand, victory still crowned their efforts, and converts were daily added to the faith. (LP 55.2)

In Lystra there was no Jewish synagogue, though there were a few Jews in the place. The temple of Jupiter occupied a conspicuous position there. Paul and Barnabas appeared in the city together, teaching the doctrine of Christ with great power and eloquence. The credulous people believed them to be gods come down from Heaven. As the apostles gathered the people about them, and explained their strange belief, the worshippers of Jupiter sought to connect these doctrines, as far as they were able, with their own superstitious faith. (LP 55.3)

Paul addressed them in the Greek language, presenting for their consideration such subjects as would lead them to a correct knowledge of Him who should be the object of their adoration. He directed their attention to the firmament of the heavens—the sun, moon, and stars—the beautiful order of the recurring seasons, the mighty mountains whose peaks were capped with snow, the lofty trees, and the varied wonders of nature, which showed a skill and exactitude almost beyond finite comprehension. Through these visible works of the Almighty, the apostle led the minds of the heathen to the contemplation of the great Mind of the universe. (LP 55.4)

He then told them of the Son of God, who came from Heaven to our world because he loved the children of men. His life and ministry were presented before them; his rejection by those whom he came to save; his trial and crucifixion by wicked men; his resurrection from the dead to finish his work on earth; and his ascension to Heaven to be man's Advocate in the presence of the Maker of the world. With the Spirit and power of God, Paul and Barnabas declared the gospel of Christ. (LP 56.1)

As Paul recounted the works of Christ in healing the afflicted, he perceived a cripple whose eyes were fastened upon him, and who received and believed his words. Paul's heart went out in sympathy toward the afflicted man, whose faith he discerned; and he eagerly grasped the hope that he might be healed by that Saviour, who, although he had ascended to Heaven, was still man's Friend and Physician, having more power even than when he was upon earth. (LP 56.2)

In the presence of that idolatrous assembly, Paul commanded the cripple to stand upright upon his feet. Hitherto he had only been able to take a sitting posture; but he now grasped with faith the words of Paul, and instantly obeyed his command, and stood on his feet for the first time in his life. Strength came with this effort of faith; and he who had been a cripple walked and leaped as though he had never experienced an infirmity. (LP 56.3)

This work performed on the cripple was a marvel to all beholders. The subject was so well known, and the cure was so complete, that there was no room for scepticism on their part. The Lycaonians were convinced that supernatural power attended the labours of the apostles, and they cried out with great enthusiasm that the gods had come down to them from Heaven in the likeness of men.

This belief was in harmony with their traditions that gods visited the earth. They conceived the idea that the great heathen deities, Jupiter and Mercury, were in their midst in the persons of Paul and Barnabas. The former they believed to be Mercury; for Paul was active, earnest, quick, and eloquent with words of warning and exhortation. Barnabas was believed to be Jupiter, and father of gods, because of his venerable appearance, his dignified bearing, and the mildness and benevolence expressed in his countenance. (LP 57.1)

The news of the miraculous cure of the cripple was soon noised throughout all that region, until a general excitement was aroused, and priests from the temple of the gods prepared to do the apostles honour, as visitants from the courts of Heaven, to sacrifice beasts to them, and to bring offerings of garlands and precious things. The apostles had sought retirement and rest in a private dwelling, when their attention was attracted by the sound of music, and the enthusiastic shouting of a vast assembly, who had come to the gate of the house where they were abiding. (LP 57.2)

When these ministers of God ascertained the cause of this visit and its attendant excitement, they were filled with indignation and horror. They rent their clothing, and rushed in among the multitude to prevent further proceedings. Paul, in a loud, ringing voice that rose above the noise of the multitude, demanded their attention; and, as the tumult was suddenly quelled, he inquired,— (LP 58.1)

"Sirs, why do ye these things? We also are men of like passions with you, and preach unto you that ye should turn from these vanities unto the living God, which made heaven, and earth, and the sea, and all things that are therein; who in times past suffered all nations to walk in their own ways. Nevertheless, he left not himself without witness, in that he did good, and gave us rain from heaven, and fruitful seasons, filling our hearts with food and gladness." (LP 58.2)

The people listened to the words of Paul with manifest impatience. Their superstition and enthusiasm had been so great in regard to the apostles that they were loth to acknowledge their error, and have their expectations and purposes thwarted. Notwithstanding the apostles positively denied the divinity attributed to them by the heathen, and Paul endeavoured to direct their minds to the true God as the only object worthy of worship, it was still most difficult to turn them from their purpose. (LP 58.3)

They reasoned that they had with their own eyes beheld the miraculous power exercised by the apostles; that they had seen a cripple who had never before used his limbs, made to leap and rejoice in perfect health and strength, through the exercise of the marvellous power possessed by these strangers. But, after much persuasion on the part of Paul, and explanation as to the true mission of the apostles, the people were reluctantly led to give up their purpose. They were not satisfied, however, and led away the sacrificial beasts in great disappointment that their traditions of divine beings visiting the earth could not be strengthened by this example of their favour in coming to confer upon them special blessings which would exalt them and their religion in the estimation of the world. (LP 58.4)

And now a strange change came upon the fickle, excitable people, because their faith was not anchored in the true God. The opposing Jews of Antioch, through whose influence the apostles were driven from that district, united with certain Jews of Iconium, and followed upon the track of the apostles. The miracle wrought upon the cripple, and its effect upon those who witnessed it, stirred up their envy, and led them to go to the scene of the apostles' labour, and put their false version upon the work. They denied that God had any part in it, and claimed that it was accomplished through the demons whom these men served. (LP 59.1)

The same class had formerly accused the Saviour of casting out devils through the power of the prince of devils; they had denounced him as a deceiver; and they now visited the same unreasoning wrath upon his apostles. By means of falsehoods they inspired the people of Lystra with the bitterness of spirit by which they were themselves actuated. They claimed to be thoroughly acquainted with the history and faith of Paul and Barnabas, and so misrepresented their characters and work that these heathen, who had been ready to worship the apostles as divine beings, now considered them worse than murderers, and that whoever should put them out of the world would do God and mankind good service. (LP 59.2)

Those who believe and teach the truths of God's word in these last days, meet with similar opposition from unprincipled persons who will not accept the truth, and who do not hesitate to prevaricate, and even to circulate the most glaring falsehoods in order to destroy the influence and hedge up the way of those whom God has sent with a message of warning to the world. While one class make the falsehoods and circulate them, another class are so blinded by the delusions of Satan as to receive them as the words of truth. They are in the toils of the arch-enemy, while they flatter themselves that they are the children of God. "For this cause God shall send them strong delusion, that they should believe a lie; that they all might be damned who believed not the truth, but had pleasure in unrighteousness." (LP 60.1)

The disappointment experienced by the idolaters in being refused the privilege of offering sacrifices to the apostles, prepared them to turn against these ministers of God with a zeal which approached that of the enthusiasm with which they had hailed them as gods. The malicious Jews did not hesitate to take full advantage of the

32

superstition and credulity of this heathen people, to carry out their cruel designs. They incited them to attack the apostles by force; and they charged them not to allow Paul an opportunity to speak, alleging that if they did so he would bewitch the people. (LP 60.2) The Lystrians rushed upon the apostles with great rage and fury. They hurled stones violently; and Paul, bruised, battered, and fainting, felt that his end had come. The martyrdom of Stephen was brought vividly to his mind, and the cruel part he had acted on that occasion. He fell to the ground apparently dead, and the infuriated mob dragged his insensible body through the gates of the city, and threw it beneath the walls. The apostle mentions this occurrence in the subsequent enumeration of his sufferings for the truth's sake: "Thrice was I beaten with rods; once was I stoned; thrice I suffered shipwreck; a night and a day I have been in the deep; in journeyings often; in perils of waters; in perils of robbers; in perils by mine own countrymen; in perils by the heathen; in perils in the city; in perils in the wilderness; in perils in the sea; in perils among false brethren." (LP 60.3)

The disciples stood around the body of Paul, lamenting over him whom they supposed to be dead, when he suddenly lifted his head, and arose to his feet with the praise of God upon his lips. To the disciples this seemed like a resurrection from the dead, a miracle of God to preserve the life of his faithful servant. They rejoiced with inexpressible gladness over his restoration, and praised God with renewed faith in the doctrine preached by the apostles. (LP 61.1)

These disciples had been newly converted to the faith, through the teachings of Paul, and had stood steadfast notwithstanding the misrepresentation and malignant persecution of the Jews. In fact, the unreasoning opposition of those wicked men had only confirmed these devoted brethren in the faith of Christ; and the restoration of Paul to life seemed to set the signet of God upon their belief. (LP 61.2)

Timothy had been converted through the ministration of Paul, and was an eye-witness of the sufferings of the apostle upon this occasion. He stood by his apparently dead body, and saw him arise, bruised and covered with blood, not with groans or murmurings upon his lips, but with praises to Jesus Christ, that he was permitted to suffer for his name. In one of the epistles of Paul to Timothy he refers to his personal knowledge of this occurrence. Timothy became the most important help to Paul and to the church. He was the faithful companion of the apostle in his trials and in his joys. The father of Timothy was a Greek; but his mother was a Jewess, and he had been thoroughly educated in the Jewish religion. (LP 62.1)

Jew and Gentile

The next day after the stoning of Paul, the apostles left the city, according to the direction of Christ: "When they persecute you in this city, flee ye into another." They departed for Derbe, where their labours were blessed, and many souls were led to embrace the truth. But both Paul and Barnabas returned again to visit Antioch, Iconium, and Lystra, the fields of labour where they had met such opposition and persecution. In all those places were many that believed the truth; and the apostles felt it their duty to strengthen and encourage their brethren who were exposed to reproach and bitter opposition. They were determined to securely bind off the work which they had done, that it might not ravel out. Churches were organized in the places mentioned, elders appointed in each church, and the proper order established there. (LP 62.2)

Paul and Barnabas soon after returned to Antioch in Syria, where they again laboured for some time; and many Gentiles there embraced the doctrine of Christ. But certain Jews from Judea raised a general consternation among the believing Gentiles by agitating the question of circumcision. They asserted with great assurance, that none could be saved without being circumcised and keeping the entire ceremonial law. (LP 63.1)

This was an important question, and one which affected the church in a very great degree. Paul and Barnabas met it with promptness, and opposed introducing the subject to the Gentiles. They were opposed in this by the believing Jews of Antioch, who favoured the position of those from Judea. The matter resulted in much discussion and want of harmony in the church, until finally the church of Antioch, apprehending that a division among them would occur from any further discussion of the question, decided to send Paul and Barnabas, together with some responsible men of Antioch, to Jerusalem, to lay the matter before the apostles and elders. There they were to meet delegates from the different churches, and those who had come to attend the approaching annual festivals. Meanwhile all controversy was to cease until a final decision should be made by the responsible men of the church. This decision was then to be universally accepted by the various churches throughout the country. (LP 63.2)

The apostles, in making their way to Jerusalem, called upon the brethren of the cities through which they passed, and encouraged them by relating their experience in the work of God, and the conversion of the Gentiles to the faith. Upon arriving at Jerusalem, the delegates from Antioch related before the assembly of the churches the success that had attended the ministry with them, and the confusion that had resulted from the fact that certain converted Pharisees declared that the Gentile converts must be circumcised and keep the law of Moses in order to be saved. (LP 63.3)

The Jews were not generally prepared to move as fast as the providence of God opened the way. It was evident to them from the result of the apostles' labours among the Gentiles, that the converts among the latter people would far exceed the Jewish converts; and that if the restrictions and ceremonies of the Jewish law were not made obligatory upon their accepting the faith of Christ, the national peculiarities of the Jews, which kept them distinct from all other people, would finally disappear from among those who embraced the gospel truths. (LP 64.1)

The Jews had prided themselves upon their divinely appointed services; and they concluded that as God once specified the Hebrew manner of worship, it was impossible that he should ever authorize a change in any of its specifications. They decided that Christianity must connect itself with the Jewish laws and ceremonies. They were slow to discern to the end of that which had been abolished by the death of Christ, and to perceive that all their sacrificial offerings had but prefigured the death of the Son of God, in which type had met its antitype rendering valueless the divinely appointed ceremonies and sacrifices of the Jewish religion. (LP 64.2)

Paul had prided himself upon his Pharisaical strictness; but after the revelation of Christ to him on the road to Damascus, the mission of the Saviour, and his own work in the conversion of the Gentiles, were plain to his mind; and he fully comprehended the difference between a living faith and a dead formalism. Paul still claimed to be one of the children of Abraham, and kept the ten commandments in letter and in spirit as faithfully as he had ever done before his conversion to Christianity. But he knew that the typical ceremonies must soon altogether cease, since that which they had shadowed forth had come to pass, and the light of the gospel was shedding its glory upon the Jewish religion, giving a new significance to its ancient rites. (LP 65.1) The question of circumcision was warmly discussed in the assembly. The Gentile converts lived in a community of idolaters. Sacrifices and offerings were made to senseless idols, by these ignorant and superstitious people. The priests of these gods carried on an extensive merchandise with the offerings brought to them; and the Jews feared that the Gentile converts would bring Christianity into disrepute by purchasing those things which had been offered to idols, and thereby sanctioning, in some measure, an idolatrous worship. (LP 65.2)

Also, the Gentiles were accustomed to eat the flesh of animals that had been strangled; while the Jews had been divinely instructed with regard to the food they should use. They were particular, in killing beasts, that the blood should flow from the body, else it was not regarded as healthful meat. God had given these injunctions to the Jews for the purpose of preserving their health and strength. The Jews considered it sinful to use blood as an article of diet. They considered that the blood was the life; and that the shedding of blood was in consequence of sin. (LP 65.3)

The Gentiles, on the contrary, practised catching the blood which flowed from the victim of sacrifice, and drinking it, or using it in the preparation of their food. The Jews could not change the customs which they had so long observed, and which they had adopted under the special direction of God. Therefore, as things then stood, if Jew and Gentile came to eat at the same table, the former would be shocked and outraged by the habits and manners of the latter. (LP 66.1)

The Gentiles, and especially the Greeks, were extremely licentious; and many, in accepting Christianity, had united the truth to their unsanctified natures, and continued to practice fornication. The Jewish Christians could not tolerate such immorality, which was not even regarded as criminal by the Greeks. The Jews, therefore, held it highly proper that circumcision, and the observance of the ceremonial law, should be brought to the Gentile converts as a test of their sincerity and devotion. This they believed would prevent the accession to the church of those who were carried away by mere feeling, or who adopted the faith without a true conversion of heart, and who might afterward disgrace the cause by immorality and excesses. (LP 66.2)

The questions thus brought under the consideration of the council seemed to present insurmountable difficulties, viewed in whatever light. But the Holy Ghost had, in reality, already settled this problem, upon the decision of which depended the prosperity, and even the existence, of the Christian church. Grace, wisdom, and sanctified judgment were given to the apostles to decide the vexed question. (LP 66.3)

Peter reasoned that the Holy Ghost had decided the matter by descending with equal power upon the uncircumcised Gentiles and the circumcised Jews. He recounted his vision, in which God had presented before him a sheet filled with all manner of four-footed beasts, and had bidden him kill and eat; that when he had refused, affirming that he had never eaten that which was common or unclean, God had said, "What God hath cleansed, that call not thou common." (LP 67.1)

He related the plain interpretation of these words, which was given to him almost immediately in his summons to go to the Gentile centurion, and instruct him in the faith of Christ. This message showed that God was no respecter of persons, but accepted and acknowledged those who feared him, and worked righteousness. Peter told of his astonishment, when, in speaking the words of truth to the Gentiles, he witnessed the Holy Spirit take possession of his hearers, both Jews and Gentiles. The same light and glory that was reflected upon the circumcised Jews, shone also upon the countenances of the uncircumcised Gentiles. This was the warning of God that he should not regard the one as inferior to the other; for the blood of Jesus Christ could cleanse from all uncleanness. (LP 67.2)

Peter had reasoned once before, in like manner, with his brethren, concerning the conversion of Cornelius and his friends, and his fellowship with them. On that occasion he had related how the Holy Ghost fell on them, and had said, "Forasmuch then as God gave them the like gift as he did unto us, who believed on the Lord Jesus Christ, what was I that I could withstand God?" Now, with equal fervour and force, he said, "God, which knoweth the hearts, bare them witness, giving them the Holy Ghost, even as he did unto us, and put no difference between us and them, purifying their hearts by faith. Now, therefore, why tempt ye God, to put a yoke upon the neck of the disciples, which neither our fathers nor we were able to bear?" (LP 67.3)

This yoke was not the law of ten commandments, as those who oppose the binding claim of the law assert; but Peter referred to the law of ceremonies, which was made null and void by the crucifixion of Christ. This address of Peter brought the assembly to a point where they could listen with reason to Paul and Barnabas, who related their experience in working among the Gentiles. "Then all the multitude kept silence, and gave audience to Barnabas and Paul, declaring what miracles and wonders God had wrought among the Gentiles by them." (LP 68.1)

James bore his testimony with decision—that God designed to bring in the Gentiles to enjoy all the privileges of the Jews. The Holy Ghost saw good not to impose the ceremonial law on the Gentile converts; and the apostles and elders, after careful investigation of the subject, saw the matter in the same light, and their mind was as the mind of the Spirit of God. James presided at the council, and his final decision was, "Wherefore my sentence is, that we trouble not them which from among the Gentiles are turned to God." (LP 68.2)

This ended the discussion. In this instance we have a refutation of the doctrine held by the Roman Catholic Church—that Peter was the head of the church. Those who, as popes, have claimed to be his successors, have no foundation for their pretensions. Nothing in the life of Peter gives sanction to those pretended claims. If the professed successors of Peter had imitated his example, they would have taken no authoritative position, but one on an equality with that of their brethren. (LP 69.1)

James, in this instance, seems to have been chosen to decide the matter which was brought before the council. It was his sentence that the ceremonial law, and especially the ordinance of circumcision, be not in any wise urged upon the Gentiles, or even recommended to them. James sought to impress the fact upon his brethren that the Gentiles, in turning to God from idolatry, made a great change in their faith; and that much caution should be used not to trouble their minds with perplexing and doubtful questions, lest they be discouraged in following Christ. (LP 69.2)

The Gentiles, however, were to take no course which should materially conflict with the views of their Jewish brethren, or which would create prejudice in their minds against them. The apostles and elders therefore agreed to instruct the Gentiles by letter to abstain from meats offered to idols, from fornication, from things strangled, and from blood. They were required to keep the commandments, and to lead holy lives. The Gentiles were assured that the men who had urged circumcision upon them were not authorized to do so by the apostles. (LP 69.3)

Paul and Barnabas were recommended to them as men who had hazarded their lives for the Lord. Judas and Silas were sent with these apostles to declare to the Gentiles, by word of mouth, the decision of the council: "For it seemed good to the Holy Ghost, and to us, to lay upon you no greater burden than these necessary things; that ye abstain from meats offered to idols, and from blood, and from things strangled, and from fornication; from which if ye keep yourselves, ye shall do well." The four servants of God were sent to Antioch with the epistle and message, which put an end to all controversy; for it was the voice of the highest authority upon earth. (LP 69.4)

The council which decided this case was composed of the founders of the Jewish and Gentile Christian churches. Elders from Jerusalem, and deputies from Antioch, were present; and the most influential churches were represented. The council did not claim infallibility in their deliberations, but moved from the dictates of enlightened judgment, and with the dignity of a church established by the divine will. They saw that God himself had decided this question by favourings the Gentiles with the Holy Ghost; and it was left for them to follow the guidance of the Spirit. (LP 70.1)

The entire body of Christians were not called to vote upon the question. The apostles and elders—men of influence and judgment—framed and issued the decree, which was thereupon generally accepted by the Christian churches. All were not pleased, however, with this decision; there was a faction of false brethren who assumed to engage in a work on their own responsibility. They indulged in murmuring and fault-finding, proposing new plans, and seeking to pull down the work of the experienced men whom God had ordained to teach the doctrine of Christ. The church has had such obstacles to meet from the first, and will ever have them to the close of time. (LP 70.2)

Jerusalem was the metropolis of the Jews, and there were found the greatest exclusiveness and bigotry. The Jewish Christians who lived in sight of the temple would naturally allow their minds to revert to the peculiar privileges of the Jews as a nation. As they saw Christianity departing from the ceremonies and traditions of Judaism, and perceived that the peculiar sacredness with which the Jewish customs had been invested would soon be lost sight of in the light of the new faith, many grew indignant against Paul, as one who had, in a great measure, caused this change. Even the disciples were not all prepared to willingly accept the decision of the council. Some were zealous for the ceremonial law, and regarded Paul with jealousy, because they thought his principles were lax in regard to the obligation of the Jewish law. (LP 71.1)

When Peter, at a later date, visited Antioch, he acted in accordance with the light given him from Heaven, and the decision of the council. He overcame his natural prejudice so far as to sit at table with the Gentile converts. But when certain Jews who were most zealous for the ceremonial law came from Jerusalem, he changed his deportment toward the converts from paganism in so marked a degree that it left a most painful impression upon their minds. Quite a number followed Peter's example. Even Barnabas was influenced by the injudicious course of the apostle; and a division was threatened in the church. But Paul, who saw the wrong done the church through the double part acted by Peter, openly rebuked him for thus disguising his true sentiments. (LP 71.2)

Peter saw the error into which he had fallen, and immediately set about repairing it as far as possible. God, who knoweth the end from the beginning, permitted Peter to exhibit this weakness of character, in order that he might see that there was nothing in himself whereof he might boast. God also saw that in time to come some would be so deluded as to claim for Peter and his pretended successors, exalted prerogatives which belong only to God; and this history of the apostle's weakness was to remain as a proof of his human fallibility, and of the fact that he stood in no way above the level of the other apostles. (LP 72.1)

Imprisonment of Paul and Silas

In company with Silas, Paul again visited Lystra, where he had been greeted as a god by the heathen; where the opposing Jews had followed on his track, and by their misrepresentation had turned the reverence of the people into insult, abuse, and a determination to kill him. Yet we find him again on the scene of his former danger, looking after the fruit of his labours there. (LP 72.2)

He found that the converts to Christ had not been intimidated by the violent persecution of the apostles; but, on the contrary, were confirmed in the faith, believing that the kingdom of Christ would be reached through trial and suffering. (LP 72.3)

Paul found that Timothy was closely bound to him by the ties of Christian union. This man had been instructed in the Holy Scriptures from his childhood, and educated for a strictly religious life. He had witnessed the sufferings of Paul upon his former visit to Lystra, and the bonds of Christian sympathy had knit his heart firmly to that of the apostle. Paul accordingly thought best to take Timothy with him to assist in his labours. (LP 72.4)

The extreme caution of Paul is manifested in this act. He had refused the companionship of Mark, because he dared not trust him in an emergency. But in Timothy he saw one who fully appreciated the ministerial work, who respected his position, and was not appalled at the prospect of suffering and persecution. Yet he did not venture to accept Timothy, an untried youth, without diligent inquiry with regard to his life and character. After fully satisfying himself on these points, Paul received Timothy as his fellow-labourer and son in the gospel. (LP 73.1)

Paul, with his usual good judgment, caused Timothy to be circumcised; not that God required it, but in order to remove from the minds of the Jews an obstacle to Timothy's ministration. Paul was to labour from place to place in the synagogues, and there to preach Christ. If his companion should be known as an uncircumcised heathen, the work of both would be greatly hindered by the prejudice and bigotry of the people, The apostle everywhere met a storm of persecution. He desired to bring the Jews to Christianity, and sought, as far as was consistent with the faith, to remove every pretext for opposition. Yet while he conceded this much to Jewish prejudice, his faith and teachings declared that circumcision or uncircumcision was nothing, but the gospel of Christ was everything. (LP 73.2)

At Philippi, Lydia, of the city of Thyatira, heard the apostles, and her heart was open to receive the truth. She and her household were converted and baptized, and she entreated the apostles to make her house their home. (LP 74.1)

Day after day, as they went to their devotions, a woman with the spirit of divination followed them, crying, "These men are the servants of the most high God, which show unto us the way of salvation." This woman was a special agent of Satan; and, as the devils were troubled by the presence of Christ, so the evil spirit which possessed her was ill at ease in the presence of the apostles. Satan knew that his kingdom was invaded, and took this way of opposing the work of the ministers of God. The words of recommendation uttered by this woman were an injury to the cause, distracting the minds of the people from the truths presented to them, and throwing disrepute upon the work by causing people to believe that the men who spoke with the Spirit and power of God were actuated by the same spirit as this emissary of Satan. (LP 74.2)

The apostles endured this opposition for several days; then Paul, under inspiration of the Spirit of God, commanded the evil spirit to leave the woman. Satan was thus met and rebuked. The immediate and continued silence of the woman testified that the apostles were the servants of God, and that the demon had acknowledged them to be such, and had obeyed their command. When the woman was dispossessed of the spirit of the devil, and restored to herself, her masters were alarmed for their craft. They saw that all hope of receiving money from her divinations and soothsayings was at an end, and perceived that, if the apostles were allowed to continue their work, their own source of income would soon be entirely cut off. (LP 74.3)

A cry was therefore raised against the servants of God, for many were interested in gaining money by Satanic delusions. They brought Paul and Silas before the magistrates with the charge that "these men, being Jews, do exceedingly trouble our city, and teach customs which are not lawful for us to receive, neither to observe, being Romans." (LP 75.1)

Satan stirred up a frenzy among the people. A mob spirit prevailed, and was sanctioned by the authorities, who, with their official hands, tore the clothes from the apostles, and commanded them to be scourged. "And when they had laid many stripes upon them, they cast them into prison, charging the jailer to keep them safely; who, having received such a charge, thrust them into the inner prison, and made their feet fast in the stocks." (LP 75.2)

The apostles were left in a very painful condition. Their lacerated and bleeding backs were in contact with the rough stone floor, while their feet were elevated and bound fast in the stocks. In this unnatural position they suffered extreme torture; yet they did not groan nor complain, but conversed with and encouraged each other, and praised

God with grateful hearts that they were found worthy to suffer shame for his dear name. Paul was reminded of the persecution he had been instrumental in heaping upon the disciples of Christ, and he was devoutly thankful that his eyes had been opened to see, and his heart to feel, the glorious truths of the gospel of the Son of God, and that he had been privileged to preach the doctrine which he had once despised. (LP 75.3)

There in the pitchy darkness and desolation of the dungeon, Paul and Silas prayed, and sung songs of praise to God. The other prisoners heard with astonishment the voice of prayer and praise issuing from the inner prison. They had been accustomed to hear shrieks and moans, cursing and swearing, breaking at night upon the silence of the prison; but they had never before heard the words of prayer and praise ascending from that gloomy cell. The guards and prisoners marvelled who were these men who, cold, hungry, and tortured, could still rejoice and converse cheerfully with each other. (LP 76.1)

Meanwhile the magistrates had returned to their homes congratulating themselves upon having quelled a tumult by their prompt and decisive measures. But upon their way home they heard more fully concerning the character and work of the men whom they had sentenced to scourging and imprisonment. They also saw the woman who had been freed from Satanic influence, and who had been a very troublesome subject to them. They were sensibly struck by the change in her countenance and demeanour. She had become quiet, peaceful, and possessed of her right mind. They were indignant with themselves when they discovered that in all probability they had visited upon two innocent men the rigorous penalty of the Roman law against the worst criminals. They decided that in the morning they would command them to be privately released, and escorted in safety from the city, beyond the danger of violence from the mob. (LP 76.2)

But while men were cruel and vindictive, or criminally negligent of the solemn responsibilities devolving upon them, God had not forgotten to be gracious to his suffering servants. An angel was sent from Heaven to release the apostles. As he neared the Roman prison, the earth trembled beneath his feet, the whole city was shaken by the earthquake, and the prison walls reeled like a reed in the wind. The heavily bolted doors flew open; the chains and fetters fell from the hands and feet of every prisoner. (LP 76.3)

The keeper of the jail had heard with amazement the prayers and singing of the imprisoned apostles. When they were led in, he had seen their swollen and bleeding wounds, and he had himself caused their feet to be fastened in the instruments of torture. He had expected to hear bitter wailing, groans, and imprecations; but lo! his ears were greeted with joyful praise. He fell asleep with these sounds in his ears;

but was awakened by the earthquake, and the shaking of the prison walls. (LP 77.1)

Upon awakening he saw all the prison doors open, and his first thought was that the prisoners had escaped. He remembered with what an explicit charge the prisoners had been intrusted to his care the night before, and he felt sure that death would be the penalty of his apparent unfaithfulness. He cried out in the bitterness of his spirit that it was better for him to die by his own hand than to submit to a disgraceful execution. He was about to kill himself, when Paul cried out with a loud voice, "Do thyself no harm; for we are all here." (LP 77.2)

The severity with which the jailer had treated the apostles had not roused their resentment, or they would have allowed him to commit suicide. But their hearts were filled with the love of Christ, and they held no malice against their persecutors. The jailer dropped his sword, and called for a light. He hastened into the inner dungeon, and fell down before Paul and Silas, begging their forgiveness. He then brought them into the open court, and inquired of them, "Sirs, what must I do to be saved?" (LP 77.3)

He had trembled because of the wrath of God expressed in the earthquake; he had been ready to die by his own hand for fear of the penalty of the Roman law, when he thought the prisoners had escaped; but now all these things were of little consequence to him compared with the new and strange dread that agitated his mind, and his desire to possess that tranquillity and cheerfulness manifested by the apostles under their extreme suffering and abuse. He saw the light of Heaven mirrored in their countenances; he knew that God had interposed in a miraculous manner to save their lives; and the words of the woman possessed by the power of divination came to his mind with peculiar force: "These men are the servants of the most high God, which show unto us the way of salvation." (LP 78.1)

He saw his own deplorable condition in contrast with that of the disciples, and with deep humility and reverence asked them to show him the way of life. "And they said, Believe on the Lord Jesus Christ, and thou shalt be saved, and thy house. And they spake unto him the word of the Lord, and to all that were in his house." The jailer then washed the wounds of the apostles, and ministered unto them; and was baptized by them. A sanctifying influence spread among the inmates of the prison, and the hearts of all were opened to receive the truths uttered by the apostles. They were convinced also that the living God, whom these men served, had miraculously released them from bondage. (LP 78.2)

The citizens had been greatly terrified by the earthquake. When the officers informed the magistrates in the morning of what had occurred at the prison, they were alarmed, and sent the sergeants to liberate the apostles from prison. "But Paul said unto them, They have beaten us openly, uncondemned, being Romans, and have cast us into prison; and now do they thrust us out privily? nay, verily; but let them come themselves and fetch us out." (LP 79.1)

Paul and Silas felt that to maintain the dignity of Christ's church, they must not submit to the illegal course proposed by the Roman magistrates. The apostles were Roman citizens, and it was unlawful to scourge a Roman, save for the most flagrant crime, or to deprive him of his liberty without a fair trial and condemnation. They had been publicly thrust into prison, and now refused to be privately released, without proper acknowledgments on the part of the magistrates. (LP 79.2)

When this word was brought to the authorities, they were alarmed for fear the apostles would make complaint of their unlawful treatment to the emperor, and cause the magistrates to lose their positions. They accordingly visited the prison, apologized to the apostles for their injustice and cruelty, and themselves conducted them out of the prison, and entreated them to depart out of the city. Thus the Lord wrought for his servants in their extremity. (LP 79.3)

The magistrates entreated them to depart, because they feared their influence over the people, and the power of Heaven that had interposed in behalf of those innocent men who had been unlawfully scourged and imprisoned. Acting upon the principles given them by Christ, the apostles would not urge their presence where it was not desired. They complied with the request of the magistrates, but did not hasten their departure precipitously. They went rejoicing from the prison to the house of Lydia, where they met the new converts to the faith of Christ, and related all the wonderful dealings of God with them. They related their night's experience, and the conversion of the keeper of the prison, and of the prisoners. (LP 79.4)

The apostles viewed their labours in Philippi as not in vain. They there met much opposition and persecution; but the intervention of Providence in their behalf, and the conversion of the jailer and all his house, more than atoned for the disgrace and suffering they had endured. The Philippians saw represented in the deportment and presence of mind of the apostles the spirit of the religion of Jesus Christ. The apostles might have fled when the earthquake opened their prison doors and loosened their fetters; but that would have been an acknowledgment that they were criminals, which would have been a disgrace to the gospel of Christ; the jailer would have been exposed to the penalty of death, and the general influence would have been bad. As it was, Paul controlled the liberated prisoners so perfectly that not one attempted to escape. (LP 80.1)

The Philippians could but acknowledge the nobility and generosity of the apostles in their course of action, especially in forbearing to appeal to a higher power against the magistrates who had persecuted them. The news of their unjust imprisonment and miraculous deliverance, was noised about through all that region, and brought the apostles and their ministry before the notice of a large number who would not otherwise have been reached. (LP 80.2)

Paul's labours at Philippi resulted in the establishment of a church there, whose numbers steadily increased. His example of zeal and devotion, above all, his willingness to suffer for Christ's sake, exerted a deep and lasting influence upon the converts to the faith. They highly prized the precious truths for which the apostle had sacrificed so much, and they gave themselves, with whole-hearted devotion, to the cause of their Redeemer. (LP 81.1)

This church did not escape persecution. Says Paul, in his Epistle to the Philippians: "Unto you it is given in the behalf of Christ, not only to believe on him, but also to suffer for his sake; having the same conflict which ye saw in me." Yet such was their steadfastness in the faith that he declares: "I thank my God upon every remembrance of you, always in every prayer of mine for you all making request with joy, for your fellowship in the gospel from the first day until now." (LP 81.2)

Opposition at Thessalonica

After leaving Philippi, Paul and Silas made their way to Thessalonica. They were there privileged to address a large concourse of people in the synagogue, with good effect. Their appearance bore evidence of their recent shameful treatment, and necessitated an explanation of what they had endured. This they made without exalting themselves, but magnified the grace of God, which had wrought their deliverance. The apostles, however, felt that they had no time to dwell upon their own afflictions. They were burdened with the message of Christ, and deeply in earnest in his work. (LP 81.3)

Paul made the prophecies in the Old Testament relating to the Messiah, and the agreement of those prophecies with the life and teachings of Christ, clear in the minds of all among his hearers who would accept evidence upon the subject. Christ in his ministry had opened the minds of his disciples to the Old-Testament scriptures; "beginning at Moses and all the prophets, he expounded unto them in all the scriptures the things concerning himself." Peter, in preaching Christ, produced his evidence from the Old-Testament scriptures, beginning with Moses and the prophets. Stephen pursued the same course, and Paul followed these examples, giving inspired proof in regard to the mission, suffering, death, resurrection, and ascension of Christ. He clearly proved his identity with the Messiah, through the testimony of Moses and the prophets; and showed that it was the voice of Christ which spoke through the prophets and patriarchs from the days of Adam to that time. (LP 82.1)

He showed how impossible it was for them to explain the passover without Christ as revealed in the Old Testament; and how the brazen serpent lifted up in the wilderness symbolized Jesus Christ, who was lifted up upon the cross. He taught them that all their religious services and ceremonies would have been valueless if they should now reject the Saviour, who was revealed to them, and who was represented in those ceremonies. He showed them that Christ was the key which unlocked the Old Testament, and gave access to its rich treasures. (LP 82.2)

Thus Paul preached to the Thessalonians three successive Sabbaths, reasoning with them from the Scriptures, upon the life, death, and resurrection of Christ. He showed them that the expectation of the Jews with regard to the Messiah was not according to prophecy, which had foretold a Saviour to come in humility and poverty, to be rejected, despised, and slain. (LP 83.1)

He declared that Christ would come a second time in power and great glory, and establish his kingdom upon the earth, subduing all authority, and ruling over all nations. Paul was an Adventist; he presented the important event of the second coming of Christ with such power and reasoning that a deep impression, which never wore away, was made upon the minds of the Thessalonians. (LP 83.2)

They had strong faith in the second coming of Christ, and greatly feared that they might not live to witness the event. Paul, however, did not give them the impression that Christ would come in their day. He referred them to coming events which must transpire before that time should arrive. Writing to them afterwards, he warned them that they should "be not soon shaken in mind, or be troubled, neither by spirit, nor by word, nor by letter as from us, as that the day of Christ is at hand. Let no man deceive you by any means; for that day shall not come, except there come a falling away first, and that man of sin be revealed, the son of perdition." (LP 83.3)

Paul foresaw that there was danger of his words being misinterpreted, and that some would claim that he, by special revelation, warned the people of the immediate coming of Christ. This he knew would cause confusion of faith; for disappointment usually brings unbelief. He therefore cautioned the brethren to receive no such message as coming from him. (LP 83.4)

In his Epistle to the Thessalonians, Paul reminds them of his manner of labouring among them. 1 Thess. 2:1-4. He declares that he did not seek to win souls through flattery, deception, or guile. "But as we were allowed of God to be put in trust with the gospel, even so we speak; not as pleasing men, but God, which trieth our hearts." Paul rebuked and warned his converts with the faithfulness of a father to his children, while, at the same time, he cherished them as tenderly as a fond mother would her child. (LP 84.1)

When the Jews saw that the apostles were successful in obtaining large congregations; that many were accepting their doctrines—among them the leading women of the city, and multitudes of Gentiles—they were filled with envy and jealousy. These Jews were not then in favour with the Roman power, because they had raised an insurrection in the metropolis not long previous to this time. They were regarded with suspicion, and their liberty was, in a measure, restricted. They now saw an opportunity to take advantage of circumstances to re-establish themselves in favour, and, at the same time, to throw reproach upon the apostles and the converts to Christianity. (LP 84.2)

This they set about doing by representing that the leaders in the new doctrine were raising a tumult among the people. They accordingly excited the passions of the worthless mob by cunningly devised falsehoods, and incited them to make an uproarious assault upon the house of Jason, the temporary home of the apostles. This they did with a fury more like that of wild beasts than of men. They had been instructed by the Jews to bring out Paul and Silas, and drag them to the authorities, accusing them of creating all this uproar, and of raising an insurrection. (LP 84.3)

When they had broken into the house, however, they found that the apostles were not there. Friends who had apprehended what was about to occur, had hastened them out of the city, and they had departed for Berea. In their mad disappointment at not finding Paul and Silas, the mob seized Jason and his brother, and dragged them before the authorities with the complaint: "These that have turned the world upside down are come hither also; whom Jason hath received; and these all do contrary to the decrees of Caesar, saying that there is another king, one Jesus." (LP 85.1)

The Jews interpreted the words of Paul to mean that Christ would come the second time in that generation, and reign upon the earth as king over all nations. The charge was brought against the apostles with so much determination that the magistrates credited it, and put Jason under bonds to keep the peace, as Paul and Silas were not to be found. The persecuting Jews flattered themselves that by their course toward the Christians they had regained the confidence of the magistrates, and had established their reputation as loyal citizens, while they had, at the same time, gratified their malice toward the apostles, and transferred to the converts to Christianity the suspicion which had heretofore rested upon themselves. (LP 85.2)

In his first Epistle to the Thessalonians, Paul says, "For our gospel came not unto you in word only, but also in power, and in the Holy Ghost, and in much assurance; as ye know what manner of men we were among you for your sake. And ye became followers of us, and of the Lord, having received the word in much affliction, with joy of the Holy Ghost; so that ye were ensamples to all that believe in Macedonia and Achaia." (LP 86.1)

Those who preach unpopular truth in our day meet with determined resistance, as did the apostles. They need expect no more favourable reception from a large majority of professed Christians than did Paul from his Jewish brethren. There will be a union of opposing elements against them; for however diverse from each other different organizations may be in their sentiments and religious faith, their forces are united in trampling under foot the fourth commandment in the law of God. (LP 86.2)

Those who will not themselves accept the truth are most zealous that others shall not receive it; and those are not wanting who perseveringly manufacture falsehoods, and stir up the base passions of the people to make the truth of God of none effect. But the messengers

48

of Christ must arm themselves with watchfulness and prayer, and move forward with faith, firmness, and courage, and, in the name of Jesus, keep at their work, as did the apostles. They must sound the note of warning to the world, teaching the transgressors of the law what sin is, and pointing them to Jesus Christ as its great and only remedy. (LP 86.3)

Paul at Berea and Athens

At Berea Paul again commenced his work by going into the synagogue of the Jews to preach the gospel of Christ. He says of them, "These were more noble than those in Thessalonica, in that they received the word with all readiness of mind, and searched the Scriptures daily, whether those things were so. Therefore many of them believed; also of honourable women which were Greeks, and of men, not a few." (LP 87.1)

In the presentation of the truth, those who honestly desire to be right will be awakened to a diligent searching of the Scriptures. This will produce results similar to those that attended the labours of the apostles in Berea. But those who preach the truth in these days meet many who are the opposite of the Bereans. They cannot controvert the doctrine presented to them, yet they manifest the utmost reluctance to investigate the evidence offered in its favour, and assume that even if it is the truth it is a matter of little consequence whether or not they accept it as such. They think that their old faith and customs are good enough for them. But the Lord, who sent out his ambassadors with a message to the world, will hold the people responsible for the manner in which they treat the words of his servants. God will judge all according to the light which has been presented to them, whether it is plain to them or not. It is their duty to investigate as did the Bereans. The Lord says through the prophet Hosea: "My people are destroyed for lack of knowledge; because thou hast rejected knowledge, I will also reject thee." (LP 87.2)

The minds of the Bereans were not narrowed by prejudice, and they were willing to investigate and receive the truths preached by the apostles. If the people of our time would follow the example of the noble Bereans, in searching the Scriptures daily, and in comparing the messages brought to them with what is there recorded, there would be thousands loyal to God's law where there is one today. But many who profess to love God have no desire to change from error to truth, and they cling to the pleasing fables of the last days. Error blinds the mind and leads from God; but truth gives light to the mind, and life to the soul. (LP 88.1)

The unbelieving Jews of Thessalonica, filled with jealousy and hatred of the apostles, and not content with having driven them from their labours among the Thessalonians, followed them to Berea, and again stirred up the excitable passions of the lower class to do them violence. The teachers of the truth were again driven from their field of labour. Persecution followed them from city to city. This hasty retreat from Berea deprived Paul of the opportunity he had anticipated of again visiting the brethren at Thessalonica. (LP 88.2)

Although the opposers of the doctrine of Christ could not hinder its actual advancement, they still succeeded in making the work of the apostles exceedingly hard. God, in his providence, permitted Satan to hinder Paul from returning to the Thessalonians. Yet the faithful apostle steadily pressed on through opposition, conflict, and persecution, to carry out the purpose of God as revealed to him in the vision at Jerusalem: "I will send thee far hence unto the Gentiles." (LP 88.3) From Berea Paul went to Athens. He was accompanied on his journey by some of the Bereans who had been newly brought into the faith, and who were desirous of learning more from him of the way of life. When the apostle arrived at Athens, he sent these men back with a message to Silas and Timothy to join him immediately in that city. Timothy had come to Berea previously to Paul's departure, and with Silas had remained to carry on the work so well begun there, and to instruct the new converts in the principles of their holy faith. (LP 89.1)

The city of Athens was the metropolis of heathendom. Paul did not here meet with an ignorant, credulous populace, as at Lystra; but he encountered a people famous for their intelligence and education. Statues of their gods and the deified heroes of history and poetry met the eye in every direction; while magnificent architecture and paintings also represented the national glory and the popular worship of heathen deities. (LP 89.2)

The senses of the people were entranced by the beauty and glory of art. Sanctuaries and temples, involving untold expense, reared their lofty forms on every hand. Victories of arms, and deeds of celebrated men, were commemorated by sculptures, shrines, and tables. All these things made this renowned city like a vast gallery of art. And as Paul looked upon the beauty and grandeur surrounding him, and saw the city crowded with idols, his spirit was stirred with jealousy for God, whom he saw dishonoured on every side. (LP 89.3)

His heart was drawn out in deep pity for the citizens of that grand metropolis, who, notwithstanding their intellectual greatness, were given to idolatry. Paul was not deceived by the grandeur and beauty of that which his eyes rested upon, nor by the material wisdom and philosophy which encountered him in this great centre of learning. He perceived that human art had done its best to deify vice and make falsehood attractive by glorifying the memory of those whose whole lives had been devoted to leading men to deny God. (LP 89.4)

The moral nature of the apostle was so alive to the attraction of heavenly things, that the joy and splendour of those riches that will never fade occupied his mind, and made valueless the earthly pomp and glory with which he was surrounded. As he saw the magnificence of the city, with its costly devices, he realized its seductive power over the minds of the lovers of art and science. His mind was deeply impressed with the importance of the work before him in Athens. His solitude in that great city where God was not worshipped was oppressive; and he longed for the sympathy and aid of his fellow-labourers. As far as human fellowship was concerned, he felt himself to be utterly isolated. In his Epistle to the Thessalonians he expresses his feelings in these words: "Left at Athens alone." (LP 90.1)

Paul's work was to bear the tidings of salvation to a people who had no intelligent understanding of God and his plans. He was not travelling for the purpose of sight-seeing, nor to gratify a morbid desire for new and strange scenes. His dejection of mind was caused by the apparently insurmountable obstacles which presented themselves against his reaching the minds of the people of Athens. Grieved at the idolatry everywhere visible about him, he felt a holy zeal for his Master's cause. He sought out his Jewish brethren, and, in their synagogue at Athens, proclaimed the doctrine of Christ. But the principal work of Paul in that city was to deal with paganism. (LP 90.2)

The religion of the Athenians, of which they made great boast, was of no value, for it was destitute of the knowledge of the true God. It consisted, in great part, of art worship, and a round of dissipating amusement and festivities. It wanted the virtue of true goodness. Genuine religion gives men the victory over themselves; but a religion of mere intellect and taste is wanting in the qualities essential to raise its possessor above the evils of his nature, and to connect him with God. On the very stones of the altar in Athens this great want was expressed by the inscription, "To the Unknown God." Yes; though boasting of their wisdom, wealth, and skill in art and science, the learned Athenians could but acknowledge that the great Ruler of the universe was unknown to them. (LP 91.1)

The great men of the city seemed hungering for subjects of discussion, in which they would have opportunity to display their wisdom and oratory. While waiting for Silas and Timothy to meet him, Paul was not idle. "He disputed in the synagogue with the Jews, and with the devout persons, and in the market daily with them that met with him." The great men of Athens were not long in finding out this singular teacher, who presented to the people doctrines so new and strange. (LP 91.2)

Some who prided themselves upon the extent of their intellectual culture entered into conversation with him. This soon drew a crowd of listeners about them. Some were prepared to ridicule the apostle as one far beneath them, socially and intellectually, and said jeeringly among themselves, "What will this babbler say? Other some, He seemeth to be a setter forth of strange gods; because he preached unto them Jesus and the resurrection." (LP 91.3)

The Stoics and the Epicureans encountered him; but they, and all others who came in contact with him, soon saw that he had a store of knowledge even greater than their own. His intellectual power commanded the respect and attention of the more intellectual and learned; while his earnest, logical reasoning, and his power of oratory, held the promiscuous audience. Thus the apostle stood undaunted, meeting his opposers on their own ground, matching logic with logic, and philosophy with philosophy. (LP 92.1)

They reminded him of Socrates, a great philosopher, who was condemned to death because he was a setter forth of strange gods. Paul was counselled not to endanger his life in the same way. But the apostle's discourse riveted the attention of the people; and his unaffected wisdom commanded their respect and admiration. He was not silenced by the science or irony of the philosophers; and, after exchanging many words with him, and satisfying themselves that he was determined to accomplish his errand among them, and tell his story at all hazards, they decided to give him a fair opportunity to speak to the people. (LP 92.2)

They accordingly conducted him to Mars' Hill. This was the most sacred spot in all Athens, and its recollections and associations were such as to cause it to be regarded with superstitious awe and reverence, that with some amounted to dread. Here, the most solemn court of justice had long been held to determine upon criminal cases, and to decide difficult religious questions. The judges sat in the open air, upon seats hewn out in the rock, on a platform which was ascended by a flight of stone steps from the valley below. At a little distance was a temple of the gods; and the sanctuaries, statues, and altars of the city were in full view. (LP 92.3)

Here, away from the noise and bustle of crowded thoroughfares, and the tumult of promiscuous discussion, the apostle could be heard without interruption; for the frivolous, thoughtless class of society did not care to follow him to this place of highest reverence. Around him here were gathered poets, artists, and philosophers,—the scholars and sages of Athens,—who thus addressed him: "May we know what this new doctrine, whereof thou speakest, is? for thou bringest certain strange things to our ears; we would know, therefore, what these things mean." (LP 93.1)

The apostle stood calm and self-possessed in that hour of solemn responsibility, relying upon the divine assurance, designed for such a time as this, "It shall be given you what ye ought to say." His heart was burdened with his important message, and the words that fell from his lips convinced his hearers that he was no idle babbler: "Ye men of

Athens, I perceive that in all things ye are too superstitious. For as I passed by and beheld your devotions, I found an altar with this inscription, To the Unknown God. Whom therefore ye ignorantly worship, him declare I unto you." With all their intelligence and general knowledge, they were ignorant of the true God. The inscription upon their altar showed the strong cravings of the soul for greater light. They were reaching out for Infinity. (LP 93.2)

With earnest and fervid eloquence, the apostle continued: "God that made the world and all things therein, seeing that he is Lord of Heaven and earth, dwelleth not in temples made with hands; neither is worshipped with men's hands, as though he needed anything, seeing he giveth to all life, and breath, and all things; and hath made of one blood all nations of men for to dwell on all the face of the earth, and hath determined the times before appointed, and the bounds of their habitation; that they should seek the Lord, if haply they might feel after him, and find him, though he be not far from every one of us." (LP 94.1)

Thus, in the most impressive manner, with hand outstretched toward the temple crowded with idols, Paul poured out the burden of his soul, and ably exposed the fallacies of the religion of the Athenians. The wisest of his hearers were astonished as they listened to his reasoning. His words could not be controverted. He showed himself familiar with their works of art, their literature, and their religion. Pointing to their statuary and idols, he declared to them that God could not be likened to forms of man's device. The works of art could not, in the faintest sense, represent the glory of the infinite God. He reminded them that their images had no breath nor life. They were controlled by human power; they could move only as the hands of men moved them; and those who worshipped them were in every way superior to that which they worshipped. Pointing to noble specimens of manhood about him, he declared, "Forasmuch, then, as we are the offspring of God, we ought not to think that the Godhead is like unto gold, or silver, or stone, graven by art and man's device." (LP 94.2)

Man was created in the image of this infinite God, blessed with intellectual power and a perfect and symmetrical body. The heavens are not large enough to contain God; how much less could those temples made with hands contain him. Paul, under the inspiration of his subject, soared above the comprehension of the idolatrous assembly, and sought to draw their minds beyond the limits of their false religion to correct views of the true Deity, whom they had styled the "Unknown God." This Being, whom he now declared unto them, was independent of man, needing nothing from human hands to add to his power and glory. (LP 94.3)

The people were carried away with admiration of Paul's

eloquence. The Epicureans began to breathe more freely, believing that he was strengthening their position, that everything had its origin in blind chance; and that certain ruling principles controlled the universe. But his next sentence brought a cloud to their brows. He asserted the creative power of God, and the existence of his overruling providence. He declared unto them the true God, who is the living centre of government. (LP 95.1)

This divine Ruler had, in the dark ages of the world, passed lightly over heathen idolatry; but now he had sent them the light of truth, through his Son; and he exacted from all men repentance unto salvation; not only from the poor and humble, but from the proud philosopher, and the princes of the earth. "Because He hath appointed a day, in the which he will judge the world in righteousness by that Man whom he hath ordained; whereof he hath given assurance unto all men, in that he hath raised him from the dead." (LP 95.2)

As Paul thus spoke of the resurrection from the dead, his speech was interrupted. Some mocked; others put his words aside, saying, "We will hear thee again of this matter." Thus closed the labours of the apostle at Athens; for the Athenians persistently clung to their idolatry, and turned away from the light of a true and reasonable religion. When a people are wholly satisfied with their own attainments, little more need be expected of them. Highly educated, and boasting of their learning and refinement, the Athenians were constantly becoming more corrupt, and having less desire for anything better than the vague mysteries of idolatry. (LP 95.3)

Many who listened to the words of Paul were convinced of the truths presented, but they would not humble themselves to acknowledge God, and to accept the plan of salvation. No eloquence of words, no force of argument, can convert the sinner. The Spirit and power of God can alone apply the truth to the heart of the impenitent. Of the Athenians it may be said, "The preaching of the cross is to them that perish foolishness, but to them that are saved it is the power of God." (LP 96.1)

In their pride of intellect and human wisdom may be found the reason why the gospel message met with so little success among that people. Our Saviour rejoiced that God had hid the things of eternal interest from the wise and prudent, and had revealed them unto babes in knowledge. All worldly wise men who come to Christ as poor, lost sinners, will become wise unto salvation; but those who come as distinguished men, extolling their own wisdom, will fail to receive the light and knowledge which he alone can give. (LP 96.2)

The labours of Paul in Athens were not wholly in vain. Dionysius, one of the most prominent citizens, and some others, became converts to Christianity, and joined themselves to him. The words of the apostle, and the description of his attitude and surroundings, as traced by the pen of inspiration, were to be handed down through all coming generations, bearing witness of his unshaken confidence, his courage in loneliness and adversity, and the victory he gained for Christianity, even in the very heart of paganism. (LP 96.3)

Inspiration has given us this glance at the life of the Athenians, with all their knowledge, refinement, and art, yet sunken in vice, that it might be seen how God, through his servant, rebuked idolatry, and the sins of a proud, self-sufficient people. The words of Paul become a memorial of the occasion, and give a treasure of knowledge to the church. He was in a position where he might easily have spoken that which would irritate his proud listeners, and bring himself into difficulty. Had his oration been a direct attack upon their gods, and the great men of the city who were before him, he would have been in danger of meeting the fate of Socrates. But he carefully drew their minds away from heathen deities, by revealing to them the true God, whom they were endeavouring to worship, but who was to them unknown, as they themselves confessed by a public inscription. (LP 97.1)

Paul at Corinth

Paul did not wait at Athens for his brethren, Silas and Timothy, but leaving word for them to follow him, went at once to Corinth. Here he entered upon a different field of labour from that which he had left. Instead of the curious and critical disciples of schools of philosophy, he came in contact with the busy, changing population of a great centre of commerce. Greeks, Jews, and Romans, with travellers from every land, mingled in its crowded streets, eagerly intent on business and pleasure, and having little thought or care beyond the affairs of the present life. (LP 98.1)

Corinth was one of the leading cities, not only of Greece, but of the world. Situated upon a narrow neck of land between two seas, it commanded the trade of both the east and the west. Its position was almost impregnable. A vast citadel of rock, rising abruptly and perpendicularly from the plain to the height of two thousand feet above the level of the sea, was a strong natural defence to the city and its two sea-ports. Corinth was now more prosperous than Athens, which had once taken the lead. Both had experienced severe vicissitudes; but the former had risen from her ruins, and was far in advance of her former prosperity, while the latter had not reached to her past magnificence. Athens was the acknowledged centre of art and learning; Corinth, the seat of government and trade. (LP 98.2)

This large mercantile city was in direct communication with Rome, while Thessalonica, Ephesus, Alexandria, and Antioch were all easy of access, either by land or water. An opportunity was thus presented for the spread of the gospel. Once established at Corinth, it would be readily communicated to all parts of the world. (LP 98.3)

Yet the apostle saw on every hand serious obstacles to the progress of his work. The city was almost wholly given up to idolatry. Venus was the favourite goddess; and a great number of dissolute women were employed in connection with the worship of this reigning deity, for the purpose of attracting the devotees of popular vice. The Corinthians had become conspicuous, even among the heathen, for their gross immorality. (LP 99.1)

There was now a much larger number of Jews in Corinth than at any previous time. This people had been generally favoured by the ruling powers. and treated with much consideration. But for some time they had been growing arrogant and insubordinate, and after they had rejected and crucified Christ, the light of the world, they followed their own darkened understanding, manifested more openly their envy and hatred of the powers that governed them, and proudly boasted of a king of the Jews who was to come with great power, overthrow their enemies, and establish a magnificent kingdom. It was in view of this vague belief that they had rejected the Saviour. The same malignant spirit that actuated them in their persecution of the Son of God led them to rebel against the Roman government. They were continually creating seditions and insurrections, until they were finally driven from Rome because of their turbulent spirit. Many of them found refuge in Corinth. (LP 99.2)

Among the Jews who took up their residence here were many who were innocent of the wrongs that prevailed among them as a people. Of this class were Aquila and Priscilla, who afterward became distinguished as believers in Christ. Paul, becoming acquainted with the character of these excellent persons, abode with them; and having in his youth learned their trade of making tents, which were much used in that warm climate, he worked at this business for his own support. (LP 99.3)

The Hebrews had been instructed of God, by his servant Moses, to train up their children to industrious habits. That people were thus led to look upon indolence as a great sin, and their children were all required to learn some trade by which, if necessary, they could gain a livelihood. Those who neglected to do this were regarded as departing from the instruction of the Lord. Labour was considered elevating in its nature, and the children were taught to combine religion and business. In the time of Christ, the Jews, though wealthy, still followed their ancient custom. (LP 100.1)

Paul was highly educated, and was admired for his genius and eloquence. He was chosen by his countrymen as a member of the Sanhedrim, and was a Rabbi of distinguished ability; yet his education had not been considered complete, until he had served an apprenticeship at some useful trade. He rejoiced that he was able to support himself by manual labour, and frequently declared that his own hands had ministered to his necessities. While in a city of strangers, he would not be chargeable to any one. When his means had been expended to advance the cause of Christ, he resorted to his trade in order to gain a livelihood. (LP 100.2)

No man ever lived who was a more earnest, energetic, and self-sacrificing disciple of Christ than was Paul. He was one of the world's greatest teachers. He crossed the seas, and travelled far and near, until a large portion of the world had learned from his lips the story of the cross of Christ. He possessed a burning desire to bring perishing men to a knowledge of the truth through a Saviour's love. His whole soul was engaged in the work of the ministry; but he seated himself to the labour of his humble trade that he might not be burdensome to the churches that were pressed with poverty. Although he had planted many churches, he refused to be supported by them, fearing that his usefulness and success as a minister of Christ might be injured by suspicions that he was preaching the gospel for gain. He would remove from his enemies all occasion to misrepresent him, and thus to detract from the force of his message. (LP 100.3)

As a labourer in the gospel, Paul might have claimed support, instead of sustaining himself; but this right he was willing to forego. Although feeble in health, he laboured during the day in serving the cause of Christ, and then toiled a large share of the night, and frequently all night, that he might make provision for his own and others' necessities. The apostle would also give an example to the Christian ministry, dignifying and honouring industry. While thus preaching and working, he presented the highest type of Christianity. He combined teaching with his labour; and while toiling with those of his trade, he instructed them concerning the way of salvation. In pursuing this course, he had access to many whom he could not otherwise have reached. (LP 101.1)

When ministers feel that they are suffering great hardships and privations in the cause of Christ, let them in imagination visit the workshop of the apostle Paul, bearing in mind that while this chosen man of God is fashioning the canvas, he is working for bread which he has justly earned by his labours as an apostle of Christ. At the call of duty, he would meet the most violent opponents, and silence their proud boasting, and then he would resume his humble employment. His zeal and industry should be a rebuke to indolence or selfish ease in the minister of Christ. Any labour that will benefit humanity or advance the cause of God, should be regarded as honourable. (LP 101.2)

In preaching the gospel at Corinth, the apostle adopted a different course of action from that which had marked his labours at Athens. While in the latter place, he had adapted his style to the character of his audience; and much of his time had been devoted to the discussion of natural religion, matching logic with logic, and science with science. But when he reviewed the time and labour which he had there devoted to the exposition of Christianity, and realized that his style of teaching had not been productive of much fruit, he decided upon a different plan of labour in the future. He determined to avoid elaborate arguments and discussions of theories as much as possible, and to urge upon sinners the doctrine of salvation through Christ. In his epistle to his Corinthian brethren, he afterward described his manner of labouring among them:— (LP 102.1)

"And I, brethren, when I came to you, came not with excellency of speech or of wisdom, declaring unto you the testimony of God. For I determined not to know anything among you, save Jesus Christ, and him crucified. And I was with you in weakness, and in fear, and in much trembling. And my speech and my preaching was not with enticing words of man's wisdom, but in demonstration of the Spirit and of power; that your faith should not stand in the wisdom of men, but in the power of God." (LP 102.2)

Here the apostle has given the most successful manner of converting souls from ignorance and the darkness of error, to the light of truth. If ministers would follow more closely the example of Paul in this particular, they would see greater success attending their efforts. If all who minister in word and doctrine would make it their first business to be pure in heart and life, and to connect themselves closely with Heaven, their teaching would have greater power to convict souls. (LP 103.1)

When Christ was upon earth, the Jews all over the land were notified to watch his movements, for their religion was not safe where his influence was felt. He was continually followed by spies, who caught up every word and act which they could use against him. Paul had to meet the same spirit of opposition and blind prejudice. He preached first in the synagogue, reasoning from Moses and the prophets, showing what sins the Lord had most severely punished in olden times, and that murmuring and rebellion was the grievous crime that had brought God's displeasure upon the people of his choice. (LP 103.2) He brought his hearers down through the types and shadows of the ceremonial law to Christ,—to his crucifixion, his priesthood, and the sanctuary of his ministry,—the great object that had cast its shadow backward into the Jewish age. He, as the Messiah, was the Antitype of all the sacrificial offerings. The apostle showed that according to the prophecies and the universal expectation of the Jews, the Messiah would be of the lineage of Abraham and David. He then traced his descent from the great patriarch Abraham, through the royal psalmist. He proved from Scripture what were to have been the character and works of the promised Messiah, and also his reception and treatment on earth, as testified by the holy prophets. He then showed that these predictions also had been fulfilled in the life, ministry, and death of Jesus, and hence that he was indeed the world's Redeemer. (LP 103.3)

The most convincing proof was given that the gospel was but the development of the Hebrew faith. Christ was to come for the special benefit of the nation that was looking for his coming as the consummation and glory of the Jewish system. The apostle then endeavoured to bring home to their consciences the fact that repentance for their rejection of Christ could alone save the nation from impending ruin. He rebuked their ignorance concerning the meaning of those Scriptures which it was their chief boast and glory that they fully understood. He exposed their worldliness, their love of station, titles, and display, and their inordinate selfishness. (LP 104.1)

But the Jews of Corinth closed their eyes to all the evidence so clearly presented by the apostle, and refused to listen to his appeals. The same spirit which had led them to reject Christ, filled them with wrath and fury against Paul. They would have put an end to his life, had not God guarded his servant, that he might do his work, and bear the gospel message to the Gentiles. (LP 104.2)

"And when they opposed themselves, and blasphemed, he shook his raiment, and said unto them, Your blood be upon your own heads; I am clean; from henceforth I will go unto the Gentiles. And he departed thence, and entered into a certain man's house, named Justus, one that worshipped God, whose house joined hard to the synagogue." Silas and Timothy had joined Paul, and together they now laboured for the Gentiles. (LP 104.3)

Paul did not bind himself nor his converts to the ceremonies and customs of the Jews, with their varied forms, types, and sacrifices; for he recognized that the perfect and final offering had been made in the death of the Son of God. The age of clearer light and knowledge had now come. And although the early education of Paul had blinded his eyes to this light, and led him to bitterly oppose the work of God, yet the revelation of Christ to him while on his way to Damascus had changed the whole current of his life. His character and works had now become a remarkable illustration of those of his divine Lord. His teaching led the mind to a more active spiritual life, that carried the believer above mere ceremonies. "For thou desirest not sacrifice, else would I give it. Thou delightest not in burnt-offering. The sacrifices of God are a broken spirit. A broken and a contrite heart, O God, thou wilt not despise." (LP 105.1)

The apostle did not labour to charm the ear with oratory, nor to engage the mind with philosophic discussions, which would leave the heart untouched. He preached the cross of Christ, not with laboured eloquence of speech, but with the grace and power of God; and his words moved the people. "And Crispus, the chief ruler of the synagogue, believed on the Lord, with all his house; and many of the Corinthians, hearing, believed and were baptized." (LP 105.2)

The feelings of hatred with which many of the Jews had regarded the apostle were now intensified. The conversion and baptism of Crispus had the effect to exasperate instead of to convince these stubborn opposers. They could not bring arguments to show that he was not preaching the truth, and for lack of such evidence, they resorted to deception and malignant attack. (LP 105.3)

They blasphemed the truth and the name of Jesus of Nazareth. No words were too bitter, no device too low, for them to use in their blind anger and opposition. They could not deny that Christ had worked miracles; but they declared that he had performed them through the power of Satan; and they now boldly affirmed that the wonderful works of Paul were accomplished through the same agency. (LP 106.1)

Those who preach unpopular truth in our day are often met by the professed Christian world with opposition similar to that which was brought against the apostle by the unbelieving Jews. Many who make the most exalted profession, and who should be light-bearers to the world, are the most bitter and unreasonable in opposing the work of the chosen servants of God. Not satisfied with choosing error and fables for themselves, they wrest the Scriptures from the true meaning in order to deceive others and hinder from accepting the truth. (LP 106.2)

Though Paul had a measure of success, yet he became very weary of the sight of his eyes and the hearing of his ears in the corrupt city of Corinth, He doubted the wisdom of building up a church from the material he found there. He considered Corinth a very questionable field of labour, and determined to leave it. The depravity which he witnessed among the Gentiles, and the contempt and insult which he received from the Jews, caused him great anguish of spirit. (LP 106.3)

As he was contemplating leaving the city for a more promising field, and feeling very anxious to understand his duty in the case, the Lord appeared to him in a vision of the night, and said, "Be not afraid, but speak, and hold not thy peace; for I am with thee, and no man shall set on thee to hurt thee; for I have much people in this city." Paul understood this to be a command to remain in Corinth, and a guarantee that the Lord would give increase to the seed sown. Strengthened and encouraged, he continued to labour there with great zeal and perseverance for one year and six months. A large church was enrolled under the banner of Jesus Christ. Some came from among the most dissipated of the Gentiles; and many of this class were true converts, and became monuments of God's mercy and the efficacy of the blood of Christ to cleanse from sin. (LP 107.1)

The increased success of Paul in presenting Christ to the people, roused the unbelieving Jews to more determined opposition. They arose in a body with great tumult, and brought him before the judgment-seat of Gallio, who was then deputy of Achaia. They expected, as on former occasions of a similar character, to have the authorities on their side; and with loud and angry voices they preferred their complaints against the apostle, saying, "This fellow persuadeth men to worship God contrary to the law." (LP 107.2)

The proconsul, disgusted with the bigotry and self-righteousness of the accusing Jews, refused to take notice of the charge. As Paul prepared to speak in self-defence, Gallio informed him that it was not necessary. Then, turning to the angry accusers, he said, "If it were a matter of wrong or wicked lewdness, O ye Jews, reason would that I should bear with you. But if it be a question of words and names, and of your law, look ye to it; for I will be no judge of such matters. And he drove them from the judgment-seat." (LP 107.3)

The decided course of Gallio opened the eyes of the clamorous crowd who had been abetting the Jews. For the first time during Paul's labours in Europe, the mob turned on the side of the minister of truth; and, under the very eye of the proconsul, and without interference from him, the people violently beset the most prominent accusers of the apostle. "Then all the Greeks took Sosthenes, the chief ruler of the synagogue, and beat him before the judgment-seat. And Gallio cared for none of those things." (LP 108.1)

Gallio was a man of integrity, and would not become the dupe of the jealous and intriguing Jews. Unlike Pilate, he refused to do injustice to one whom he knew to be an innocent man. The Jewish religion was under the protection of the Roman power; and the accusers of Paul thought that if they could fasten upon him the charge of violating the laws of their religion, he would probably be given into their hands for such punishment as they saw fit to inflict. They hoped thus to compass his death. (LP 108.2)

Both Greeks and Jews had waited eagerly for the decision of Gallio; and his immediate dismissal of the case, as one that had no bearing upon the public interest, was the signal for the Jews to retire, baffled and enraged, and for the mob to assail the ruler of the synagogue. Even the ignorant rabble could but perceive the unjust and vindictive spirit which the Jews displayed in their attack upon Paul. Thus Christianity obtained a signal victory. If the apostle had been driven from Corinth at this time because of the malice of the Jews, the whole community of converts to the faith of Christ would have been placed in great danger. The Jews would have endeavoured to follow up the advantage gained, as was their custom, even to the extermination of Christianity in that region. (LP 108.3)

It is recorded that Paul laboured a year and six months in Corinth. His efforts, however, were not exclusively confined to that city, but he availed himself of the easy communication by land and water with adjacent cities, and laboured among them both by letter and personal effort. He made Corinth his headquarters, and his long tarry and successful ministry there gave him influence abroad as well as at home. Several churches were thus raised up under the efforts of the apostle and his co-labourers. The absence of Paul from the churches of his care was partially supplied by communications weighty and powerful, which were received generally as the word of God to them through his obedient servant. These epistles were read in the churches. (LP 109.1)

Epistles to the Thessalonians

While Paul was still at Corinth, labouring in word and doctrine, and also in the work-shop, Silas and Timothy came from Macedonia. The pleasure of meeting these two faithful co-labourers gave him fresh zeal and courage to withstand the continually increasing opposition, which had greatly hindered his labours. The apostle himself acknowledged that he was in Corinth "in weakness, and in fear, and in much trembling;" but God, "who comforteth those that are cast down," comforted him by the arrival of his friends. God designs that fellow-labourers in the gospel shall have their hearts knit closely together in the bonds of Christian love, so that their presence shall greatly cheer and encourage one another. (LP 109.2)

Paul had sent Timothy to revisit the places of his former labours, and to confirm and establish the church at Thessalonica. Timothy's report was encouraging, and refreshed the spirit of Paul. He was thus prompted to write to these beloved brethren. His first and second epistles to the church are given us. His heart was drawn out in love to those who had embraced the doctrine of Christ, which subjected them to reproach and persecution heretofore unknown to them. (LP 110.1)

There was still another reason for Paul's communication to these brethren. Some who were newly brought into the faith had fallen into errors in regard to those who had died since their conversion. They had hoped that all would witness the second coming of Christ; but they were in great sorrow as one after another of the believers fell under the power of death, making it impossible for them to behold that desirable event,—the coming of Christ in the clouds of heaven. (LP 110.2)

Some, who had fallen into the error that Christ was to come in their day, imbibed the fanatical idea that it was praiseworthy to show their faith by giving up all business, and resigning themselves to idle waiting for the great event which they thought was near. Others despised the gift of prophecy, exalting all other gifts above that. (LP 110.3)

Paul wrote to the church at Thessalonica, greeting them, and invoking in their behalf the blessing of God and the Lord Jesus Christ. He reminded them of his own labours among them, and their acceptance of the word, turning away from idols "to serve the living and true God, and to wait for his Son from Heaven, whom he raised from the dead, even Jesus, which delivered us from the wrath to come." (LP 111.1) He further referred to his work and that of his fellow-labourers among them, reminding them of the boldness with which they had preached the gospel unto them, in the midst of opposition, abuse, and discouragement, "not as pleasing men, but God, which trieth our hearts." (LP 111.2)

Paul then endeavoured to inform his Thessalonian brethren concerning the true state of the dead. He speaks of them as asleep,—in a state of unconsciousness: "I would not have you to be ignorant, brethren, concerning them which are asleep, that ye sorrow not, even as others which have no hope. For if we believe that Jesus died and rose again, even so them also which sleep in Jesus will God bring with him..... For the Lord himself shall descend from Heaven with a shout, with the voice of the archangel, and with the trump of God; and the dead in Christ shall rise first. Then we which are alive and remain shall be caught up together with them in the clouds, to meet the Lord in the air; and so shall we ever be with the Lord. Wherefore comfort one another with these words." (LP 111.3)

The friends of the righteous dead should not sorrow as those who lose their loved ones and have no hope in Jesus Christ, and who are not cheered by the immortal future beyond the resurrection of the just. Paul addressed the Thessalonians as those who had turned from the practices of heathen idolatry to the service of Christ. Vague heathen ideas concerning the state of the dead were more or less mingled with the new faith. But those who clearly saw the truth of the resurrection from the dead, in the doctrine preached by Paul, were greatly comforted. The cheering hope which they thus received, that the righteous dead would rise from their graves to a holy, happy immortal life, was in marked contrast with their former pagan ideas of death. For they had believed that there was no future life, no happy meeting with those whom they had loved and lost on earth. (LP 111.4)

The Thessalonians had eagerly grasped the idea that Christ was coming to change the faithful who were alive, and take them to himself. They had carefully guarded the lives of their friends, lest they should die, and lose the blessing which they anticipated at the coming of their Lord. But, one after another, death had laid their loved ones low; and they had buried them from their sight with fear and trembling. All their ancestors had thus been buried, and with anguish the Thessalonians looked upon the faces of their dead for the last time, never expecting to meet them again in a future life. (LP 112.1)

The reception of Paul's epistle was to them a great event. Written communications passing between friends were of very rare occurrence in those times. There was great joy in the church as the epistle was opened and read. What consolation was afforded them by those words which revealed the true state of the dead. Paul therein showed them that those who should be alive when Christ should come would not go to meet their Lord in advance of those who should be asleep in Jesus. For the voice of the archangel and the trump of God should reach the sleeping ones, and the dead in Christ should rise first, before the touch of immortality should be given to the living. "Then we which are alive and remain shall be caught up together with them in the clouds, to meet the Lord in the air; and so shall we ever be with the Lord. Wherefore comfort one another with these words." (LP 112.2)

The hope and joy which this assurance gave to the young church at Thessalonica can scarcely be understood by us. That letter, coming from their father in the gospel, was believed and cherished by them, and their hearts went out in love to him who had brought them the precious light of truth. He had told them these things before; but at that time their minds were grasping doctrines new and surpassingly strange to them, and it is not surprising that the force of some points had not been vividly impressed upon their minds. But they were hungering for truth, and Paul's epistle gave to their souls new hope and strength, a firmer faith in, and a deeper affection for, the Redeemer who had brought life and immortality to light through his death. (LP 113.1)

The darkness that had enshrouded the sepulchre of the dead was dispelled; for they now knew that their believing friends would be resurrected from the grave, and enjoy immortal life in the kingdom of God. A new splendour now crowned the Christian faith, and they saw a new glory in the life, sufferings, death, and resurrection of Christ. (LP 113.2)

Paul wrote, "Even so, them also which sleep in Jesus will God bring with him." Many interpret this passage to mean that the sleeping ones are brought with Christ from Heaven; but Paul designed to be understood that in like manner as Christ was raised from the dead, so will God bring up the sleeping saints with him from their graves, and take them with him to Heaven. Precious consolation! glorious hope! not only to the church of Thessalonica, but to all true Christians who live upon the earth. (LP 113.3)

Paul had previously so fully canvassed the subject of the signs of the times, showing what events would transpire prior to the revelation of the Son of man in the clouds of heaven, that he did not consider it necessary to enter largely upon those particulars again on this occasion. He, however, pointedly referred to his former teachings on that subject: "But of the times and the seasons, brethren, ye have no need that I write unto you; for yourselves know perfectly that the day of the Lord so cometh as a thief in the night. For when they shall say, Peace and safety, then sudden destruction cometh upon them." (LP 114.1)

The careless and unbelieving close their eyes to the evidence which Christ has given to warn men of his coming. They seek to quiet all apprehension, while, at the same time, the signs of the end are rapidly fulfilling, and the world is hastening to the period of the revelation of the Son of man in the clouds of heaven. But those who receive the light of truth as it shines upon their pathway, are not in darkness that this great event should come upon them unawares. Paul teaches that it would be sinful to be indifferent to the signs which should precede the second coming of Christ. Those who should be guilty of this neglect, he calls children of the night and of darkness. He encourages the vigilant and watchful with these words: "But ye, brethren, are not in darkness, that that day should overtake you as a thief. Ye are all the children of light, and the children of the day; we are not of the night, nor of darkness. Therefore let us not sleep, as do others; but let us watch and be sober." (LP 114.2)

The teachings of the apostle upon this point are especially important to the church in our time. Above all others, those who are living so near to the great consummation, should be sober and watchful. The watchful Christian is a working Christian, seeking zealously to purify his life, and to do all in his power for the cause of God. As his love for his Redeemer increases, so also does his love for his fellow-creatures increase. He has severe trials, as did his Master; and, like him, he is to some extent a man of sorrows, mourning because of the abominations done in the land. But this grief does not sour his temper, nor destroy his peace of mind. His afflictions, if well borne, refine and purify his nature. He is thus brought into closer fellowship with Christ; and inasmuch as he, through fierce opposition, is a partaker of the sufferings of Christ, he will also be a partaker of his consolation, and finally a sharer of his glory. (LP 115.1)

Paul continued his admonition to the church: "We beseech you, brethren, to know them which labour among you, and are over you in the Lord, and admonish you; and to esteem them very highly in love for their work's sake. And be at peace among yourselves." (LP 115.2)

The Thessalonians were greatly annoyed by persons coming among them with fanatical ideas and doctrines. The church had been properly organized, and officers had been appointed to act as ministers and deacons. But some would not be subordinate to those who held authoritative positions in the church. Ardent, self-willed persons claimed not only the right of private judgment, but to be heard publicly in urging their views upon the church. Paul, therefore, earnestly called the attention of his brethren to the respect and deference due those who had authority in the church, and who had been intrusted with the responsibilities connected with it. (LP 115.3)

He cautions the Thessalonians not to despise the gift of prophecy, and enjoins a careful discrimination in distinguishing the false manifestation from the true: "Quench not the Spirit; despise not prophesyings; prove all things; hold fast that which is good." He prays that God will sanctify them wholly, that their "whole spirit and soul and body be preserved blameless unto the coming of our Lord Jesus Christ;" and in closing, adds the assurance, "Faithful is He that calleth you, who also will do it." (LP 116.1)

In this First Epistle to the Thessalonians, Paul's teachings concerning the second coming of Christ were in perfect harmony with his former instructions to the church. Yet his words were misapprehended by some of the Thessalonian brethren. They understood him to express the hope that he himself would live to witness the Saviour's advent. This belief served to increase their enthusiasm and excitement. Those who had previously neglected their cares and duties, now considered themselves sustained by the apostle; hence they became more persistent than before in urging their erroneous views. (LP 116.2)

In his second letter to this church, Paul seeks to correct their misapprehensions, and to set before them his true position. He expresses his confidence in their Christian integrity, and his gratitude to God that their faith was not waning, and that love abounded toward one another, and for the cause of their divine Master. He also states that he presents them to other churches as furnishing a sample of the patient and persevering faith which bravely withstands the persecution and tribulation brought upon them by the opposition of the enemies of God. He carries them forward to hope for rest from all their cares and perplexities, when the Lord Jesus shall be revealed, "in flaming fire taking vengeance on them that know not God, and that obey not the gospel of our Lord Jesus Christ." (LP 116.3)

He then showed that great events were to transpire in the future, as foretold in prophecy, before Christ should come. Said the apostle: "Be not soon shaken in mind, nor be troubled, neither by spirit, nor by word, nor by letter as from us, as that the day of Christ is at hand. Let no man deceive you by any means; for that day shall not come, except there come a falling away first, and that man of sin be revealed." The papal power, so clearly described by the prophet Daniel, was yet to rise, and wage war against God's people, and trample upon his law. Until this power should have performed its deadly and blasphemous work, it would be vain for the church to look for the coming of their Lord. (LP 117.1)

Thus Paul put to naught the arguments of those who represented him as teaching that the day of Christ was at hand. He charged his brethren not to neglect their duties and resign themselves to idle waiting. After their glowing anticipations of immediate deliverance, the round of daily life and the opposition which they must expect to meet, would appear doubly forbidding. He therefore exhorted them to steadfastness in the faith. Their work had been appointed them of God;

by their faithful adherence to the truth they were to communicate to others the light which they had received. He bade them not to become weary in well-doing, and pointed them to his own example of diligence in temporal matters while labouring with untiring zeal in the cause of Christ. He reproved those who had given themselves up to sloth and aimless excitement, and directed that "with quietness they work, and eat their own bread." He also enjoined upon the church to separate from their fellowship any who should persist in disregarding his instructions. "Yet," he added, "count him not as an enemy, but admonish him as a brother." He concluded this epistle also with a prayer, that amid life's toils and trials the peace of God and the grace of the Lord Jesus Christ might be their consolation and support. (LP 117.2)

Apollos at Corinth

After leaving Corinth, Paul's next scene of labour was at Ephesus. He was on his way to Jerusalem to celebrate the approaching festival; and his stay at Ephesus was necessarily brief. He reasoned with the Jews in the synagogue, and produced so favourable an impression that he was entreated to continue his labours among them. His plan to visit Jerusalem prevented him from tarrying; but he promised to labour with them on his return. He had been accompanied to Ephesus by Aquila and Priscilla, and he now left them to carry forward the good work which he had begun. (LP 118.1)

It was at this time that Apollos, an Alexandrian Jew, visited Ephesus. He had received the highest Grecian culture, and was a scholar and an orator. He had heard the teachings of John the Baptist, had received the baptism of repentance, and was a living witness that the work of the prophet was not in vain. Apollos was a thorough student of the prophecies, and an able expounder of the Scriptures, publicly proclaiming his faith in Christ, as far as he himself had received the light. (LP 119.1)

Aquila and Priscilla listened to him, and saw that his teachings were defective. He had not a thorough knowledge of the mission of Christ, his resurrection and ascension, and of the work of his Spirit, the Comforter which he sent down to remain with his people during his absence. They accordingly sent for Apollos, and the educated orator received instruction from them with grateful surprise and joy. Through their teachings he obtained a clearer understanding of the Scriptures, and became one of the ablest defenders of the Christian church. Thus a thorough scholar and brilliant orator learned the way of the Lord more perfectly from the teachings of a Christian man and woman whose humble employment was that of tent-making. (LP 119.2)

Apollos, having become better acquainted with the doctrine of Christ, now felt anxious to visit Corinth, and the Ephesian brethren wrote to the Corinthians to receive him as a teacher in full harmony with the church of Christ. He accordingly went to Corinth, and laboured with the very Jews who had rejected the truth as preached to them by Paul. He reasoned with them from house to house, both publicly and privately, showing them Christ in prophecy; that he was Jesus whom Paul had preached, and that their expectations of another Messiah to come were in vain. Thus Paul planted the seed of truth, and Apollos watered it; and the fact that Apollos supported the mission of Paul gave character to the past labours of the great apostle among them. (LP 119.3)

His success in preaching the gospel led some of the church to exalt his labours above those of Paul, while he himself was working in harmony with Paul for the advancement of the cause. This rival spirit threatened to greatly hinder the progress of truth. Paul had purposely presented the gospel to the Corinthians in its veriest simplicity. Disappointed with the result of his labours at Athens, where he had brought his learning and eloquence to bear upon his hearers, he determined to pursue an entirely different course at Corinth. He presented there the plain, simple truth, unadorned with worldly wisdom, and studiously dwelt upon Christ, and his mission to the world. The eloquent discourses of Apollos, and his manifest learning, were contrasted by his hearers with the purposely simple and unadorned preaching of Paul. (LP 120.1)

Many declared themselves to be under the leadership of Apollos, while others preferred the labours of Paul. Satan came in to take advantage of these imaginary differences in the Corinthian church, tempting them to hold these Christian ministers in contrast. Some claimed Apollos as their leader, some Paul, and some Peter. Thus Paul, in his efforts to establish Christianity, met with conflicts and trials in the church as well as outside of it. (LP 120.2)

Factions also were beginning to rise through the influence of Judaizing teachers, who urged that the converts to Christianity should observe the ceremonial law in the matter of circumcision. They still maintained that the original Israel were the exalted and privileged children of Abraham, and were entitled to all the promises made to him. They sincerely thought that in taking this medium ground between Jew and Christian, they would succeed in removing the odium which attached to Christianity, and would gather in large numbers of the Jews. (LP 121.1)

They vindicated their position, which was in opposition to that of Paul, by showing that the course of the apostle, in receiving the Gentiles into the church without circumcision, prevented more Jews from accepting the faith than there were accessions from the Gentiles. Thus they excused their opposition to the results of the calm deliberations of God's acknowledged servants. (LP 121.2)

They refused to admit that the work of Christ embraced the whole world. They claimed that he was the Saviour of the Hebrews alone; therefore they maintained that the Gentiles should receive circumcision before being admitted to the privileges of the church of Christ. (LP 121.3)

After the decision of the council at Jerusalem concerning this question, many were still of this opinion, but did not then push their opposition any farther. The council had, on that occasion, decided that the converts from the Jewish church might observe the ordinances of the Mosaic law if they chose, while those ordinances should not be made obligatory upon converts from the Gentiles. The opposing class now took advantage of this, to urge a distinction between the observers of the ceremonial law and those who did not observe it, holding that the latter were farther from God than the former. (LP 121.4)

Paul's indignation was stirred. His voice was raised in stern rebuke: "If ye be circumcised, Christ shall profit you nothing." The party maintaining that Christianity was valueless without circumcision arrayed themselves against the apostle, and he had to meet them in every church which he founded or visited; in Jerusalem, Antioch, Galatia, Corinth, Ephesus, and Rome. God urged him out to the great work of preaching Christ, and him crucified; circumcision or uncircumcision was nothing. The Judaizing party looked upon Paul as an apostate, bent upon breaking down the partition wall which God had established between the Israelites and the world. They visited every church which he had organized, creating divisions. Holding that the end would justify the means, they circulated false charges against the apostle, and endeavoured to bring him into disrepute. As Paul, in visiting the churches, followed after these zealous and unscrupulous opposers, he met many who viewed him with distrust, and some who even despised his labours. (LP 122.1)

These divisions in regard to the ceremonial law, and the relative merits of the different ministers teaching the doctrine of Christ, caused the apostle much anxiety and hard labour. In his Epistle to the Corinthians, he thus addresses them on the latter subject:— (LP 122.2)

"Now I beseech you, brethren, by the name of our Lord Jesus Christ, that ye all speak the same thing, and that there be no divisions among you; but that ye be perfectly joined together in the same mind and in the same judgment. For it hath been declared unto me of you, my brethren, by them which are of the house of Chloe, that there are contentions among you. Now this I say, that every one of you saith, I am of Paul; and I of Apollos; and I of Cephas; and I of Christ. Is Christ divided? was Paul crucified for you? or were ye baptized in the name of Paul?" (LP 122.3)

He also explains the reason of his manner of labour among them: "And I, brethren, could not speak unto you as unto spiritual, but as unto carnal, even as unto babes in Christ. I have fed you with milk, and not with meat; for hitherto ye were not able to bear it, neither yet now are ye able. For ye are yet carnal; for whereas there is among you envying, and strife, and divisions, are ye not carnal, and walk as men?" (LP 123.1)

He thus shows them that he could not, when with them, address them as those who had an experience in spiritual life and the mystery of godliness. However wise they might have been in the worldly knowledge, they were but babes in the knowledge of Christ; and it was his work to instruct them in the rudiments, the very alphabet, of Christian faith and doctrine. It was his part to sow the seed, which another must water. It was the business of those who followed him, to carry forward the work from the point where he had left it, and to give spiritual light and knowledge in due season, as the church were able to bear. (LP 123.2)

When he came to them, they had no experimental knowledge of the way of salvation, and he was obliged to present the truth in its simplest form. Their carnal minds could not discern the sacred revealings of God; they were strangers to the manifestations of the divine power. Paul had spoken to them as those who were ignorant of the operations of that power upon the heart. They were carnal-minded, and the apostle was aware that they could not comprehend the mysteries of salvation; for spiritual things must be spiritually discerned. He knew that many of his hearers were proud believers in human theories, and reasoners of false systems of theology, groping with blind eyes in the book of nature for a contradiction of the spiritual and immortal life revealed in the Book of God. (LP 123.3)

He knew that criticism would set about converting the Christian interpretation of the revealed word, and scepticism would treat the gospel of Christ with scoffing and derision. It behoved him to introduce most carefully the great truths he wished to teach them. True Christianity is a religion of progress. It is ever giving light and blessing, and has in reserve still greater light and blessing to bestow to those who receive its truths. The illuminating influence of the gospel of Christ, and the sanctifying grace of God, can alone transform the carnal mind to be in harmony with spiritual things. (LP 124.1)

Paul did not venture to directly rebuke the licentious, and to show them how heinous was their sin in the sight of a holy God. His work was, as a wise instructor, to set before them the true object of life, impressing upon their minds the lessons of the divine Teacher, which were designed to bring them up from worldliness and sin to purity and immortal life. The spiritual senses must be matured by continual advancement in the knowledge of heavenly things. Thus the mind would learn to delight in them; and every precept of the word of God would shine forth as a priceless gem. (LP 124.2)

The apostle had dwelt especially upon practical godliness, and the character of that holiness which must be gained in order to make sure of the kingdom of Heaven. He wished the light of the gospel of Christ to pierce the darkness of their minds, that they might discern how offensive their immoral practices were in the sight of God. Therefore the burden of Paul's preaching among them had been Christ, and him crucified. He wished them to understand that the theme for their most earnest study, and greatest joy, should be the grand truth of salvation through repentance toward God, and faith in our Lord Jesus Christ. (LP 124.3)

The philosopher turns aside from the light of salvation, because it puts his proud theories to shame. The worldling refuses to receive it, because it would separate him from his earthly idols, and draw him to a holier life, for which he has no inclination. Paul saw that the character of Christ must be understood, before men could love him, and view the cross with the eye of faith. Here must begin that study which shall be the science and the song of the redeemed through all eternity. In the light of the cross alone can the true value of the human soul be estimated. (LP 125.1)

The refining influence of the grace of God changes the natural disposition of man. Heaven would not be desirable to the carnal-minded; their natural, unsanctified hearts would feel no attraction toward that pure and holy place; and if it were possible for them to enter, they would find nothing there congenial to them, in their sinful condition. The propensities which reign in the natural heart must be subdued by the grace of Christ, before fallen man can be elevated to harmonize with Heaven, and enjoy the society of the pure and holy angels. When man dies to sin, and is quickened to new life in Christ Jesus, divine love fills his heart; his understanding is sanctified; he drinks from an inexhaustible fountain of joy and knowledge; and the light of an eternal day shines upon his path, for he has the Light of life with him continually. (LP 125.2)

Paul sought to impress upon his Corinthian brethren the fact that he himself, and the ministers associated with him, were only men, commissioned of God to teach the truth; that they were individually engaged in the same work, which was given them by their Heavenly Father; and that they were all dependent upon him for the success which attended their labours. "For while one saith, I am of Paul; and another, I am of Apollos; are ye not carnal? Who then is Paul, and who is Apollos, but ministers by whom ye believed, even as the Lord gave to every man? I have planted, Apollos watered; but God gave the increase." (LP 126.1)

The consciousness of being God's servant should inspire the minister with energy and diligence perseveringly to discharge his duty, with an eye single to the glory of his Master. God has given to each of his messengers his distinctive work; and while there is a diversity of gifts, all are to blend harmoniously in carrying forward the great work of salvation. They are only instruments of divine grace and power. (LP 126.2)

Paul says: "So, then, neither is he that planteth anything, neither he that watereth; but God that giveth the increase. Now he that planteth and he that watereth are one; and every man shall receive his own reward according to his own labour. For we are labourers together with God; ye are God's husbandry, ye are God's building." The teacher of Christ's truth must be near the cross himself, in order to bring sinners to it. His work should be to preach Christ, and studiously to avoid calling attention to himself, and thus encumbering the sacred truth, lest he hinder its saving power. (LP 126.3)

There can be no stronger evidence in churches that the truths of the Bible have not sanctified the receivers, than their attachment to some favourite minister, and their unwillingness to accept the labours of some other teacher, and to be profited by them. The Lord sends help to his church as they need, not as they choose; for short-sighted mortals cannot discern what is for their highest good. It is seldom that one minister has all the qualifications necessary to perfect any one church in all the requirements of Christianity; therefore God sends other ministers to follow him, one after another, each possessing some qualifications in which the others were deficient. (LP 127.1)

The church should gratefully accept these servants of Christ, even as they would accept the Master himself. They should seek to derive all the benefit possible from the instruction which ministers may give them from the word of God. But the ministers themselves are not to be idolized; there should be no religious pets and favourites among the people; it is the truths they bring which are to be accepted and appreciated in the meekness of humility. (LP 127.2)

In the apostles' day, one party claimed to believe in Christ, yet refused to give due respect to his ambassadors. They claimed to follow no human teacher, but to be taught directly from Christ, without the aid of ministers of the gospel. They were independent in spirit, and unwilling to submit to the voice of the church. Another party claimed Paul as their leader, and drew comparisons between him and Peter, which were unfavourable to the latter. Another declared that Apollos far exceeded Paul in address, and power of oratory. Another claimed Peter as their leader, affirming that he had been most intimate with Christ when he was upon the earth, while Paul had been a persecutor of the believers. There was danger that this party spirit would ruin the Christian church. (LP 127.3)

Paul and Apollos were in perfect harmony. The latter was disappointed and grieved because of the dissension in the church; he took no advantage of the preference shown himself, nor did he encourage it, but hastily left the field of strife. When Paul afterward urged him to visit Corinth, he declined, and did not again labour there until long after, when the church had reached a better spiritual state. (LP 128.1)

Paul at Ephesus

While Apollos was preaching at Corinth, Paul fulfilled his promise to return to Ephesus. He had made a brief visit to Jerusalem, and had spent some time at Antioch, the scene of his early labours. Thence he had travelled through Asia Minor, visiting the churches which he had himself established, and strengthening the faith of the disciples. (LP 128.2)

The city of Ephesus was the capital of the province of Asia, * and the great commercial centre of Asia Minor. Its harbour was crowded with shipping from all parts of the known world, and its streets thronged with the people of every country. It therefore presented, like Corinth, a favourable missionary field. (LP 128.3)

The Jews, now widely dispersed in all civilized lands, were generally expecting the speedy advent of the Messiah. In their visits to Jerusalem at the annual feasts, many had gone out to the banks of the Jordan to listen to the preaching of John the Baptist. From him they had heard the proclamation of Christ as the Promised One, and on their return home they had carried the tidings to all parts of the world. Thus had Providence prepared the way for the apostle's labours. (LP 129.1)

On his arrival at Ephesus, Paul found twelve brethren, who, like Apollos, had been disciples of John the Baptist, and like him had gained an imperfect knowledge of the life and mission of Christ. They had not the ability of Apollos, but with the same sincerity and faith they were seeking to spread the light which they had received. (LP 129.2)

These disciples were ignorant of the mission of the Holy Spirit, that Jesus promised to his believing people, to be the life and power of the church. When asked by Paul if they had received the Holy Ghost, they answered, "We have not so much as heard whether there be any Holy Ghost." Paul inquired, "Unto what then were ye baptized?" and they said, "Unto John's baptism." The apostle then proceeded to set before them the great truths which are the foundation of the Christian's hope. (LP 129.3)

He told them of the life of Christ on earth, and of his cruel and shameful death. He told them how the Lord of life had broken the barriers of the tomb, and risen triumphant over death. He repeated the

---

* As used in the New Testament, the word Asia does not apply to the continent of Asia, but to a Roman province which embraced the western part of Asia Minor, and of which Ephesus was the capital.

Saviour's commission to his disciples: "All power is given unto me in Heaven and in earth. Go ye, therefore, and teach all nations, baptizing them in the name of the Father, and of the Son, and of the Holy Ghost." He told them also of Christ's promise to send the Comforter, through whose power mighty signs and wonders would be wrought, and described the glorious fulfilment of that promise on the day of Pentecost. (LP 129.4)

With deep interest, and grateful, wondering joy, the disciples listened to the words of Paul. By faith they grasped the atoning sacrifice of Christ, and acknowledged him as their Redeemer. They were then baptized "in the name of Jesus;" and as Paul laid his hands upon them, they received also the baptism of the Holy Spirit, by which they were enabled to speak the languages of other nations and to prophesy. Thus these men were qualified to act as missionaries in the important field of Ephesus and its vicinity, and also from this centre to spread the gospel of Christ in Asia Minor. (LP 130.1)

It was by cherishing a humble and teachable spirit that these brethren gained their precious experience. Their example presents a lesson of great value to Christians of every age. There are many who make but little progress in the divine life, because they are too self-sufficient to occupy the position of learners. They are content to remain in ignorance of God's word; they do not wish to change their faith or their practice, and hence make no effort to obtain greater light. (LP 130.2)

If the followers of Christ were but earnest seekers after divine wisdom, they would be led into rich fields of truth, as yet wholly unknown to them. Whoever will give himself to God as fully as did Moses, will be guided by the divine hand as verily as was the great leader of Israel. He may be lowly and apparently ungifted; yet if with a loving, trusting heart he obeys every intimation of God's will, his powers will be purified, ennobled, energized; his capabilities increased. As he treasures the lessons of divine wisdom, a sacred commission is intrusted to him; he is enabled to make his life an honour to God and a blessing to the world. "The entrance of Thy words giveth light; it giveth understanding unto the simple." (LP 130.3)

A mere intellectual knowledge of religious truth is not enough. There are today many as ignorant as those men of Ephesus of the Holy Spirit's work upon the heart. Yet no truth is more clearly taught in the word of God. Prophets and apostles have dwelt upon this theme. Christ himself calls our attention to the growth of the vegetable world to illustrate the agency of his Spirit in sustaining religious life. (LP 131.1)

The juices of the vine, ascending from the root, are diffused to the branches sustaining growth, and producing blossoms and fruit. So the life-giving power of the Holy Spirit, proceeding from Christ, and imparted to every disciple, pervades the soul, renews the motives and affections, and even the most secret thoughts, and brings forth the precious fruit of holy deeds. The life attests the union with the true and living Vine. (LP 131.2)

The Author of this spiritual life is unseen, and the precise method by which it is imparted and sustained is beyond the power of human philosophy to explain. It is the mystery of godliness. Yet the operations of the Spirit are always in harmony with the written word. As in the natural, so in the spiritual world. Human life is preserved, moment by moment, by divine power; yet it is not sustained by a direct miracle, but through the use of blessings placed within our reach. So the life of the Christian is sustained by the use of those means which Providence has supplied. He must eat of the bread of life, and drink of the waters of salvation. He must watch, he must pray, he must work, in all things giving heed to the instructions of the word of God, if he would "grow up to the full measure of the stature of a man in Christ Jesus." (LP 131.3)

There is still another lesson for us in the experience of those Jewish converts. When they received baptism at the hand of John, they were holding serious errors. But with clearer light they gladly accepted Christ as their Redeemer; and with this advance step came a change in their obligations. As they received a purer faith, there was a corresponding change in their life and character. In token of this change, and as an acknowledgment of their faith in Christ, they were rebaptised, in the name of Jesus. (LP 132.1)

Many a sincere follower of Christ has had a similar experience. A clearer understanding of God's will, places man in a new relation to him. New duties are revealed. Much which before appeared innocent, or even praiseworthy, is now seen to be sinful. The apostle Paul states that though he had, as he supposed, rendered obedience to the law of God, yet when the commandment was urged upon his conscience by the Holy Spirit, "sin revived, and I died." He saw himself a sinner, and conscience concurred with the sentence of the law. (LP 132.2)

There are many at the present day who have unwittingly violated one of the precepts of God's law. When the understanding is enlightened, and the claims of the fourth commandment are urged upon the conscience, they see themselves sinners in the sight of God. "Sin is the transgression of the law," and "he that shall offend in one point is guilty of all." (LP 133.1)

The honest seeker after truth will not plead ignorance of the law as an excuse for transgression. Light was within his reach. God's word is plain, and Christ has bidden him search the Scriptures. He reveres God's law as holy, just, and good, and he repents of his transgression.

78

By faith he pleads the atoning blood of Christ, and grasps the promise of pardon. His former baptism does not satisfy him now. He has seen himself a sinner, condemned by the law of God. He has experienced anew a death to sin, and he desires again to be buried with Christ by baptism, that he may rise to walk in newness of life. Such a course is in harmony with the example of Paul in baptizing the Jewish converts. That incident was recorded by the Holy Spirit as an instructive lesson for the church. (LP 133.2)

As was his custom, Paul had begun his work at Ephesus by teaching in the synagogue of the Jews. He continued to labour there for three months, "disputing and persuading the things concerning the kingdom of God." He at first met with a favourable reception; but as in other fields of labour, he was soon violently opposed by the unbelieving Jews. As they persisted in their rejection of the gospel, the apostle ceased preaching in the synagogue. (LP 133.3)

The Spirit of God had wrought with and through Paul in his labours for his countrymen. Sufficient evidence had been presented to convince all who honestly desired to know the truth. But many permitted themselves to be controlled by prejudice and unbelief, and refused to yield to the most conclusive evidence. Fearing that the faith of the believers would be endangered by continued association with these opposers of the truth, Paul separated the disciples as a distinct body, and himself continued his public instructions in the school of one Tyrannus, a teacher of some note. (LP 134.1)

Paul saw that "a great door and effectual" was open before him, though there were "many adversaries." Ephesus was not only the most magnificent, but the most corrupt, of the cities of Asia. Superstition and sensual pleasure held sway over her teeming population. Under the shadow of her idol temples, criminals of every grade found shelter, and the most degrading vices flourished. (LP 134.2)

The city was famed for the worship of the goddess Diana and the practice of magic. Here was the great temple of Diana, which was regarded by the ancients as one of the wonders of the world. Its vast extent and surpassing magnificence made it the pride, not only of the city, but of the nation. Kings and princes had enriched it by their donations. The Ephesians vied with one another in adding to its splendour, and it was made the treasure-house for a large share of the wealth of Western Asia. (LP 134.3)

The idol enshrined in this sumptuous edifice was a rude, uncouth image, declared by tradition to have fallen from the sky. Upon it were inscribed mystic characters and symbols, which were believed to possess great power. When pronounced, they were said to accomplish wonders. When written, they were treasured as a potent charm to guard their possessor from robbers, from disease, and even from death.

Numerous and costly books were written by the Ephesians to explain the meaning and use of these symbols. (LP 134.4)

As Paul was brought in direct contact with the idolatrous inhabitants of Ephesus, the power of God was strikingly displayed through him. The apostles were not always able to work miracles at will. The Lord granted his servants this special power as the progress of his cause or the honour of his name required. Like Moses and Aaron at the court of Pharaoh, the apostle had now to maintain the truth against the lying wonders of the magicians; hence the miracles he wrought were of a different character from those which he had heretofore performed. As the hem of Christ's garment had communicated healing power to her who sought relief by the touch of faith, so on this occasion, garments were made the means of cure to all that believed; "diseases departed from them, and evil spirits went out of them." Yet these miracles gave no encouragement to blind superstition. When Jesus felt the touch of the suffering woman, he exclaimed, "Virtue is gone out of me." So the scripture declares that the Lord wrought miracles by the hand of Paul, and that the name of the Lord Jesus was magnified, and not the name of Paul. (LP 135.1)

The manifestations of supernatural power which accompanied the apostle's work, were calculated to make a deep impression upon a people given to sorcery, and priding themselves upon their intercourse with invisible beings. The miracles of Paul were far more potent than had ever before been witnessed in Ephesus, and were of such a character that they could not be imitated by the skill of the juggler or the enchantments of the sorcerer. Thus the Lord exalted his servant, even in the estimation of the idolaters themselves, immeasurably above the most favoured and powerful of the magicians. (LP 135.2)

But He to whom all the spirits of evil were subject, and who had given his servants authority over them, was about to bring still greater shame and defeat upon those who despised and profaned his holy name. Sorcery had been prohibited in the Mosaic law, on pain of death, yet from time to time it had been secretly practised by apostate Jews. At the time of Paul's visit to Ephesus, there were in the city certain Jewish exorcists, who, seeing the wonders wrought by him, claimed to possess equal power. Believing that the name of Jesus acted as a charm, they determined to cast out evil spirits by the same means which the apostle had employed. (LP 136.1)

An attempt was made by seven brothers, the sons of one Sceva, a Jewish priest. Finding a man possessed with a demon, they addressed him, "We adjure thee by Jesus, whom Paul preacheth." But the evil spirit answered with scorn, "Jesus I know, and Paul I know; but who are ye?" and the one possessed sprang on them with frantic violence, and beat and bruised them, so that they fled out of the house, naked and wounded. (LP 136.2)

The discomfiture and humiliation of those who had profaned the name of Jesus, soon became known throughout Ephesus, by Jews and Gentiles. Unmistakable proof had been given of the sacredness of that name, and the peril which they incurred who should invoke it while they had no faith in Christ's divine mission. Terror seized the minds of many, and the work of the gospel was regarded by all with awe and reverence. (LP 136.3)

Facts which had previously been concealed were now brought to light. In accepting Christianity, some of the brethren had not fully renounced their heathen superstitions. The practice of magic was still to some extent continued among them. Convinced of their error by the events which had recently occurred, they came and made a full confession to Paul, and publicly acknowledged their secret arts to be deceptive and Satanic. Many sorcerers also abjured the practice of magic, and received Christ as their Saviour. They brought together the costly books containing the mysterious "Ephesian letters," and the secrets of their art, and burned them in the presence of all the people. When the books had been consumed, they proceeded to reckon up the value of the sacrifice. It was estimated at fifty thousand pieces of silver, equal to about ten thousand dollars. (LP 137.1)

The influence of these events was more widespread than even Paul then realized. The manifestation of the power of Christ was a grand victory for Christianity in the very stronghold of superstition. From Ephesus the news was widely circulated, and a strong impetus was given to the cause of Christ. These scenes in the ministry of Paul lived in the memory of men, and were the means of converting many to the gospel, long after the apostle himself had finished his course. (LP 137.2)

When the Ephesian converts burned their books on magic, they showed that the things in which they had once most delighted were now the most abhorred. It was by and through magic that they had especially offended God and imperilled their souls, and it was against magic that they showed such indignation. Here was given the best evidence of true conversion. (LP 138.1)

Those treatises on divination contained rules and forms of communication with evil spirits. They were the regulations of the worship of Satan,—directions for soliciting his help and obtaining information from him. By retaining these books, the disciples would have exposed themselves to temptation; by selling them they would have placed temptation in the way of others. They had renounced the kingdom of darkness, and they did not hesitate at any sacrifice to destroy its power. Thus the truth triumphed over men's prejudices, their favourite pursuits, and their love of money. (LP 138.2)

It is fondly supposed that heathen superstitions have disappeared before the civilization of the nineteenth century. But the word of God and the stern testimony of facts declare that sorcery is practised in this Christian age and Christian nation as verily as by the old-time magicians. The ancient system of magic is, in reality, the same as that which is now known as modern Spiritualism. Satan is finding access to thousands of minds by presenting himself under the guise of departed friends. The Scriptures of truth declare that "the dead know not anything." Their thoughts, their love, their hatred, have perished. The dead do not hold communion with the living. But true to his early cunning, when in the form of a serpent he deceived the mother of our race, Satan employs this device to gain control of the minds of men. (LP 138.3)

The heathen oracles have their counterpart in the spiritualistic mediums, the clairvoyants, and fortune-tellers of today. The mystic voices that spoke at Endor and Ephesus, are still by their lying words misleading the children of men. The mysteries of heathen worship are replaced by the secret associations and séances, the obscurities and wonders, of the sorcerers of our time. Their disclosures are eagerly received by thousands who refuse to accept light from God's word or from his Spirit. While they speak with scorn of the magicians of old, the great deceiver laughs in triumph as they yield to his arts in a different form. (LP 139.1)

His agents still claim to cure disease. They profess to employ electricity, magnetism, or the so-called "sympathetic remedies;" but in truth the magnetic power of which they boast is directly attributable to the sorcery of Satan. By this means he casts his spell over the bodies and souls of men. (LP 139.2)

The sick, the bereaved, the curious, are communicating with evil spirits. All who venture here are on dangerous ground. The word of truth declares how God regards them. In ancient times he pronounced judgments upon one who sent for counsel to a heathen oracle: "Is it not because there is not a God in Israel that thou sendest to inquire to Baal-zebub, the god of Ekron? therefore thou shalt not come down from that bed on which thou art gone up, but shalt surely die." (LP 139.3)

The visible and the invisible world are in close contact. Could the veil be lifted, we would see evil angels employing all their arts to deceive and destroy. Wherever an influence is exerted to cause men to forget God, there Satan is exercising his bewitching power. All who venture into scenes of dissipation or irreligious pleasure, or seek the society of the sensualist, the sceptic, or the blasphemer, by personal intercourse or through the medium of the press, are tampering with sorcery. Ere they are aware, the mind is bewildered and the soul polluted. The apostle's admonition to the Ephesian church should be heeded by the people of God today: "Have no fellowship with the unfruitful works of darkness, but rather reprove them." (LP 140.1)

Trials and Victories of Paul

For upwards of three years, Ephesus was the centre of Paul's work. A flourishing church was raised up here, and from this city the gospel spread throughout the province of Asia, among both Jews and Gentiles. (LP 140.2)

The apostle had for some time contemplated another missionary journey. He desired again to visit the churches in Macedonia and Achaia, and after spending some time at Corinth, to go to Jerusalem, after which he hoped to preach the gospel at Rome. In pursuance of his plan, he sent Timothy and Erastus before him into Macedonia; but feeling that the cause in Ephesus still demanded his presence, he decided to remain till after Pentecost. An event soon occurred, however, which hastened his departure. (LP 140.3)

The month of May was specially devoted to the worship of the goddess of Ephesus. The universal honour in which this deity was held, the magnificence of her temple and her worship, attracted an immense concourse of people from all parts of the province of Asia. Throughout the entire month the festivities were conducted with the utmost pomp and splendour. The gods were represented by persons chosen for the purpose, who were regarded as objects of worship, and were honoured by processions, sacrifices, and libations. Musical contests, the feats of athletes, and the fierce combats of men and beasts, drew admiring crowds to the vast theatres. The officers chosen to conduct this grand celebration were the men of highest distinction in the chief cities of Asia. They were also persons of vast wealth, for in return for the honour of their position, they were expected to defray the entire expense of the occasion. The whole city was a scene of brilliant display and wild revelry. Imposing processions swept to the grand temple. The air rung with sounds of joy. The people gave themselves up to feasting, drunkenness, and the vilest debauchery. (LP 141.1)

This gala season was a trying occasion to the disciples who had newly come to the faith. The company of believers who met in the school of Tyrannus were an inharmonious note in the festive chorus. Ridicule, reproach, and insult were freely heaped upon them. By the labours of Paul at Ephesus, the heathen worship had received a telling blow. There was a perceptible falling-off in attendance at the national festival, and in the enthusiasm of the worshippers. The influence of his teachings extended far beyond the actual converts to the faith. Many who had not openly accepted the new doctrines, became so far enlightened as to lose all confidence in heathen gods. The presence of

Paul in the city called special attention to this fact, and curses loud and deep were uttered against him. (LP 141.2)

Another cause of dissatisfaction existed. It had long been customary among heathen nations to make use of small images or shrines to represent their favourite objects of worship. Portable statues were modelled after the great image of Diana, and were widely circulated in the countries along the shores of the Mediterranean. Models of the temple which enshrined the idol were also eagerly sought. Both were regarded as objects of worship, and were carried at the head of processions, and on journeys and military expeditions. An extensive and profitable business had grown up at Ephesus from the manufacture and sale of these shrines and images. (LP 142.1)

Those who were interested in this branch of industry found their gains diminishing. All united in attributing the unwelcome change to Paul's labours. Demetrius, a manufacturer of silver shrines, called together the workmen of his craft, and by a violent appeal endeavoured to stir up their indignation against Paul. He represented that their traffic was endangered, and pointed out the great loss which they would sustain if the apostle were allowed to turn the people away from their ancient worship. He then appealed to their ruling superstition, saying: "Moreover ye see and hear, that not alone at Ephesus, but almost throughout all Asia, this Paul hath persuaded and turned away much people, saying that they be no gods which are made with hands; so that not only this our craft is in danger to be set at naught, but also that the temple of the great goddess Diana should be despised, and her magnificence should be destroyed, whom all Asia and the world worshippeth." This speech acted as fire to the stubble. The excited passions of the people were roused, and burst forth in the cry, "Great is Diana of the Ephesians!" (LP 142.2)

A report of the speech of Demetrius was rapidly circulated. The uproar was terrific. The whole city seemed in commotion. An immense crowd soon collected, and a rush was made to the workshop of Aquila, in the Jewish quarters, with the object of securing Paul. In their insane rage they were ready to tear him in pieces. But the apostle was not to be found. His brethren, receiving an intimation of the danger, had hurried him from the place. Angels of God were sent to guard the faithful apostle. His time to die a martyr's death had not yet come. (LP 143.1)

Failing to find the object of their wrath, the mob seized two of his companions, Gaius and Aristarchus, and with them hurried on to the theatre. Paul's place of concealment was not far distant, and he soon learned of the peril of his beloved brethren. His courage was in keeping with the occasion. He was ever ready to press to the front in the battle for his Master. Forgetful of his own safety, he desired to go at once to the theatre, to address the rioters. But his friends refused to permit him thus to sacrifice himself. Gaius and Aristarchus were not the prey that the people sought; no serious harm to them was apprehended. But should the apostle's pale, care-worn face be seen, it would arouse at once the worst passions of the mob, and there would not be the least human possibility of saving his life. (LP 143.2)

Paul was still eager to defend the truth before the multitude; but he was at last deterred by a message of warning from the theatre. Several of the most honourable and influential among the magistrates sent him an earnest request not to venture into a situation of so great peril. This proof of the regard in which Paul was held by the leading men of Asia was no mean tribute to the sterling integrity of his character. (LP 144.1)

The tumult at the theatre was continually increasing. "Some cried one thing, and some another; and the more part knew not wherefore they had come together." From the fact that Paul and some of his companions were of Hebrew extraction, the Jews felt that odium was cast upon them, and that their own safety might be endangered. Wishing it to be understood that they had no sympathy with the Christians, they thrust forward one of their own number to set the matter before the people. The speaker chosen was Alexander, one of the craftsmen, a coppersmith, to whom Paul afterward referred as having done him much evil. Alexander was a man of considerable ability, and he bent all his energies to direct the wrath of the people exclusively against Paul and his companions. But the crowd were in no mood to make nice distinctions. Seeing that Alexander was a Jew, they thrust him aside, the uproar continually increasing as all with one voice cried out, "Great is Diana of the Ephesians!" This cry continued for two hours. (LP 144.2)

At last there came a momentary silence, from sheer exhaustion. Then the recorder of the city arrested the attention of the crowd, and by virtue of his office obtained a hearing. By his prudence and good judgment he soon succeeded in quieting the excitement. (LP 145.1)

He met the people on their own ground, and showed that there was no cause for the present tumult. He appealed to their reason to decide whether the strangers who had come among them could change the opinions of the whole world regarding their ruling goddess. Said he: "Ye men of Ephesus, what man is there that knoweth not how that the city of Ephesus is a worshipper of the great goddess Diana, and of the image which fell down from Jupiter? Seeing then that these things cannot be spoken against, ye ought to be quiet, and to do nothing rashly." He bade them consider that Paul and his companions had not profaned the temple of Diana, nor outraged the feelings of any by reviling the goddess. (LP 145.2)

He then skilfully turned the subject, and reproved the course of

Demetrius: "Wherefore if Demetrius and the craftsmen which are with him have a matter against any man, the law is open, and there are deputies; let them implead one another. But if ye inquire anything concerning other matters, it shall be determined in a lawful assembly." He closed by warning them that such an uproar, raised without apparent cause, might subject the city of Ephesus to the censure of the Romans, thus causing a restriction of her present liberty, and intimating that there must not be a repetition of the scene. Having by this speech completely tranquillised the disturbed elements, the recorder dismissed the assembly. (LP 145.3)

The words of Demetrius reveal the real cause of the tumult at Ephesus, and also the cause of much of the persecution which followed the apostles in their work of promulgating the truth. "This, our craft, is in danger." With Demetrius and his fellows, the profitable business of image-making was endangered by the teaching and spread of the gospel. The income of pagan priests and artisans was at stake; and for this reason they instituted the most bitter opposition to the apostle, and refused to receive or investigate the new religion, which would have made them wise unto salvation. (LP 146.1)

Paul's labours in Ephesus were at length concluded. He felt that the excitement which prevailed was unfavourable to the preaching of the gospel. His heart was filled with gratitude to God that his life had been preserved, and that Christianity had not been brought into disrepute by the tumult at Ephesus. The decision of the recorder and of others holding honourable offices in the city, had set Paul before the people as one innocent of any unlawful act. This was another triumph of Christianity over error and superstition. God had raised up a great magistrate to vindicate his apostle, and hold the tumultuous mob in check. (LP 146.2)

Paul parted from his children in the faith with an affectionate farewell. He set out on his journey to Macedonia, designing on the way thither to visit Troas. He was accompanied by Tychicus and Trophimus, both Ephesians, who remained his faithful companions and fellow-labourers to the close of his life. (LP 146.3)

Paul's ministry in Ephesus had been a season of incessant labour. of many trials, and deep anguish. He taught the people in public and from house to house, instructing and warning them with many tears. He was continually opposed by the unbelieving Jews, who lost no opportunity to stir up the popular feeling against him. Again and again he was attacked by the mob, and subjected to insult and abuse. By every means which they could employ, the enemies of truth sought to destroy the effects of his labour for the salvation of men. (LP 147.1)

And while thus battling against opposition, and with untiring zeal pushing forward the gospel work and guarding the interests of a church yet young in the faith, Paul was bearing upon his soul the burden of all the churches. Nor was he released even from the tax of physical labour. Here, as at Corinth, he worked with his own hands to supply his necessities. In weariness and painfulness from unceasing toil and constant danger, enfeebled by disease, and at times depressed in spirits, he steadfastly pursued his work. (LP 147.2)

The news which he received, of apostasy in churches of his own planting, caused him deep anguish. He greatly feared that his efforts in their behalf would prove to have been in vain. Many a sleepless night was spent in prayer and earnest thought, as he learned of the new and varied methods employed to counteract his work. As he had opportunity, he wrote to the churches, giving reproof, counsel, admonition, and encouragement, as their state demanded. In his epistles the apostle does not dwell on his own trials, yet there are occasional glimpses of his labours and sufferings in the cause of Christ. Stripes and imprisonment, cold and hunger and thirst, perils by land and sea, in the city and in the wilderness, from his own countrymen, from the heathen, and from false brethren,—all these he endured for the truth's sake. He was defamed, reviled, "made the offscouring of all things," "perplexed, persecuted, troubled on every side," "in jeopardy every hour," "alway delivered unto death for Jesus' sake." (LP 147.3)

Amid the constant storm of opposition, the clamour of enemies, and the desertion of friends, the intrepid apostle at times almost lost heart. But he looked back to Calvary, and with new ardour pressed on to spread the knowledge of the Crucified. He was but treading the blood-stained path which Christ had trodden before him. He sought no discharge from the warfare till he should lay off his armour at the feet of his Redeemer. (LP 148.1)

Eighteen centuries have passed since the apostle rested from his labours; yet the history of his toils and sacrifices for Christ's sake are among the most precious treasures of the church. That history was recorded by the Holy Spirit, that the followers of Christ in every age might thereby be incited to greater zeal and faithfulness in the cause of their Master. (LP 148.2)

How does this hero of faith tower above the self-indulgent, ease-loving men who are today crowding the ranks of the ministry. When subjected to the ordinary difficulties and trials of life, many feel that their lot is hard. But what have they done or suffered for the cause of Christ? How does their record appear when compared with that of this great apostle? What burden of soul have they felt for the salvation of sinners? They know little of self-denial or sacrifice. They are indebted to the grace of Christ for all the excellences of character which they possess, for every blessing which they enjoy. All that they are, and all that they have, is the purchase of the blood of Christ. As the servants of

Christ encounter opposition and persecution, they should not permit their faith to grow dim or their courage to fail. With Christ as a helper, they can resist every foe, and overcome every difficulty. The same obligation rests upon them which impelled the apostle to his unwearied labours. Only those who emulate his fidelity, will share with him the crown of life. (LP 148.3)

Paul to the Corinthians

The First Epistle to the Corinthians was written by the apostle Paul during the latter part of his stay in Ephesus. For no church had he felt a deeper interest or put forth more earnest effort than for the believers at Corinth. The good seed sown by him had seemed to promise an abundant harvest; but tares were planted by the enemy among the wheat, and ere long these sprung up, and brought forth their evil fruit. The period of Paul's absence was a time of severe temptation to the Corinthian church. They were surrounded by idolatry and sensualism under the gayest and most alluring aspect. While the apostle was with them, these influences had little power. With his firm faith, his fervent prayers, and words of instruction, and, above all, his own example to inspire and encourage, they could gladly choose to suffer affliction for Christ's sake, rather than to enjoy the pleasures of sin. But when Paul departed, natural tastes and inclinations would assert control. It is not in a day that the education and habits of a life are to be overcome. Little by little, many departed from the faith. (LP 149.1)

For three years the voice which had urged them Heavenward had been silent. Like the children of Israel when Moses was hid from view by the clouds of Sinai, they sat down to eat and drink, and rose up to play. Not a few returned to the debasing sins of heathenism, as though they had never heard the heavenly message; some practised iniquity in secret, others openly, and with a spirit of bravado, perverting the Scriptures to justify their course. (LP 150.1)

Paul had written briefly to the church, announcing a plan which he for a time cherished, of visiting them immediately upon leaving Ephesus, and again upon his return from Macedonia. In the same letter he had admonished them to cease all communication with members who should persist in their profligacy. But the Corinthians perverted the apostle's meaning, quibbled over his words, and excused themselves for disregarding his instructions. (LP 150.2)

A letter was sent to Paul by the church, revealing nothing of the enormous sins that existed among them, but in a self-complacent manner asking counsel from him concerning various matters. He was, however, forcibly impressed by the Holy Spirit, that the true state of the church had been concealed, and that this letter was an attempt to draw from him statements which the writers could construe to serve their own purposes. There had come to Ephesus about this time several members of the household of Chloe, a Christian family of high repute in Corinth. In answer to the questions of the apostle, these brethren

90

reluctantly gave him a statement of facts as they existed. The church was rent in factions; the dissensions that arose at the time of Apollos' visit had greatly increased. False teachers were leading the brethren to despise the instructions of Paul. The doctrines and the ordinances of the gospel had been perverted. Pride, idolatry, and sensualism were steadily increasing among those who had once been disciples of Christ. (LP 150.3)

The apostle's worst fears were more than realized. He was filled with horror at the picture thus presented before him. But he did not even now yield to despair. He did not conclude that his work had been a failure. With a heart throbbing with anguish, and eyes blinded with tears, he sought counsel from God, and made his plans. His immediate visit to Corinth must be given up. In the present state of the church they were not prepared to profit by his labours. He sent Titus to Corinth to inform them of his change of plans, and to do what he could to correct the existing evils. Then, summoning all the courage of his nature, and keeping his soul stayed upon God, stifling all feelings of indignation at the ingratitude which he had received, and throwing his whole soul into the work, he dictated to the faithful Sosthenes one of the richest, most instructive, and most powerful of all his letters,—the first extant Epistle to the Corinthians. (LP 151.1)

With marvellous clearness and energy, he proceeded to answer the various questions proposed by the church, and to lay down general principles, which, if heeded, would produce a better spiritual condition. His letter is no long-studied production of the intellect. He did not seek by polished sentences to please the ear of his brethren. Their souls were in peril. He warned them of their dangers, and faithfully reproved their sins. He pointed them again to Christ, and sought to kindle anew the fervour of their early devotion. (LP 152.1)

After a tender greeting to the church, he refers to their experience under his ministry, by which they have been led to turn from idolatry to the service and worship of the true God. He reminds them of the gifts of the Holy Spirit which they have received, and presents before them their duty to make continual advancement in the Christian life, that they may attain to the purity and holiness of Christ. Having thus prepared the way, he speaks plainly of the dissensions among them, and exhorts his brethren, in the name and by the authority of Christ, to cease from their strife, and to seek earnestly for Christian unity and love. (LP 152.2)

Paul was free to mention how and by whom he had been informed of the divisions in the church: "It hath been declared unto me of you, my brethren, by them which are of the house of Chloe, that there are contentions among you." Though Paul was an inspired apostle, the Lord did not reveal to him at all times just the condition of his people. Those who were interested in the prosperity of the church, and saw evils creeping in, presented the matter before him, and from the light which he had previously received, he was prepared to judge of the character of these developments. Because the Lord had not given him a new revelation for that special time, those who were really seeking light did not cast aside his message as only a common letter. The Lord had shown him the difficulties and dangers which would arise in the churches, that when they should develop, he might know how to treat them. He was set for the defence of the church; he was to watch for souls as one who must render account to God; and should he not take notice of the reports concerning their state of anarchy and division? Most assuredly; and the reproof he sent them was written as much under the inspiration of the Spirit of God as were any of his epistles. (LP 152.3)

The apostle made no mention of the false teachers who were seeking to destroy the fruit of his labour. Because of the darkness and division in the church, he wisely forbore to irritate them by such references, for fear of turning some entirely from the truth. But he called the attention of the Corinthians to his own work among them, saying: "According to the grace of God which is given unto me, as a wise master-builder, I have laid the foundation, and another buildeth thereon. But let every man take heed how he buildeth thereupon. For other foundation can no man lay than that is laid, which is Jesus Christ." (LP 153.1)

Paul, as a champion of the faith, did not hesitate to declare the character of his work. But he did not thereby exalt himself when he asserted that he was a wise master-builder, who had laid the foundation for another to build upon. He stated, "For we are labourers together with God." He claimed no wisdom of his own; but divine power, uniting with his human efforts, had enabled him to present the truth in a manner pleasing to God. He was a co-labourer with Christ, a diligent worker in bringing spiritual knowledge from the word of God and the works of Christ, to all whose hearts were open to evidence. United with Christ, who was the greatest of all teachers, Paul had been enabled to communicate lessons of divine wisdom, which met the necessities of all classes and conditions of men, and which were to apply to all times, all places, and all people. In so doing, the apostle took no glory to himself, as a humble instrument in the hands of God. (LP 153.2)

The Lord gave Paul the wisdom of a skilful architect, that he might lay the foundation of the church of Christ. This figure of the erection of a temple is frequently repeated in the Scriptures, as forcibly illustrating the building up of the true Christian church. Zechariah refers to Christ as the Branch that should build the temple of the Lord.

He also refers to the Gentiles as helping in this work: "And they that are far off shall come and build in the temple of the Lord." (LP 154.1)

Paul had now been working in the Gentile quarry, to bring out valuable stones to lay upon the foundation, which was Jesus Christ, that by coming in contact with that living stone, they might also become living stones. In writing to the Ephesians, he says: "Now, therefore, ye are no more strangers and foreigners, but fellow-citizens with the saints, and of the household of God; and are built upon the foundation of the apostles and prophets, Jesus Christ himself being the chief corner-stone; in whom all the building, fitly framed together, groweth unto an holy temple in the Lord. In whom ye also are builded together for an habitation of God." (LP 154.2)

In his letter to the Corinthians, he writes, further: "If any man build upon this foundation, gold, silver, precious stones, wood, hay, stubble, every man's work shall be made manifest; for the day shall declare it." Some ministers, through their labours, furnish the most precious material, gold, silver, and precious stones, which represent true moral worth in those gained to the cause by them. The false material, gilded to imitate the true,—that is, a carnal mind, and unsanctified character, glossed over with seeming righteousness,—may not be readily detected by mortal eye; but the day of God will test the material. (LP 155.1)

The precious stones represent the most perfect Christians, who have been refined and polished by the grace of God, and by affliction which they have endured with much prayer and patience. Their obedience and love resemble those of the great Pattern. Their lives are beautified and ennobled by self-sacrifice. They will endure the test of the burning day, for they are living stones. "Him that overcometh will I make a pillar in the temple of my God, and he shall go no more out." (LP 155.2)

From worldly policy, many endeavour, by their own efforts, to become as polished stones; but they cannot be living stones, because they are not built upon the true foundation. The day of God will reveal that they are, in reality, only wood, hay, and stubble. The great temple of Diana was ruined; her magnificence utterly perished; those who shouted, "Great is Diana of the Ephesians!" perished with their goddess and the temple which enshrined her. Their religion is forgotten, or seems like an idle tale. That temple was built upon a false foundation, and when tried, it was found to be worthless. But the stones that Paul quarried out from Ephesus were found to be precious and enduring. (LP 155.3)

Paul laid himself upon the true foundation, and brought every stone, whether large or small, polished or unhewn, common or precious, to be connected with the living foundation-stone, Christ

Jesus. Thus slowly ascended the temple of the church of God. The apostle says, "Know ye not that ye are the temple of God, and that the Spirit of God dwelleth in you? If any man defile the temple of God, him shall God destroy; for the temple of God is holy, which temple ye are." (LP 156.1)

Paul had, in vision, a view of the city of God, with its foundations; and he represents the true Christian converts to be gold, silver, and precious stones. But the Jews made the work of Paul exceedingly difficult. They were continually claiming to be the only true children of Abraham, and therefore the only legitimate building-stones for God's house; and when the Gentiles accepted the gospel, and were brought to the true foundation, the Jews murmured about this material. Thus they hindered the work of God; nevertheless, the apostle unflinchingly continued his labours. (LP 156.2)

Paul and his fellow-workmen were skilful architects, because they had learned from Christ and his works. They had not only to build, but to tear down. They had to contend with the bigotry, prejudice, and violence of men who had built upon a false foundation. Through the power of God, the apostles became mighty in pulling down these strongholds of the enemy. Many who wrought as builders of the temple of Christ's church could be likened to the builders of the wall in Nehemiah's day: "They which builded on the wall, and they that bore burdens, with those that laded, every one with one of his hands wrought in the work, and with the other held a weapon." (LP 156.3)

One after another of the noble builders fell at his work by the hand of the enemy. Stephen was stoned; James was slain by the sword; Paul was beheaded; Peter was crucified; John was exiled. And yet stone after stone was added to the building, the church increased in the midst of the terrible persecutions that afflicted her, and new workers on the wall took the place of the fallen. (LP 157.1)

These faithful builders sought diligently to bring precious material to the living foundation. Paul laboured to have his own heart and character in harmony with the law of God, and then earnestly sought to bring about the same result with his converts. He exhorted Timothy, "Take heed unto thyself, and unto the doctrine." This is the duty of every teacher of Bible truth,— to illustrate in his own life the active Christian virtues, to be pure in heart, given to holy conversation, to be good, and to do good. (LP 157.2)

God will not accept the most brilliant talent or the most able service, unless it is laid upon the living foundation stone, and connected with it; for this alone gives true value to ability, and makes the labour a living service to God. We may look back through centuries, and see the living stones gleaming like jets of light through the darkness of error and superstition. These precious jewels will shine with continually increasing lustre throughout eternity. Although dead, the righteous of all ages testify, by the record of their words and deeds, to the truth of God. The names of the martyrs for Christ's sake are immortalized among the angels in Heaven; and a bright reward awaits them when the Lifegiver shall call them from their graves. (LP 157.3)

The flashing light of these polished stones, set for beauty in Christ's temple, has ever been exceedingly annoying to the world; for their brightness in the midst of surrounding darkness shows the strong contrast between righteousness and sin,—the gold of truth and the dross of error and tradition. Those who refuse to obey the truth themselves are unwilling that others should obey it; for the course of the faithful is a continual reproof to the unbelieving and disobedient. (LP 158.1)

Christ himself, the foundation and the crowning glory of God's temple, became "a rock of offense to them that stumble at the word." Yet that chief foundation stone, "disallowed indeed of men," was "chosen of God and precious." Though rejected by the Jewish builders, it became the head of the corner. Christ was put to death; but the work of building did not cease. He was honoured in Heaven and by the faithful on earth as the true foundation. (LP 158.2)

The servants of Christ have ever been greatly hindered in their labours by the errors which have from time to time corrupted the church. Carnal minds wrest the word of God to make it pander to their follies and superstitions. That unerring word, the rule by which every stone brought to the foundation must be tested, has been virtually set aside by many who appeared to be zealous builders on the temple of Christ's church. Thus wood, hay, and stubble have been laid upon the foundation stone by heedless workmen as precious acquisitions. (LP 158.3)

When emperors, kings, popes, and priests sought to defile and destroy this temple of God with sacrilegious idolatry and persecution of the faithful, God's eye never for a moment left his building and his workmen. In the face of gaping prisons, torture, and flames, the work grew under the hands of faithful men; the structure arose, beautiful and symmetrical. The workmen were at times almost blinded by the mists of superstition that settled dense and dark around them, and they were beaten back by the violence of their opponents; yet, like Nehemiah and his co-labourers, they still urged forward the work. Their language was, The God of Heaven liveth and reigneth; he will prosper his own work. Therefore we, his servants, will arise and build. (LP 159.1)

The figure which Paul uses of the temple erected on the foundation stone is to represent the work of God's servants to the end of time. To all who are building for God, the apostle addresses words of encouragement and warning: "If any man's work abide, which he have built thereupon, he shall receive a reward. If any man's work shall be burned, he shall suffer loss; but he himself shall be saved, yet so as by fire." The Christian teacher who faithfully presents the word of truth, leading his converts to holiness of heart and life, is bringing precious material to the foundation; and in the kingdom of God he will be honoured as a wise builder. He who neglects to teach the truth in its purity, will gather converts who are not holy in heart and life. He is bringing material that will not stand the test. In the day of God he will suffer loss. Though it is possible that those who have spent the best of life in teaching error may, by repentance and faith, be saved at last, yet their work is lost. Their life has failed of the good results that might have been secured. Souls have gone down to ruin, who, by a faithful presentation of the truth, might have been saved. Says the apostle, "Let every man take heed how he buildeth." (LP 159.2)

Paul writes to the Corinthians: "Though I be free from all men, yet have I made myself servant unto all, that I might gain the more." The apostle desired that his Corinthian brethren might be led to see the selfish ambition and intolerance which they had cherished. Hence he presents before them his own course of action, that they may by contrast perceive the sinfulness of their conduct. He laboured for men of every nation, tongue, and people, and sought to meet the varied classes on their own ground. He avoided making prominent the difference between himself and them. He strove to lay aside his personal feelings, and to bear with the prejudices of the persons for whom he was labouring. (LP 160.1)

When working for the unconverted Jews, he did not at once begin to preach that which they regarded as dangerous heresy, but commenced with doctrines upon which they could agree. Beginning with Moses and the prophets, he led them gradually from point to point, comparing scripture with scripture, tracing down the fulfilment of prophecy, showing the evidence that Messiah was to have come, and the manner of his coming. He then clearly presented before them the object of his coming, and what he was to have done upon earth, and how he was to have been received. (LP 160.2)

When he had given many discourses upon these subjects, he testified that the Messiah had indeed come, and then preached the simple gospel of Jesus Christ. This was the craft which Paul mentions, saying that he caught them with guile. He thus tried to allay prejudice, and win souls to the truth. He refrained from urging upon the Jews the fact that the ceremonial laws were no longer of any force. He cautioned Timothy to remove any occasion for them to reject his labours. He complied with their rules and ordinances as far as was consistent with his mission to the Gentiles. He would not mislead the Jews nor practice

96

deception upon them; but he waived his personal feelings, for the truth's sake. (LP 161.1)

With the Gentiles his manner of labour was different. He plainly informed them that the sacrificial offerings and ceremonies of the Jews were no longer to be observed, and preached to them Christ and him crucified. (LP 161.2)

The apostle in his labours encountered a class who claimed that the moral law had been made void, with the precepts of the ceremonial system. He vindicated the law of ten commandments, and held it up before the people as a rule of life. He showed that all men are under the most solemn obligation to obey that law, which Christ came to make honourable. He taught that Christ is the only one who can release men from the consequences of breaking the divine law; and that it is only by repentance for their past transgressions, faith in the atoning sacrifice of Christ, and a life of obedience, that men can hope to receive the favour of God. (LP 161.3)

Paul did not make light of the conscientious scruples of those who were weak in faith or dull of comprehension. He did not display his superior knowledge, and show contempt for their ignorance; but he placed himself as nearly as possible on a level with them, manifesting for them true sympathy and love, and leading them to nobler and more elevated views. He says, "I am made all things to all men, that I might by all means save some." By cheerful, patient kindness and Christian courtesy, he won the hearts of the people, quieted their prejudices, and endeavoured to teach them the truth without exciting their combativeness. All this he did because he loved the souls of men, and desired to bring them to Christ that they might be saved. (LP 162.1)

Paul endeavoured to impress upon the minds of his Corinthian brethren the importance of firm self-control, strict temperance, and unflagging zeal in the service of Christ. To illustrate the Christian warfare, he compared it with the games celebrated near Corinth, and always attended by vast multitudes of spectators. This illustration was calculated to make a vivid impression upon the minds of those whom he addressed, as it referred to that with which they were intimately acquainted. Various games were instituted among the Greeks and Romans for the purpose of amusement, and also with the design of training young men to personal vigour and activity, and thus qualifying them for warfare. The foot-races were the most ancient and the most highly esteemed of these games. They were held at stated times and places with great pomp, and were patronized by kings, nobles, and statesmen. Persons of rank and wealth engaged in these exercises, and shrank from no effort or discipline necessary to obtain the honour won by the victors. (LP 162.2)

The contest was governed by strict regulations, from which there was no appeal. Before the names of candidates could be entered upon the list as competitors for the prize, they were required to undergo a severe preparatory training. Every indulgence of appetite, or other gratification which could in the least affect their mental or physical vigour, was strictly forbidden. The muscles were kept strong and supple. Every nerve must be under control, every movement certain, every step swift and unswerving, and all the powers kept up to the highest mark, to give any hope of success in the grand trial of strength and speed. (LP 163.1)

As the contestants in the race made their appearance before the eager and waiting crowd, their names were heralded, and the rules of the race expressly stated. The prize was placed in full view before the competitors, and they all started together, the fixed attention of the spectators inspiring them with zeal and determination to win. The judges were seated near the goal, that they might watch the race from its beginning to its close, and award the prize to the victor. If a man came off victorious through taking any unlawful advantage, the prize was not awarded to him. (LP 163.2)

Great risks were run in these contests; it was not unusual for one of the contestants to drop dead as he was about to seize the prize in triumph. But this was not considered too great a risk to run for the sake of the honour awarded to the conqueror. As he reached the goal, shout after shout of applause from the vast multitude rent the air and wakened the echoes of the surrounding hills and mountains. The judge, in full view of the spectators, presented him with the emblems of victory, the perishable laurel crown, and a palm branch to carry in his right hand. This crown was worn by the victor with great pride. His praise was extravagantly heralded, and sung throughout the land. His parents received their share of honour, and even the city where he lived was held in high esteem for having produced so great an athlete. (LP 164.1)

Paul presents these races as a striking figure of the Christian warfare: "Know ye not that they which run in a race run all, but one receiveth the prize? So run, that ye may obtain. And every man that striveth for the mastery is temperate in all things. Now they do it to obtain a corruptible crown; but we an incorruptible." (LP 164.2)

To run the Christian course in triumph, it is as necessary for us to exercise fortitude, patience, and self-denial, as it was for the contestants in the games and races of the Greeks and Romans. Like them the Christian must not allow his attention to be attracted by the spectators, nor diverted by amusements, luxuries, or love of ease. All his habits and passions must be brought under the strictest discipline. Reason, enlightened by the teachings of God's word, and guided by his Spirit, must hold the reins of control. Every hindrance must be laid aside; no weight must impede his course. And after this has been done, the utmost exertion is required in order to gain the victory. (LP 164.3)

"Now they do it to obtain a corruptible crown; but we an incorruptible." The chaplet of fading laurel is presented before us in the strongest contrast with the enduring honour and the crown of immortal glory which he will receive who runs with triumph the Christian race, and becomes a victor in the spiritual warfare. There must be no flagging of zeal, no wavering steps, or the effort will be lost. The last few strides of the contestants in the race were always made with agonizing effort to keep up undiminished speed. So the Christian, as he nears the goal, must press on with even more zeal and determination than at the first part of his course. (LP 165.1)

Paul carries the illustration back to the preparation necessary to the success of the contestants in the race,—to the preliminary discipline, the careful and abstemious diet, the temperance in all things. These were unflinchingly practised in order to win the small recompense of earthly honour. How much more important that the Christian, whose eternal interest is at stake, be trained to put appetite and passion under subjection to reason and the will of God. If men will voluntarily submit to hardships, privations, and self-denial to secure the perishable reward of worldly distinction, how much more should the Christian be willing to do and to suffer for the sake of obtaining the crown of glory that fadeth not away, and the life which runs parallel with the life of God. (LP 165.2)

The competitors in the ancient games, after they had submitted to self-denial and rigid discipline, were not even then sure of the victory. The prize could be awarded to but one. Some might put forth the utmost effort to obtain this crowning honour, but, as they reached forth the hand to secure it, another, an instant before them, might grasp the coveted treasure. Such is not the case in the Christian warfare. Those who comply with the conditions are not to be disappointed at the end of the race. They all may gain the prize, and win and wear the crown of immortal glory. (LP 165.3)

Multitudes in the world are witnessing this game of life, the Christian warfare. The Monarch of the universe and myriads of heavenly angels are watching with intense interest the efforts of those who engage to run the Christian race. The reward given to every man will be in accordance with the persevering energy and faithful earnestness with which he has performed his part in the great contest. (LP 166.1)

Paul himself practised self-denial and endured severe hardships and privations that he might win the prize of eternal life, and, by his example and teachings, lead others also to be gainers of the same reward. He says: "I therefore so run, not as uncertainly; so fight I, not as one that beateth the air; but I keep under my body, and bring it into subjection, lest that by any means, when I have preached to others, I myself should be a castaway." The apostle desired to arouse his Corinthian brethren to see the danger that menaced them through self-gratification, he therefore dwelt on the rigid discipline and abstemiousness necessary to develop soundness, vigour, and endurance in the competitors in the games. He drew a contrast between this preparation and its consequences, and the self-indulgent life of the Corinthian Christians, who had matters of eternal interest at stake, and needed the fullest strength of body and mind in order to come off victorious. He showed them that heretofore their course had been highly censurable; for not even anxiety for spiritual health and the honour of the gospel could induce them to deny the cravings of appetite and passion. (LP 166.2)

In the indulgence of depraved appetites they had even united with the heathen in their idolatrous festivals, thus endangering the faith of those newly converted from idolatry. Paul counsels them to firmly control their animal passions and appetites. The body, the master-piece of God's workmanship, like a perfect and well-stringed instrument, must be kept in soundness, in order to produce harmonious action. He says that unless he should put in practice his own exhortations, by striving for the mastery over self, observing temperance in all things, he would, after preaching to others, himself becomes a castaway. (LP 167.1)

The apostle declares that he did not run in the Christian race uncertainly, that is, indifferently, willing to be left behind; neither did he fight as the pugilist practices prior to the fray, beating the air with empty blows, having no opponent. But as, when in actual conflict, he contends for the mastery, overcomes his antagonist by repeated and well-directed blows, beats him to the ground, and holds him there till he acknowledges himself conquered, so did the apostle fight against the temptations of Satan and the evil propensities of the carnal nature. (LP 167.2)

Paul refers his brethren to the experience of ancient Israel, to the blessings which rewarded their obedience, and the judgments which followed their transgressions. He reminds them of the fact that the Hebrews were led in a miraculous manner from Egypt, under the protection of the shadowy cloud by day and the pillar of fire by night. He recounts how the whole company were thus safely conducted through the Red Sea, while the Egyptians, essaying to cross in like manner, were all drowned. God in these acts acknowledged all Israel as his church. "They did all eat the same spiritual meat, and did all drink the same spiritual drink; for they drank of that spiritual Rock that followed them; and that Rock was Christ." The Hebrews, in all their travels, had Christ as a leader. The smitten rock typified Christ, who was to be wounded for men's transgressions, that the stream of salvation might flow to them. (LP 168.1)

Notwithstanding the favour which God manifested to the Hebrews, yet because of their wicked lust for the luxuries which they had left in Egypt,—because of their sins and rebellion,— the judgments of God came upon them. The apostle enjoins upon his brethren the lesson to be learned: "Now these things were our examples, to the intent we should not lust after evil things, as they also lusted." (LP 168.2)

Paul continues, giving the most solemn warnings against the sins of idolatry, licentiousness, and presumption, which caused so many of the Israelites to fall in the wilderness. He cites examples from sacred history to show how love of ease and pleasure prepared the way for those sins which called forth the signal vengeance of God. It was when the children of Israel sat down to eat and drink, and rose up to play, that they threw off the righteous fear of God which they had felt a short time before as they listened to the law from Sinai. They made them a golden calf to represent God, and worshipped it in a festive religious gathering. Again, it was after enjoying a luxurious feast connected with the worship of Baal-peor that many of the Hebrews fell through licentiousness, and the anger of God was manifested toward them, and twenty-three thousand were slain by the sword at the command of God through Moses. (LP 168.3)

The apostle adjures the Corinthians, "Let him that thinketh he standeth, take heed lest he fall." Should they become boastful and self-confident, and neglect to watch and pray, they would fall into grievous sin, and call down upon themselves the wrath of God. Yet Paul would not have them yield to despondency or discouragement. Whatever might be their temptations or their dangers, he assures them, "God is faithful, who will not suffer you to be tempted above that ye are able; but will with the temptations also make a way to escape, that ye may be able to bear it." (LP 169.1)

Paul enjoins upon his brethren to inquire what influence their words and works will have upon others, and to do nothing, however innocent in itself, that would seem to sanction idolatry, or that would offend the scruples of those who might be weak in the faith. "Whether therefore ye eat, or drink, or whatsoever ye do, do all to the glory of God. Give none offense, neither to the Jews, nor to the Gentiles, nor to the church of God." (LP 169.2)

The apostle's words of warning to the Corinthian church are applicable to all time, and are specially adapted to the wants of our day. By idolatry he did not alone mean the worship of idols, but also selfishness, love of ease, the gratification of appetite and passion. All these come under the head of idolatry. A mere profession of faith in Christ, and a boastful knowledge of the truth, does not constitute a Christian. A religion which seeks only to gratify the eye, the ear, and the taste, or which permits any hurtful self-indulgence, is not the religion of Christ. It is in harmony with the spirit of the world, and is opposed to the teachings of the Holy Scriptures. Festivals and scenes of amusement, in which professed members of the Christian church imitate the customs and enjoy the pleasures of the world, constitute a virtual union with the enemies of God. (LP 169.3)

The Corinthians were departing widely from the simplicity of the faith and the harmony of the church. They continued to assemble for worship, but with hearts that were estranged from one another. They had perverted the true meaning of the Lord's supper, patterning in a great degree after idolatrous feasts. They came together to celebrate the sufferings and death of Christ, but turned the occasion into a period of feasting and selfish enjoyment. (LP 170.1)

It had become customary, before partaking of the communion, to unite in a social meal. Families professing the faith brought their own food to the place of meeting, and ate it without courteously waiting for the others to be ready. The holy institution of the Lord's supper was, for the wealthy, turned into a gluttonous feast; while the poor were made to blush when their meagre fare was brought in contrast with the costly viands of their rich brethren. (LP 170.2)

Paul rebukes the Corinthians for making the house of God a place of feasting and revelry, like a company of idolaters: "What! have ye not houses to eat and to drink in? or despise ye the church of God, and shame them that have not?" The public religious feasts of the Greeks had been conducted in this way, and it was by following the counsels of false teachers that the Christians had been led to imitate their example. These teachers had begun by assuring them that it was not wrong to attend idolatrous feasts, and had finally introduced similar practices into the Christian church. (LP 171.1)

Paul proceeded to give the order and object of the Lord's supper, and then warned his brethren against perverting this sacred ordinance: "As often as ye eat this bread, and drink this cup, ye do show the Lord's death till he come. Wherefore, whosoever shall eat this bread, and drink this cup of the Lord, unworthily, shall be guilty of the body and blood of the Lord....He that eateth and drinketh unworthily, eateth and drinketh damnation to himself, not discerning the Lord's body." (LP 171.2)

The apostle thus sought, in the most decided and impressive manner, to correct the false and dangerous ideas and practices which were prevailing in the Corinthian church. He spoke plainly, yet in love for their souls. In his warnings and reproofs, light from the throne of

God was shining upon them, to reveal the hidden sins that were defiling their lives and characters. Yet how would it be received? (LP 171.3)

While writing to the Corinthians, Paul had firmly controlled his feelings; but when the letter had been dispatched, a reaction came. He feared lest he should wound too deeply those whom he desired to benefit. He keenly dreaded a further alienation, and sometimes longed to recall his words. With trembling anxiety he waited to receive some tidings as to the reception of his message. (LP 171.4)

Those who, like the apostle, have felt a responsibility for beloved churches or institutions, can best appreciate his depression of spirit and self-accusings. The servants of God who bear the burden of his work for this time, share the same experience of labour, conflict, and anxious care that fell to the lot of the great apostle. Burdened by divisions in the church, meeting with ingratitude and betrayal from those to whom they look for sympathy and support, vividly impressed with the peril of churches that are harbouring iniquity, compelled to bear a close, searching testimony in reproof of sin, and then weighed down with fear that they may have dealt with too great severity,—the faithful soldiers of the cross find no rest this side of Heaven. (LP 172.1)

Second Epistle to the Corinthians

From Ephesus Paul went to Troas, with the same object which was ever before him, that of making known to the people the way of salvation through Christ. It was while visiting this city upon a former journey that the vision of the man of Macedonia and the imploring cry, "Come over and help us," had decided him to preach the gospel in Europe. His stay in Troas was thus shortened, and he was prevented from labouring there as he had purposed; but he states that a door was now open to him of the Lord, and he laid the foundation of a church, which rapidly increased. (LP 172.2)

Paul had directed Titus, on his return from Corinth, to rejoin him at Troas, and he awaited the coming of this beloved fellow-labourer, hoping to receive some tidings from the Corinthian church. But week after week passed, and Titus came not. The apostle's solicitude became almost insupportable. He says, "My spirit found no rest, because of Titus, my brother." He left Troas, and went to Philippi, where he met Timothy, his son in the gospel. (LP 173.1)

Here was a church which had proved its love for the gospel of Christ by its faith and works. The brethren had not swerved from their confidence in the Lord's messenger. Paul, in his epistle to the Philippians, does not censure them, but speaks words of warm approval. The truth of the gospel had thoroughly converted them. This church could not be prevented from making donations to the apostle for his support while preaching the gospel, although he had repeatedly refused to accept their liberality. He was very persistent in his determination to sustain himself, lest occasion might be given his enemies to say that he laboured for his personal gain. But the Philippians would not be denied the privilege of aiding the Lord's ambassador by bestowing of their means to meet his necessities. Twice while he was at Thessalonica, immediately after their conversion, they urged their gifts upon him. Again they sent him relief while he was preaching at Corinth, and working for his own support. Also when the apostle was a prisoner at Rome, the faithful love of his Philippian brethren was evinced by their kindly care for his comfort. (LP 173.2)

The church at Philippi were not wealthy. Paul says of these brethren: "In a great trial of affliction, the abundance of their joy and their deep poverty abounded unto the riches of their liberality. For to their power, I bear record, yea, and beyond their power they were willing of themselves; praying us with much entreaty that we would receive the gift, and take upon us the fellowship of the ministering to the saints. And this they did, not as we hoped, but first gave their own selves to the Lord, and unto us by the will of God." (LP 174.1)

It had been one object of the apostle, in this journey, to collect means for the relief of the poor saints at Jerusalem. He had established in the Corinthian church, as also in Galatia, a system of weekly offerings, and had enjoined upon Titus, in his visit to Corinth, to give special attention to forwarding this benevolent enterprise. Not only was the apostle actuated by a desire to relieve the sufferings of his Jewish brethren, but he hoped that this tangible expression of the love and sympathy of the Gentile converts would soften the bitter feelings cherished toward them by many of the believers in Judea. Notwithstanding the poverty of the Philippian church, they joined readily in the apostle's plan, and urged him to accept their bounty for the needy Christians at Jerusalem. They had the utmost confidence in his integrity and judgment, and considered him the proper person to take charge of their gifts. (LP 174.2)

The Philippians did not hold their small earthly possessions with a tenacious grasp, but considered them as theirs only to use in doing good. They thus experienced the truth of the words of Christ, "It is more blessed to give than to receive." They felt that the cause of Christ was one everywhere. They therefore, in their poverty, felt called out to help other churches more needy than themselves. (LP 175.1)

This spirit of unsectional liberality should characterize the churches of today. They should continually keep the burden on their souls for the advancement of the cause of God in any and every place. Benevolence is the very foundation of the universe. God is a benefactor of the human family. He is a being of inexhaustible goodness and love. The love of the Father for man was expressed in the gift of his beloved Son to save the race from ruin. (LP 175.2)

Christ gave his life for man. He was a monarch in the courts of Heaven, yet he voluntarily left his riches and honour, and came to earth, becoming poor and lowly that we might be made rich and happy in the kingdom of Heaven. The revelation of the gospel should lead all who accept its sacred truths to imitate the great Exemplar in doing good, in blessing humanity, and in living a life of self-denial and benevolence. The sin of covetousness is specially denounced in the Scriptures. Worldliness is at war with the true principles of Christianity. A life of beneficent labour is the fruit borne by the Christian tree. (LP 175.3)

A deep sadness still rested upon the mind and heart of Paul because of his apprehensions concerning the Corinthian church. While at Philippi he commenced his second epistle to them; for they hung as a heavy weight upon his soul. The depression of spirits from which the apostle suffered was, however, attributable in a great degree to bodily infirmities, which made him very restless when not engaged in active service. But when working for the salvation of souls, he rose superior to physical debility. He felt that the disease under which he suffered was a terrible impediment to him in his great work, and repeatedly besought the Lord to relieve him. God did not see fit to answer his prayers in this respect, though he gave him assurance that divine grace should be sufficient for him. (LP 175.4)

Paul's burden because of the Corinthians did not leave him until he reached Macedonia, where he met Titus. He states, "Our flesh had no rest, but we were troubled on every side; without were fightings, within were fears. Nevertheless, God that comforteth those that are cast down, comforted us by the coming of Titus." The report of this faithful messenger greatly relieved the mind of Paul. Titus assured him that the greater part of the church at Corinth had submitted to the injunctions of the apostle, and had given proof of the deepest repentance for the sins that had brought a reproach upon Christianity. They had immediately separated from their fellowship the ones who had sinned, and who had sought to justify their corrupt course. They had also nobly responded to the appeal in behalf of the poor saints at Jerusalem. (LP 176.1)

In this second epistle to the church, the apostle expressed his joy at the good work which had been wrought in them: "Though I made you sorry with a letter, I do not repent, though I did repent"—when tortured with fear that his words would be despised, and half regretting that he had written so decidedly and severely. He continues: "Now I rejoice, not that ye were made sorry, but that ye sorrowed to repentance; for ye were made sorry after a godly manner, that ye might receive damage by us in nothing. For godly sorrow worketh repentance to salvation not to be repented of." That repentance which is produced by the influence of divine grace upon the heart, will lead to the confession and forsaking of sin. Such were the fruits which the apostle declares had been manifested by the Corinthian church: "What carefulness it wrought in you, yea, what clearing of yourselves, yea, what indignation, yea, what fear, yea, what vehement desire, yea, what zeal." (LP 176.2)

Still there was a small minority of the Corinthians who stubbornly resisted all efforts of the apostle for the purification of the church; but their course was such that none could be deceived in them. They displayed a most bitter spirit, and were bold in denunciation of Paul, accusing him of mercenary motives, and craft in preaching the gospel and dealing with the churches. They charged him with receiving personal advantage from the means contributed by the brethren for various benevolent purposes. On the other hand, some challenged his claims to apostleship, because he did not demand support from the churches which he had raised up. Thus the accusations of his opposers were conflicting, and without a shadow of foundation. (LP 177.1)

Just such unreasonable persons are to be met in our times, men who set themselves against the progress of the work of God, while professing to believe the truth. They refuse to come into harmony with the body of the church, the burden of their work being to dissect the characters of their brethren, to raise dark suspicions, and circulate covert insinuations. Many honest persons are deceived by these calumniators, whose purpose are not so readily discerned as they would be if the traducer dealt in bare-faced falsehoods. (LP 177.2)

Paul, in his second epistle to the Corinthians, expresses his faith and hope in that church, that, as they had suffered reproach for Christ's sake, they would not be left in perplexities and trials without consolation. The majority of the church were true to principle, and of firm integrity; they shared in the sorrows and anxiety of their father in the gospel, and greatly deplored the sins of some who professed the Christian faith. (LP 178.1)

Paul informed the Corinthians of his trouble in Asia, where, he says, "We were pressed out of measure, above strength, insomuch that we despaired even of life." In his first epistle he speaks of fighting with beasts at Ephesus. He thus refers to the fanatical mob that clamoured for his life. They were indeed more like furious wild beasts than men. With gratitude to God, Paul reviews his danger and his deliverance. He had thought when at Ephesus, that his life of usefulness was about to close, that the promise made to him that he should at last die for his faith, was about to be fulfilled. But God had preserved him, and his remarkable to deliverance made him hope that his labours were not at an end. (LP 178.2)

The apostle mentions his distress because of the burden of the churches. The pressure was sometimes so great that he could scarcely endure it. Outward dangers and inward fears had harassed him beyond his own power to bear. False teachers had prejudiced his brethren against him; they had made false charges against him to destroy his influence among the churches which he had raised up. But, amid all his persecutions and discouragements, he could rejoice in the consolation which he found in Christ. (LP 178.3)

His conscience did not accuse him of dishonesty or unfaithfulness to his trust. It was a cause of joy to him that he had been enabled, through the grace of God, to labour in the ministry, not using his natural eloquence, to receive the praise of men, but with simplicity and pureness, in the Spirit of God, his only aim being the good of souls. The fear of God had been ever before him; the love of Christ had ever sustained him. He had not dissembled, he had not laboured to obtain honour, or a reputation for wisdom. The wisdom given him of God he had exercised to rescue souls from the darkness of error and superstition, and to strengthen and build up the churches in the most holy faith. (LP 179.1)

He had been watchful for souls as one who must give account to God. He had not been turned from his purpose by opposition, falsehoods, the prejudice of his brethren, or the persecution of his enemies. He had given his disinterested love and labours alike to all parts of the world that he had visited. He had preached Christ with sincerity and simplicity, and the church at Corinth could sustain no charges against him. (LP 179.2)

He refers to the promise which he made them, to the effect that he would visit them before going to Macedonia. He tells them that God had not permitted him to visit them according to his intention; for his presence at that time would have precipitated a crisis which might have endangered souls. Had he visited them immediately after leaving Ephesus, he could not have withheld the reproof that their course deserved. Had they then resisted him, the power of God, through him, would have been visited upon the evil workers. God saw that this course was not proper at that time, and guided his servant in another direction. He had sent his first epistle to present before them the evil of their course, that they might manifest repentance, and take action against those who were disgracing the church by their lascivious conduct. (LP 179.3)

It was through the counsel of God that he had been turned away from his original purpose of visiting them, so that when he should go to them, it would not be with the rod of correction, but with love, approval, and the spirit of meekness. He had felt that more could be gained by his letter than by his presence at that time. He had admonished them to put away the evils existing among them, before he should visit Corinth in person. (LP 180.1)

His compassion for them is evinced by his advice that the ones who had been dealt with for their sins, having given proof of their repentance, should be received with love and kindness. They were at liberty to act in his behalf toward the repenting sinner. If they could forgive and accept the penitent, he, acting in Christ's stead, would ratify their action. Thus the apostle shows his confidence in the wisdom of the church, and recognizes their authority to receive again into their fellowship those who had once injured the cause by their wicked course, but had now become truly penitent. (LP 180.2)

Paul's opposers in the church made use against him of his failure to visit Corinth according to his promise, and argued that he was inconsistent and vacillating, changing his plans according to his convenience or inclination. But the apostle solemnly assures his Corinthian brethren that the reports were untrue, and that their knowledge of him should convince them of their injustice. His change of purpose, viewed from any standpoint, was no evidence that his doctrine was uncertain. As God was true and faithful, Paul's preaching was not in uncertainty or contradiction. After he had once declared the doctrine of Christ, he had said yea in Christ, and had never after said nay; or, in other words, had never retracted a single point which he had established by the word of God. His testimony had been straightforward, uniform, and harmonious, and exemplified by his own life. (LP 180.3)

He and his fellow-labourers had been, in their teachings and doctrine, unchangeable. Their course had been consistent and unwavering. They had ever assured their hearers that salvation was to be found alone in Christ. In matters of customs and ceremonies, the apostle declared that he had wisely met the people where they were, that none might be turned from the truth by pressing upon them that which was of no vital importance. He had carefully instructed them in the truly essential matters of the faith. (LP 181.1)

The apostle declares that their belief in the truths of the gospel was not the result of wisdom of words in their teachers. No human power had worked the great change. They had not been converted from heathenism to Paul or to any other man, but to Christianity. God had accepted them and made them his children, stamping his divine image upon their hearts through the transforming power of his Spirit and grace. But it was necessary that those among them who had perverted the gospel of Christ, and corrupted the pure doctrines taught by him, should be rebuked, to prevent them from corrupting others, and that all might be warned by seeing that the frown of God was upon those enemies of the faith. (LP 181.2)

After informing his brethren of his great anxiety in their behalf, and the relief that he experienced at the coming of Titus, the apostle breaks forth with a voice of praise and triumph: "Now thanks be unto God, which always causeth us to triumph in Christ, and maketh manifest the savour of his knowledge by us in every place. For we are unto God a sweet savour of Christ, in them that are saved, and in them that perish." The figure in the apostle's mind was that of a general returning from a victorious warfare, followed by a train of captives, according to the custom of the day. On such occasions there were persons appointed as incense-bearers. As the army marched triumphantly home, the fragrant odours, the signal of victory, were to the captives appointed to die a savour of death, in that it showed them they were nearing the time of their execution. But to those of the prisoners who had found favour with their captors, and whose lives were to be spared, it was a savour of life, in that it showed them that their freedom was near. (LP 182.1)

Paul had been an ardent opposer of the gospel, but he had been conquered by light from Heaven, and had yielded himself a captive of Christ. He had become an incense-bearer, signalling the victory of Christ over his enemies. Paul was now full of hope and faith. He felt that Satan was not to triumph over the work of God. The praise and gratitude of his heart was poured forth as a precious ointment. He determined that the name and salvation of Jesus should be diffused by him as a sweet odour. He and his fellow-labourers would celebrate their victory over the enemies of Christ and the truth. They would go forth to their duties with new zeal and courage to spread the knowledge of Christ, as a stream of fragrant incense, through the world. To those who would accept Christ, the message would be a savour of life unto life; but to those who would persist in unbelief, it would be a savour of death unto death. (LP 182.2)

Paul, feeling the overwhelming magnitude of the work, exclaims, "And who is sufficient for these things?" Who is competent to preach Christ in such a way that his enemies shall have no just cause to despise him or the message which he bears? Paul would impress upon believers the solemn responsibility of the gospel ministry. Faithfulness in preaching the word, joined to a pure and consistent life, would alone make the efforts of ministers acceptable to God, and profitable to souls. Ministers of our day, burdened with a sense of the greatness of the work, may well exclaim, with the apostle, "Who is sufficient for these things?" (LP 183.1)

Paul Revisits Corinth

It was autumn when Paul again visited Corinth. As he beheld the Corinthian towers and lofty citadel in the distance, the clouds that enshrouded the mountains and cast a shadow upon the city beneath, seemed a fitting emblem of the error and immorality which threatened the prosperity of the Christian church in that place. The mind of Paul was agitated by conflicting thoughts. He was to meet his children in the faith of the gospel. Some of them had been guilty of grievous sins. Some of his former friends had forgotten his love and the sweet friendship and confidence of earlier days. They had become his enemies, and questioned and disputed whether he was a true apostle of Christ, intrusted with the gospel. Though the majority of the church had turned from their sins and submitted to the commands of Paul, yet it could not be with them entirely as it was before their immorality. There could not exist that union, love, and confidence between teacher and people, as upon the occasion of his former visit. (LP 183.2)

There were still some in the church, who, when reproved by the apostle, had persisted in their sinful course, despising his warnings and defying his authority. The time had come when he must take decisive measures to put down this opposition. He had warned the Corinthians of his purpose to come and deal in person with the obstinate offenders: "I write to them which heretofore have sinned, and to all other, that if I come again, I will not spare; since ye seek a proof of Christ speaking in me." He had delayed his coming, to give them time for reflection and repentance. But now all who continued in their course of error and sin, must be separated from the church of Christ. They had charged Paul with timidity and weakness because of his long forbearance through love for their souls. He would now be compelled to pursue a course which would disprove this charge. (LP 184.1)

As Paul thus approaches Corinth, how striking the contrast to the close of a former journey, when Saul, "breathing out threatenings and slaughter against the disciples of the Lord," drew near to Damascus! How widely different the appearance, purposes, and spirit of Saul and Paul! Then he was intrusted with the sword of secular power, he was the agent of the Sanhedrim, the Jewish inquisitor, the exterminator of heretics, seeking victims to imprison, to scourge, or to stone. Filled with pride, he rode toward Damascus, with servants at his command to convey his prisoners to Jerusalem. Now he journeys on foot, with no outward tokens of rank or power, and no officers of justice to do his bidding. The utmost that he can do to punish those who disregard his authority, is to separate them from a society whose members are everywhere regarded as ignorant and degraded. His enemies declare that his bodily presence is weak, and his speech contemptible. Yet the apostle is not so powerless as he is represented. He bears a commission from the King of kings. All Heaven is enlisted to sustain him. His weapons are not carnal, but mighty through God to overthrow the strongholds of sin and Satan. (LP 185.1)

There has been as great a change in the spirit of the apostle, as in his outward appearance. Then he was "breathing out threatenings and slaughter against the disciples;" he "made havoc of the church;" he "haled men and women to prison;" he "compelled them to blaspheme;" he was "exceedingly mad" against all who revered the name of Jesus. His heart was filled with bitterness, malice, and hatred; yet he was so deluded as to imagine himself serving God, while in reality doing the work of Satan. Now the proud, passionate nature of Saul has been transformed by the grace of Christ. His heart yearns over his most bitter opponents. The thought of causing them pain, fills him with sorrow. He wrote to his brethren, "If I cause you grief, who is there to cause me joy?" He entreated them to spare him the necessity of dealing severely with them. All that was good and noble in the character of Saul remains, the same zeal burns upon the altar of his heart; but it has been purified, and sacredly consecrated to the service of Christ. (LP 185.2)

Paul was accompanied to Corinth by a little band of fellow-labourers, some of whom had been his companions during the months spent in Macedonia, and his assistants in gathering funds for the church at Jerusalem. He could rely upon these brethren for sympathy and support in the present crisis. And though the condition of the Corinthian church was in some respects painful and discouraging, there were also reasons for joy and gratitude. Many who had once been corrupt and degraded worshippers of idols, were now sincere and humble followers of Christ. Not a few still regarded the apostle with warm affection, as the one who had first borne to them the precious light of the gospel. As he once more greeted these disciples, and saw the proof of their fidelity and zeal, he felt that his labour had not been in vain. In the society of his beloved companions and these faithful converts, his worn and troubled spirit found rest and encouragement. (LP 186.1)

For three months Paul stayed at Corinth. During this period he not only laboured unweariedly for the church in that city, but he found time to look forward to wider missions, and to prepare for new conquests. His thoughts were still occupied with his contemplated journey from Jerusalem to Rome. To see the Christian faith firmly established at the great centre of the known world, was one of his dearest hopes and most cherished plans. A church had already been raised up at Rome, and the apostle desired to secure their co-operation in the work which he hoped to accomplish. To prepare the way for his labours among these brethren, as yet strangers, he addressed them by letter, announcing his purpose to visit Rome, and also by their aid to plant the standard of the cross in Spain. (LP 186.2)

In his Epistle to the Romans, Paul set forth the great principles of the gospel which he hoped to present in person. He stated his position on the questions which were agitating the Jewish and Gentile churches, and showed that the hopes and promises which once belonged especially to the Jews were now offered to the Gentiles. With great clearness and power he presented the doctrine of justification by faith in Christ. While addressing the Roman Christians, Paul designed to instruct other churches also; but how little could he foresee the far-reaching influence of his words! The great truth of justification by faith, as set forth in this epistle, has stood through all the ages as a mighty beacon to guide the repentant sinner into the way of life. This light scattered the darkness which enveloped Luther's mind, and revealed to him the power of the blood of Christ to cleanse from sin. It has guided thousands of sin-burdened souls to the same source of pardon and peace. Every Christian has reason to thank God for that epistle to the church at Rome. (LP 187.1)

While Paul looked with interest and hope to new fields of labour in the west, he had cause for serious apprehension concerning the fields of his former labour in the east. Tidings had been received at Corinth from the churches in Galatia, revealing a state of great confusion, and even of absolute apostasy. Judaizing teachers were opposing the work of the apostle, and seeking to destroy the fruit of his labours. (LP 188.1)

In almost every church there were some members who were Jews by birth. To these converts the Jewish teachers found ready access, and through them gained a foot-hold in the churches. It was impossible, by scriptural arguments, to overthrow the doctrines taught by Paul; hence they resorted to the most unscrupulous measures to counteract his influence and weaken his authority. They declared that he had not been a disciple of Jesus, and had received no commission from him; yet he had presumed to teach doctrines directly opposed to those held by Peter, James, and the other apostles. Thus the emissaries of Judaism succeeded in alienating many of the Christian converts from their teacher in the gospel. Having gained this point, they induced them to return to the observance of the ceremonial law as essential to salvation. Faith in Christ, and obedience to the law of ten commandments, were regarded as of minor importance. Division, heresy, and sensualism were rapidly gaining ground among the believers in Galatia. (LP 188.2)

Paul's soul was stirred as he saw the evils that threatened

speedily to destroy these churches. He immediately wrote to the Galatians, exposing their false theories, and with great severity rebuking those who had departed from the faith. (LP 188.3)

In the introduction to his epistle, he asserted his own position as an apostle, "not of men, neither by man, but by Jesus Christ, and God the Father, who raised him from the dead." He had been commissioned by the highest authority, not of earth, but in Heaven. After giving his salutation to the church, he pointedly addresses them: "I marvel that ye are so soon removed from Him that called you into the grace of Christ unto another gospel, which is not another." The doctrines which the Galatians had received, could not in any sense be called the gospel; they were the teachings of men, and were directly opposed to the doctrines taught by Christ. (LP 189.1)

The apostle continues: "But there be some that trouble you, and would pervert the gospel of Christ. But though we, or an angel from Heaven, preach any other gospel unto you than that which we have preached unto you, let him be accursed." (LP 189.2)

How different from his manner of writing to the Corinthian church is the course which he pursues toward the Galatians! In dealing with the former, he manifests great caution and tenderness, while he reproves the latter with abrupt severity. The Corinthians had been overcome by temptation, and deceived by the ingenious sophistry of teachers who presented errors under the guise of truth. They had become confused and bewildered. To teach them to distinguish the false from the true, required great caution and patience in their instructor. Harshness or injudicious haste would have destroyed his influence over those whom he sought to benefit. (LP 189.3)

In the Galatian churches, open, unmasked error was supplanting the faith of the gospel. Christ, the true foundation, was virtually renounced for the obsolete ceremonies of Judaism. The apostle saw that if these churches were saved from the dangerous influences which threatened them, the most decisive measures must be taken, the sharpest warnings given, to bring them to a sense of their true condition. (LP 190.1)

To deal wisely with different classes of minds, under varied circumstances and conditions, is a work requiring wisdom and judgment, enlightened and sanctified by the Spirit of God. The minister of Christ should learn the importance of adapting his labours to the condition of those whom he seeks to benefit. Tenderness, patience, decision, and firmness are alike needful; but they are to be exercised with proper discrimination. It is only by maintaining a close connection with God that his servants can hope to meet judiciously the trials and difficulties that still arise in the churches. (LP 190.2)

Paul had presented to the Galatians the gospel of Christ in its purity. His teachings were in harmony with the Scriptures; and the Holy Spirit had witnessed to his labours. Hence he warned his brethren to listen to nothing that should contradict the truth which they had been taught. (LP 190.3)

The apostle reverts to his own experience, of which the Galatians have been previously informed. He reminds them of his proficiency in the learning of the Jews, and his zeal for their religion. Even in early manhood he had achieved distinction as an able and zealous defender of the Jewish faith. But when Christ was revealed to him, he at once renounced all his prospective honours and advantages, and devoted his life to the preaching of the cross. He appeals to his brethren to decide whether in all this he could have been actuated by any worldly or selfish motive. He then shows them that after his conversion he had no opportunity to receive instruction from man. The doctrines which he preached had been revealed to him by the Lord Jesus Christ. After the vision at Damascus, Paul retired into Arabia, for communion with God. It was not until three years had elapsed that he went up to Jerusalem; and he then made a stay of but fifteen days, thence going out to preach the gospel to the Gentiles. He declares that he was "unknown by face unto the churches of Judea which were in Christ. But they had heard only, that he which persecuted us in times past, now preacheth the faith which once he destroyed. And they glorified God in me." (LP 190.4)

In thus reviewing his history, the apostle seeks to make apparent to all that by special manifestation of divine power he had been led to perceive and to grasp the great truths of the gospel, as presented in the Old Testament scriptures and embodied in the life of Christ on earth. It was the knowledge received from God himself which led Paul to warn and admonish the Galatians in that solemn and positive manner. He did not present the gospel in hesitancy and doubt, but with the assurance of settled conviction and absolute knowledge. In his epistle he clearly marks the contrast between being taught by man and receiving instruction direct from Christ. (LP 191.1)

The apostle urged upon the Galatians, as their only safe course, to leave the false guides by whom they had been misled, and to return to the faith which they had received from the Source of truth and wisdom. Those false teachers were hypocritical, unregenerate men; unholy in heart, and corrupt in life. Their religion consisted in a round of ceremonies, by the performance of which they expected to receive the favour of God. They had no relish for a doctrine which taught, "Except a man be born again, he cannot see the kingdom of God." Such a religion required too great a sacrifice. Hence they clung to their errors, deceiving themselves, and deceiving others. (LP 192.1)

To substitute the external forms of religion for holiness of heart and life, is still as pleasing to the unrenewed nature as in the days of the apostles. For this reason, false teachers abound, and the people listen eagerly to their delusive doctrines. It is Satan's studied effort to divert the minds of men from the one way of salvation, —faith in Christ, and obedience to the law of God. In every age the arch-enemy adapts his temptations to the prejudices or inclinations of the people. In apostolic times he led the Jews to exalt the ceremonial law, and reject Christ; at the present day he induces many professed Christians, under the pretence of honouring Christ, to cast contempt upon the moral law, and teach that its precepts may be transgressed with impunity. It is the duty of every faithful servant of God, to firmly and decidedly withstand these perverters of the faith, and to fearlessly expose their errors by the word of truth. (LP 192.2)

Paul continues to vindicate his position as the apostle of Christ, not by the will of men, but by the power of God. He describes the visit which he made to Jerusalem to secure a settlement of the very questions which are now agitating the churches of Galatia, as to whether the Gentiles should submit to circumcision and keep the ceremonial law. This was the only instance in which he had deferred to the judgment of the other apostles as superior to his own. He had first sought a private interview, in which he set the matter in all its bearings before the leading apostles, Peter, James, and John. With far-seeing wisdom, he concluded that if these men could be led to take a right position, everything would be gained. Had he first presented the question before the whole council, there would have been a division of sentiment. The strong prejudice already excited because he had not enforced circumcision on the Gentiles, would have led many to take a stand against him. Thus the object of his visit would have been defeated, and his usefulness greatly hindered. But the three leading apostles, against whom no such prejudice existed, having themselves been won to the true position, brought the matter before the council, and won from all a concurrence in the decision to leave the Gentiles free from the obligations of the ceremonial law. (LP 192.3)

Paul further disproved the accusations of his enemies, by showing that his position as an apostle of Christ had been acknowledged by the council at Jerusalem, and that in his labours among the Gentiles he had complied with the decisions of that council. Those who were seeking to destroy his influence, professed to acknowledge Peter, James, and John as pillars of the church. They were constantly extolling these apostles, and endeavouring to prove them superior to Paul in position and authority. But Paul showed that his enemies could not justify their course by a pretended regard for these apostles. While he honoured them as faithful ministers of Christ, he showed that they had not attempted to instruct him, neither had they commissioned him to preach the gospel. They were convinced that God had called him to present the truth to the Gentiles, as he had designated Peter to go especially to the Jews. Hence they acknowledged before the council Paul's divine commission, and received him as a fellow-labourer of equal position with themselves. (LP 193.1)

It was not to exalt self, but to magnify the grace of God, that Paul thus presented to those who were denying his apostleship, proof that he was "not a whit behind the very chiefest apostles." Those who sought to belittle his calling and his work were fighting against Christ, whose grace and power were manifested through Paul. Hence the apostle felt that he was forced, by the opposition of his enemies, and even by the course of his brethren, to take a decided stand to maintain his position and authority. (LP 194.1)

Paul's Last Journey to Jerusalem

Paul greatly desired to reach Jerusalem before the passover, as he would thus have an opportunity to meet the people who came from all parts of the world to attend the feast. He had a continual hope that in some way he might be instrumental in removing the prejudice of his countrymen, so that they might accept the precious light of the gospel. He was also desirous of meeting the church at Jerusalem, and bearing to them the liberalities donated by other churches to the poor brethren in Judea. And he hoped, in this visit, to bring about a firmer Christian union between the Jewish and Gentile converts to the faith. (LP 194.2)

Having completed his work at Corinth, he determined to sail directly for one of the ports on the coast of Palestine. All his arrangements had been made, and he was about to step on board the ship, when he was informed of a plot laid by the Jews to take his life. These opposers of the faith had been foiled in all their efforts to put an end to the apostle's work. Since the unsuccessful attempt to secure his condemnation by Gallio, five years before, they had been unable to arouse the people or the rulers against him. The work of the gospel had advanced, despite all their opposition. From every quarter there came accounts of the spread of the new doctrine by which Jews were released from their distinctive observances, and Gentiles admitted to share equal privileges as children of Abraham. The success attending the preaching of this doctrine, which with all their hatred they could not controvert, stung the Jews to madness. Paul, in his preaching at Corinth, presented the same arguments which he urged so forcibly in his epistles. His strong statement, "There is neither Greek nor Jew, circumcision nor uncircumcision," was regarded by his enemies as daring blasphemy. They determined that his voice should be silenced. While he was under the protection of the Roman authorities, it might not be prudent to molest him; but they would have their revenge as soon as the ship had left the shore. It would not be a difficult matter to bribe captain or sailors to do any deed of violence. (LP 195.1)

Upon receiving warning of the plot, Paul decided to change his course, and go round by Macedonia, accompanied by a sufficient number of brethren to protect him. His plan to reach Jerusalem by the passover had to be given up, but he hoped to be there at Pentecost. An overruling Providence permitted the apostle to be delayed on this occasion; for had he been present at the passover, he would have been accused of instigating a riot and massacre which was caused by the pretensions of an Egyptian impostor claiming to be the Messiah. (LP 196.1)

At Philippi Paul tarried to keep the passover. Only Luke remained with him, the other members of the company passing on to Troas to await him there. The Philippians were the most loving and true-hearted of the apostle's converts, and he enjoyed a peaceful and happy visit with them during the eight days of the feast. (LP 196.2)

The passage from Philippi was hindered by contrary winds, so that five days instead of two, the usual time, were required to reach Troas. Here Paul remained seven days, and as was his custom, improved the opportunity to encourage and strengthen the believers. (LP 196.3)

Upon the last evening of his tarry with them, the brethren "came together to break bread." The fact that their beloved teacher was about to depart, had called together a larger company than usual. They assembled in an upper room on the third story, the coolest and pleasantest place for such a gathering on that warm spring evening. The nights were then dark, but many lights were burning in the chamber. Paul's mind was impressed with a sense of the perils that awaited him, and the uncertainty of again meeting with his brethren; he had matters of great interest and importance to present before them; and in the earnestness of his love and solicitude for them, he preached until midnight. (LP 196.4)

On the broad sill of a window whose shutters had been thrown open, sat a youth named Eutychus. In this perilous position he sank into a deep slumber, and at last fell from his seat into the court below. The discourse was interrupted. All was alarm and confusion. The youth was taken up dead, and many gathered about him with cries and mourning. But Paul, passing through the affrighted company, clasped him in his arms, and sent up an earnest prayer that God would restore the dead to life. The prayer was granted. Above the sound of mourning and lamentation the apostle's voice was heard, saying, "Trouble not yourselves, for his life is in him." With rejoicing, yet in deep humility at this signal manifestation of God's power and mercy, the believers again assembled in the upper chamber. They partook of the communion, and then Paul continued his discourse till the dawn of day. Eutychus was now fully restored, and they brought him into the congregation and were not a little comforted. (LP 197.1)

The time had now come when the company must separate. The brethren who accompanied Paul went on board the ship, which was about to set sail. The apostle, however, chose to take the nearer route by land between Troas and Assos, and rejoin his companions on shipboard at the latter city. The difficulties and dangers connected with his proposed visit to Jerusalem, the attitude of that church toward himself and his work, as well as the condition of the churches and the interests of the gospel work in other fields, presented subjects for earnest, anxious thought, and he chose this lonely walk that he might have opportunity for reflection and communion with God. (LP 197.2)

As the travellers sailed southward from Assos, they passed the city of Ephesus, so long the scene of the apostle's labours. He had greatly desired to visit the church there; for he had important instruction and counsel to impart to them. But upon consideration he relinquished this purpose. Any delay might render it impossible for him to reach Jerusalem by Pentecost. On arriving at Miletus, however, he learned that the ship would be detained for a short time, and he immediately sent a message to the elders of the Ephesian church to come to him. The distance was but thirty miles, and the apostle hoped to secure at least a few hours' intercourse with these men upon whom the prosperity of the church must largely depend. (LP 198.1)

When they had come, in answer to his call, he thus addressed them: "Ye know, from the first day that I came into Asia, after what manner I have been with you at all seasons, serving the Lord with all humility of mind, and with many tears, and temptations, which befell me by the lying in wait of the Jews; and how I kept back nothing that was profitable unto you, but have showed you, and have taught you publicly, and from house to house, testifying both to the Jews, and also to the Greeks, repentance toward God, and faith toward our Lord Jesus Christ." (LP 198.2)

Paul had ever exalted the divine law. He had presented before the people their great sin in transgressing its precepts, and their duty to repent of such transgression. He had showed them that there was in law no power to save them from the penalty of disobedience. While they should repent of their sins, and humble themselves before God, whose holy law they had broken, and whose just wrath they had thus incurred, they must exercise faith in the blood of Christ as their only ground of pardon. The Son of God died as their sacrifice, and ascended to Heaven to stand as their advocate before the Father. By repentance and faith they might be freed from the condemnation of sin, and through the grace of Christ be enabled henceforth to render obedience to the law of God. (LP 199.1)

The apostle continued: "And now, behold, I go bound in the spirit unto Jerusalem, not knowing the things that shall befall me there, save that the Holy Ghost witnesseth in every city, saying that bonds and afflictions abide me. But none of these things move me, neither count I my life dear unto myself, so that I might finish my course with joy, and the ministry, which I have received of the Lord Jesus, to testify the gospel of the grace of God. And now, behold, I know that ye all, among whom I have gone preaching the kingdom of God, shall see my face no more." Paul had not designed to bear this testimony; but while he was speaking, the Spirit of inspiration came upon him, confirming his former fears that this would be his last meeting with his Ephesian brethren. He therefore left with them his counsel and admonition as his will and testament to be carried out by them when they should see him no more. (LP 199.2)

"Wherefore I take you to record this day, that I am pure from the blood of all men; for I have not shunned to declare unto you all the counsel of God." No fear of giving offense, no desire for friendship or applause, could lead him to withhold the words which God had given him for their instruction, warning, or correction. The minister of Christ is not to present to the people those truths that are most pleasing, while he withholds others which might cause them pain. He should watch with deep solicitude the development of character. If he sees that any of his flock are cherishing sin, he must as a faithful shepherd give them instruction from God's word applicable to their case. Should he permit them in their self-confidence to go on in sin unwarned, he would be held responsible for their blood. The pastor who fulfils his high commission must instruct his people in every point of the Christian faith, all that they ought to be or to do, in order to stand perfect in the day of God. (LP 200.1)

The apostle admonishes his brethren: "Take heed therefore unto yourselves, and to all the flock, over the which the Holy Ghost hath made you overseers, to feed the church of God, which he hath purchased with his own blood." Could ministers of the gospel constantly bear in mind that they are dealing with the purchase of the blood of Christ, they would have a deeper sense of the solemn importance of their work. They are to take heed unto themselves and to the flock. Their own example must illustrate and enforce their instructions. Those who teach others the way of life should be careful to give no occasion for the truth to be evil spoken of. As representatives of Christ, they are to maintain the honour of his name. By their devotion, their purity of life, their godly conversation, they should prove themselves worthy of their calling. By a right example they may exert an influence which words alone could not have, to encourage faith and holiness, fervent love, devotion, and integrity among those for whom they labour. God requires of all his servants fearlessness in preaching the word, fidelity in exemplifying its precepts, however it may be despised, reviled, opposed, or persecuted. Every faithful teacher of the truth will at the close of his labours be able to say with Paul, "I am pure from the blood of all men." (LP 200.2)

The Holy Spirit revealed to the apostle the dangers which would assail the church at Ephesus: "I know this, that after my departing shall grievous wolves enter in among you, not sparing the flock. Also of your own selves shall men arise, speaking perverse things, to draw away disciples after them." Paul trembled for the church as he looked forward to the attacks which they must suffer from external and internal foes. It is while the husbandman sleeps that tares are sown; while the shepherds are neglecting their duty, the wolf finds entrance to the fold. With solemn earnestness he bids his brethren guard vigilantly their sacred trust. He points them for an example to his own unwearied labours: "Therefore watch, and remember that by the space of three years I ceased not to warn every one night and day and with tears." (LP 201.1)

"And now, brethren," he continued, "I commend you to God, and to the word of his grace, which is able to build you up, and to give you an inheritance among all them which are sanctified. I have coveted no man's silver, or gold, or apparel." Some of the Ephesian brethren were wealthy; but Paul had never sought to receive personal benefit from them. It was no part of his message to call attention to his own wants. He declares, "These hands have ministered unto my necessities, and to them that were with me." Amid his arduous labours and extensive journeys for the cause of Christ, he was able, not only to supply his own wants, but to spare something for the support of his fellow-labourers and the relief of the worthy poor. This was accomplished only by unremitting diligence and the closest economy. Well might he point to his own example, as he said, "I have showed you all things, how that so labouring ye ought to support the weak, and to remember the words of the Lord Jesus, how he said, It is more blessed to give than to receive." (LP 201.2)

"And when he had thus spoken, he kneeled down, and prayed with them all. And they all wept sore, and fell on Paul's neck, and kissed him, sorrowing most of all for the words which he spake, that they should see his face no more." By his fidelity to the truth, Paul inspired intense hatred; but he also inspired the deepest and warmest affection. Sadly the disciples followed him to the ship, their hearts filled with anxiety, both for his future and for their own. The apostle's tears flowed freely as he parted from these brethren, and after he had embarked there came to him from the shore the sound of weeping. With heavy hearts the elders turned homeward, knowing that they could expect no further help from him who had felt so deep an interest and laboured with so great zeal for them and for the church under their care. (LP 202.1)

From Miletus the travellers had a prosperous voyage to Patara, on the southwest shore of Asia Minor, where they left their ship, and took passage on another vessel bound for the coast of Phenicia. Again they enjoyed favourings winds, and, fully two weeks before the Pentecost, they landed at Tyre, where the ship was to unload its cargo. (LP 203.1)

The apostle's anxiety about reaching Jerusalem was now at an end. There were a few disciples at Tyre, and having succeeded in searching them out, he spent the next week with them. The Holy Spirit had revealed to these brethren something of the dangers which awaited Paul at Jerusalem, and they endeavoured to dissuade him from his purpose. But the same Spirit which had warned him of afflictions, bonds, and imprisonment, still urged him forward, a willing captive. When the week was over, Paul left them. So strong a hold upon their affections had he gained in this brief period, that all the brethren, with their wives and children, started with him to conduct him on his way; and before he stepped on board the ship, they knelt side by side upon the shore and prayed, he for them, and they for him. (LP 203.2)

Pursuing their journey southward, the travellers arrived at Caesarea, and "entered into the house of Philip the evangelist, which was one of the seven, and abode with him." Here Paul tarried until the very eve of the feast. These few peaceful, happy days were the last days of perfect freedom which he was for a long time to enjoy. Before he should enter upon the stormy scenes that awaited him at Jerusalem, the Lord graciously refreshed his spirit with this season of rest and happy communion. (LP 203.3)

Philip the evangelist was bound to Paul by ties of the deepest sympathy. A man of clear discernment and sterling integrity, Philip had been the first to break away from the bondage of Jewish prejudice, and thus had helped prepare the way for the apostle's work. It was Philip who preached the gospel to the Samaritans; it was Philip who had the courage to baptize the Ethiopian eunuch. For a time the history of these two workers had been closely intertwined. It was the violent persecution of Saul the Pharisee that had scattered the church at Jerusalem, and destroyed the effectiveness of the organization of the seven deacons. The flight from Jerusalem had led Philip to change his manner of labour, and resulted in his pursuing the same calling to which Paul gave his life. Precious hours were these that Paul and Philip spent in each other's society; thrilling were the memories that they recalled of the days when the light which had shone upon the face of Stephen upturned to Heaven as he suffered martyrdom, flashed in its glory upon Saul the persecutor, bringing him, a helpless suppliant, to the feet of Jesus. (LP 204.1)

Soon after the apostle's arrival at Caesarea, the prophet Agabus came down from Judea. He had been warned by the Holy Spirit, of the fate which awaited Paul, and in the symbolic manner of the ancient prophets he loosened the apostle's girdle, and with it bound his own hands and feet, saying, "So shall the Jews at Jerusalem bind the man that owneth this girdle, and shall deliver him into the hands of the Gentiles." The companions of Paul had been aware that his visit to

Jerusalem would be attended with great peril; but they had not foreseen the full extent of the danger. Now apprehension had become certainty; and to the perils to be encountered from the Jews were added the horrors of a Roman imprisonment. They earnestly entreated Paul to stay where he was, and permit them to go to Jerusalem to deliver the contributions from the Gentile churches. The brethren at Caesarea also united their prayers and tears with those of his companions: Why should he face this great peril? Why expose his precious life to the malice of the Jews? Would it not be presumptuous to go, after receiving definite warning from the Spirit of God? (LP 204.2)

The apostle was deeply moved by the entreaties of his beloved brethren. To human judgment he had sufficient reason to relinquish his plan as unwise. But he felt that he was moving in obedience to the will of God, and he could not be deterred by the voice of friends, or even the warning of the prophet. He would not swerve from the path of duty to the right hand nor to the left. He must follow Christ, if need be, to prison and to death. His tears fell not for himself, but in sympathy with his brethren, upon whom his determination had brought so great sorrow. "What mean ye to weep, and to break mine heart?" he exclaimed; "for I am ready not to be bound only, but also to die at Jerusalem, for the name of the Lord Jesus." Seeing that they caused him pain, without changing his purpose, the brethren ceased their importunity, saying only, "The will of the Lord be done." (LP 205.1)

The time soon came for the brief stay at Caesarea to end, and, accompanied by some of the Caesarean brethren, Paul and his company set out for Jerusalem, their hearts deeply shadowed by the presentiment of coming evil. The crowd at the annual feasts was so great that strangers often failed to find shelter within the city, and were obliged to resort to booths outside the walls. But, according to previous arrangements, the apostle and his attendants were to be entertained at the house of "one Mnason, of Cyprus, an old disciple." (LP 206.1)

Since his conversion, Paul's visits to Jerusalem had always been attended with anxiety, and with a feeling of remorse as he gazed upon scenes that recalled his former life. There was the school of Gamaliel, where he had received his education, the synagogue in which he worshipped, the house where the high priest had given him his commission to Damascus, the spot where the blood of Stephen had witnessed for Christ. As the apostle gazed upon the place for martyrdom, the scene in all its vividness rose up before him. Was he going forward to a similar fate? Never had he trod the streets of Jerusalem with so sad a heart as now. He knew that he would find few friends and many enemies. In the crowds around him were thousands whom the very mention of his name would excite to madness. He was in the city which had been the murderer of the prophets, which had rejected and slain the Son of God, and over which now hung the threatenings of divine wrath. Remembering how bitter had been his own prejudice against the followers of Christ, he felt the deepest pity for his deluded countrymen. And yet how little hope could he feel that he would be able to benefit them! The same blind wrath which had once burned in his own heart, was now with untold power kindling the hearts of a whole nation against him. (LP 206.2)

And he could not count upon the sympathy and support of even his own brethren in the faith. The unconverted Jews who had so closely followed upon his track, had not been slow to circulate the most unfavourable reports at Jerusalem, both personally and by letter, concerning him and his work, and some, even of the apostles and elders, had received these reports as truth, making no attempt to contradict them, and manifesting no desire to harmonize with him. Yet in the midst of discouragements, the apostle was not in despair. He trusted that the Voice which had spoken to his own heart would yet speak to the hearts of his countrymen, and that the Master whom his fellow-disciples loved and served would yet unite their hearts with his in the one work of the gospel. (LP 207.1)

Meeting with the Elders

"And when we were come to Jerusalem, the brethren received us gladly." Thus Luke describes the reception of the apostle to the Gentiles on his arrival at Jerusalem. Although Paul everywhere encountered prejudice, envy, and jealousy, he also found hearts that were open to receive the glad tidings which he brought, and that loved him for the sake of Christ and the truth. Yet, cheering as was the kindly greeting he received, it could not remove his anxiety as to the attitude of the church at Jerusalem toward himself and his work. Their real feelings would be more fully seen in the meeting with the elders of the church, to take place on the morrow. (LP 207.2)

Paul longed to be fully united with these. He had done all in his power to remove the prejudice and distrust so unjustly excited because he presented the gospel to the Gentiles without the restrictions of the ceremonial law. Yet he feared that his efforts might be in vain, and that even the liberal offerings of which he was the bearer might fail to soften the hearts of the Jewish brethren. He knew that the men whom he was to encounter were persons of great firmness and decision, and he looked forward with considerable apprehension to this meeting with them; yet he could not avoid the ordeal, trying though it might be. He had come to Jerusalem for no other purpose than to remove the barriers of prejudice and misunderstanding which had separated them, and which had so greatly obstructed his labours. (LP 208.1)

On the day following Paul's arrival, the elders of the church, with James at their head, assembled to receive him and his fellow-travellers as messengers from the Gentile churches. Paul's first act was to present the contributions with which he had been intrusted. He had been careful to guard against the least occasion for suspicion in the administration of his trust, by causing delegates to be elected by the several churches to accompany him as joint trustees of the funds collected. These brethren were now called forward, and one by one they laid at the feet of James the offerings which the Gentile churches had freely given, although often from their deepest poverty. Here was tangible proof of the love and sympathy felt by these new disciples for the mother-church, and their desire to be in harmony with the Jewish brethren. Here was evidence also, that Paul had faithfully fulfilled the promise given, when at the council years before he had been urged to remember the poor. (LP 208.2)

These contributions had cost the apostle much time and anxious thought, and much wearisome labour. They far exceeded the expectations of the Jewish elders, and might have been expected to call forth warm expressions of gratitude and appreciation. But Paul's half-acknowledged fears as to the manner in which the gift would be received were realized. He could only find comfort in the consciousness that he had done his duty, and had encouraged in his converts a spirit of generosity and love. (LP 209.1)

After the presentation of the gifts, Paul gave the brethren an account of his manner of labour, and its results. He had on former occasions stood before the same assembly, in the same city. It was before the same audience at the apostolic council (Acts 15) years before, that he related his experience in his conversion, and the great work which God had wrought through him among the Gentiles. The Spirit of the Lord then witnessed to the word spoken, and under its influence the council yielded their prejudices, and expressed themselves as in harmony with the position of the apostle, and sent an address to the churches to that effect. But the same battle was again to be fought, the same prejudices once more to be met. (LP 209.2)

Paul now gave his brethren an account of his labours since he parted with them four years before, and "declared particularly what things God had wrought among the Gentiles by his ministry." As he described the work at Ephesus, which had resulted in raising up that large church in the very stronghold of heathenism, none could listen without interest. But he necessarily touched upon points that would irritate those who had cherished prejudice against him. He could not recount his experience in Galatia without stating the difficulties which he had encountered from those Judaizing teachers who had attempted to misrepresent his teaching and pervert his converts. In describing the work at Corinth, he could but mention those who had spread confusion and strife among the church there. Yet he related all with great gentleness and courtesy, carefully avoiding everything that would unnecessarily wound his brethren, and dwelling especially upon topics where he knew they could harmonize. (LP 210.1)

The effort was not without good results. The Spirit of God impressed the minds of the brethren and affected their hearts. The tidings of the progress of the gospel, the evidence that the power of God was working with the apostle's efforts, softened their feelings toward Paul, and convinced them that their prejudice against him was unfounded; and they glorified God for the wonders of his grace. At the close of Paul's address, the brethren joined in a season of solemn praise, and the Amen, expressive of their hearty sanction of his work, was swelled by many voices. (LP 210.2)

But beneath this apparent harmony, prejudice and dissatisfaction were still smouldering. Some in the church were still striving to mould Christianity after the old customs and ceremonies that were to pass away at the death of Christ. They felt that the work of preaching the gospel must be conducted according to their opinions. If Paul would labour in accordance with these ideas, they would acknowledge and sustain his work; otherwise they would discard it. (LP 211.1)

The elders of the church had been at fault in allowing themselves to be influenced by the enemies of the apostle. But when they heard from his own lips an account of the work he had been doing, it assumed a different aspect. They could not condemn his manner of labour; they were convinced that it bore the signet of Heaven. The liberal contributions from the new churches he had raised up, testified to the power of the truth. They saw that they had been held in bondage by the Jewish customs and traditions, and that the work of the gospel had been greatly hindered by their efforts to maintain the middle wall of partition between Jew and Gentile. (LP 211.2)

Now was the golden opportunity for these leading men to frankly confess that God had wrought through Paul, and that they were wrong in permitting the reports of his enemies to create jealousy and prejudice against him. But instead of doing justice to the one whom they had injured, they still appeared to hold him responsible for the existing prejudice, as though he had given them cause for such feelings. They did not nobly stand in his defence, and endeavour to show the disaffected party their error; but they threw the burden wholly upon Paul, counselling him to pursue a course for the removal of all misapprehension. They responded to his testimony in these words: "Thou seest, brother, how many thousands of Jews there are which believe, and they are all zealous of the law. And they are informed of thee, that thou teachest all the Jews which are among the Gentiles to forsake Moses, saying that they ought not to circumcise their children, neither to walk after the customs. What is it therefore? the multitude must needs come together; for they will hear that thou art come. Do therefore this that we say to thee: We have four men which have a vow on them; them take, and purify thyself with them, and be at charges with them, that they may shave their heads; and all may know that those things, whereof they were informed concerning thee, are nothing; but that thou thyself also walkest orderly, and keepest the law. As touching the Gentiles which believe, we have written and concluded that they observe no such thing, save only that they keep themselves from things offered to idols, and from blood, and from strangled, and from fornication." (LP 211.3)

The brethren hoped that by this act Paul might give a decisive contradiction of the false reports concerning him. But while James assured Paul that the decision of the former council (Acts 15) concerning the Gentile converts and the ceremonial law still held good, the advice given was not consistent with that decision which had also

128

been sanctioned by the Holy Spirit. The Spirit of God did not prompt this advice. It was the fruit of cowardice. By non-conformity to the ceremonial law, Christians would bring upon themselves the hatred of the unbelieving Jews, and expose themselves to severe persecution. The Sanhedrim was doing its utmost to hinder the progress of the gospel. Men were chosen by this body to follow up the apostles, especially Paul, and in every possible way oppose them in their work. Should the believers in Christ be condemned before the Sanhedrim as breakers of the law, they would bring upon themselves swift and severe punishment as apostates from the Jewish faith. (LP 212.1)

Here is a decisive refutation of the claims so often made, that Christ and his apostles violated the Sabbath of the fourth commandment. Could the sin of Sabbath breaking have been fastened upon Christ or Stephen or others who died for their faith, men would not have been suborned to bear false witness against them to furnish some pretext for their condemnation. One such instance of transgression of the law would have placed the Christians in the power of their enemies. Their carefulness to show the utmost respect for customs and ceremonies of minor importance is an evidence that it would have been impossible for them to violate the Sabbath of the fourth commandment without suffering the severest penalty. (LP 213.1)

The disciples themselves yet cherished a regard for the ceremonial law, and were too willing to make concessions, hoping by so doing to gain the confidence of their countrymen, remove their prejudice, and win them to faith in Christ as the world's Redeemer. Paul's great object in visiting Jerusalem was to conciliate the church of Palestine. So long as they continued to cherish prejudice against him, they were constantly working to counteract his influence. He felt that if he could by any lawful concession on his part win them to the truth, he would remove a very great obstacle to the success of the gospel in other places. But he was not authorized of God to concede so much as they had asked. This concession was not in harmony with his teachings, nor with the firm integrity of his character. His advisers were not infallible. Though some of these men wrote under the inspiration of the Spirit of God, yet when not under its direct influence they sometimes erred. It will be remembered that on one occasion Paul withstood Peter to the face because he was acting a double part. (LP 213.2)

When we consider Paul's great desire to be in harmony with his brethren, his tenderness of spirit toward the weak in faith, his reverence for the apostles who had been with Christ, and for James, the brother of the Lord, and his purpose to become all things to all men as far as he could do this and not sacrifice principle,—when we consider all this, it is less surprising that he was constrained to deviate from his firm, decided course of action. But instead of accomplishing the desired object, these efforts for conciliation only precipitated the crisis, hastened the predicted sufferings of Paul, separated him from his brethren in his labours, deprived the church of one of its strongest pillars, and brought sorrow to Christian hearts in every land. (LP 214.1)

Paul a Prisoner

On the following day Paul proceeded to comply with the counsel of the elders. There were among the believers in Jerusalem at that time four persons who were under the Nazarite vow, (Numbers 6) the term of which had nearly expired. Certain sacrifices for purification were yet to be offered, which were so costly as to be impossible for a very poor man. It was considered by the Jews a pious act for a wealthy man to defray the necessary expenses and thus assist his poorer brethren to complete their vow. This, Paul had consented to do for the four Christian Nazarites. The apostle himself was poor, working with his own hands for his daily bread, yet he willingly incurred this expense, and accompanied the Nazarites to the temple to unite with them in the ceremonies of the seven days of purification. (LP 214.2)

Those who had counselled Paul to perform this act of concession had not fully considered the great peril to which he would be exposed. At this season, strangers from all regions of the world thronged the streets of Jerusalem, and delighted to congregate in the temple courts. As Paul, in the fulfilment of his commission, had borne the gospel to the Gentiles, he had visited many of the world's largest cities, and was well known to thousands who came from foreign parts to attend the feast. For him to enter the temple on a public occasion was to risk his life. For several days he passed in and out among the worshippers, apparently unnoticed; but before the close of the specified period, as he was conversing with the priest concerning the sacrifices to be offered, he was recognized by some of the Jews from Asia. These men had been defeated in their controversy with him in the synagogue at Ephesus, and had become more and more enraged against him as they witnessed his success in raising up a Christian church in that city. They now saw him where they had not supposed that he would trust himself,—within the very precincts of the temple. Now he was in their power, and they determined to make him suffer for his boldness. (LP 215.1)

With the fury of demons they rushed upon him, crying, "Men of Israel, help! This is the man that teacheth all men everywhere against the people, and the law, and this place." And as the people in great excitement flocked to the scene another accusation was added to excite their passions to the highest pitch,—"and further brought Greeks also into the temple, and hath polluted this holy place." (LP 216.1)

By the Jewish law, it was a crime punishable with death for an uncircumcised person to enter the inner courts of the sacred edifice. As Paul had been seen in the city in company with Trophimus, an Ephesian, it was conjectured that he had brought him into the temple.

This he had not done, and being himself a Jew, his act in entering the temple was no violation of the law. But though the charge was wholly false, it served to stir up the popular prejudice. As the cry was taken up and borne through the temple courts, the vast throngs gathered there were thrown into the wildest excitement. The news quickly spread through Jerusalem, "and all the city was moved, and the people ran together." (LP 216.2)

That an apostate from Israel should presume to profane the temple at the very time when thousands had come from all parts of the world to worship there, excited the fiercest passions of the mob. Only their reverence for the temple saved the apostle from being torn in pieces on the spot. With violent blows and shouts of vindictive triumph, they dragged him from the sacred inclosure. Now that they had him in their power, they were determined not to lose their prey. He should be stoned to death, as Stephen had been years before. They had already reached the court of the Gentiles, and the Levites had closed the gates behind them, lest the holy place should be polluted with blood, when they were interrupted in their murderous designs. (LP 216.3)

News had been carried to Claudius Lysias, the commander of the Roman garrison, that all Jerusalem was in an uproar. Lysias well knew the turbulent elements with which he had to deal, and with his officers and a strong force of armed men he rushed down to the temple court. Ignorant of the cause of the tumult, but seeing that the rage of the multitude was directed against Paul, the Roman captain concluded that he must be the Egyptian rebel who had so successfully eluded their vigilance. He commanded that Paul be seized, and bound between two soldiers, a hand being chained to each. He then questioned those who seemed to be leaders in the tumult as to who their prisoner was, and of what crime he had been guilty. Many voices were at once raised in loud and angry accusation; but on account of the uproar the chief captain could obtain no satisfactory information, and he ordered that the prisoner be removed to the castle, where were the Roman barracks. (LP 217.1)

The rage of the multitude was unbounded when they saw their prey about to be taken from their grasp; and they surged and pressed so closely about Paul that the soldiers were compelled to bear him in their arms up the staircase which led from the temple. Priests and people were actuated by the same Satanic spirit that moved them thirty years before to clamour for the blood of the Son of God. From the staircase and from the crowd below again echoed the deafening shout, "Away with him! Away with him!" (LP 217.2)

In the midst of the tumult the apostle remained calm and self-possessed. His mind was stayed upon God, and he knew that angels of Heaven were about him. He could not leave the temple without making an effort to set the truth before his countrymen. He therefore turned to the commanding officer, and in a deferential manner addressed him in Greek, saying, "May I speak with thee?" In astonishment Lysias inquired if he was indeed mistaken in supposing the prisoner to have been the ring-leader of a band of robbers and murderers in the late rebellion. In reply, Paul declared that he was no Egyptian, but a Jew of "Tarsus, a city in Cilicia, a citizen of no mean city," and begged that he might be permitted to speak to the people. The Lord had given his servant an influence over the Roman officer, and the request was granted. (LP 218.1)

"Paul stood on the stairs, and beckoned with the hand unto the people." The gesture attracted their attention, while his bearing commanded respect. The scene changed as suddenly as when Christ drove the traffickers from the temple courts. Quiet fell upon the sea of heads below, and then Paul addressed the throng in the Hebrew language, saying, "Men, brethren, and fathers, hear ye my defence which I make now unto you." At the sound of that holy tongue, there was "a great silence," and in the universal hush, he continued:— (LP 218.2)

"I am verily a man which am a Jew, born in Tarsus, a city in Cilicia, yet brought up in this city at the feet of Gamaliel, and taught according to the perfect manner of the law of the fathers, and was zealous toward God, as ye all are this day." None could deny the apostle's statements, and there were many present who could testify to their truthfulness. He then acknowledged his former zeal in persecuting "this way unto the death," and narrated the circumstances of his wonderful conversion, telling his hearers how his own proud heart had been brought to bow to the crucified Nazarene. Had he attempted to enter into argument with his opponents, they would have stubbornly refused to listen to his words; but this relation of his experience was attended with a convincing power that for the time seemed to soften and subdue their hearts. (LP 219.1)

He then endeavoured to show that his work among the Gentiles had not been from choice. He had desired to labour for his own nation; but in that very temple the voice of God had spoken to him in holy vision, directing his course "far hence, unto the Gentiles." Hitherto the people had given close attention, but when he reached the point in his history where he was appointed Christ's ambassador to the Gentiles, their fury broke forth anew. Accustomed to look upon themselves as the only people favoured of God, they could not endure the thought that the despised Gentiles should share the privilege which had hitherto belonged exclusively to themselves. National pride bore down every argument which could influence their reason or command their reverence. An outburst of rage interrupted his speech, as all with one voice cried out, "Away with such a fellow from the earth; for it is not fit that he should live!" In their excitement they flung off their garments, as they had done years before at the martyrdom of Stephen, and threw dust into the air with frantic violence. (LP 219.2)

This fresh outbreak threw the Roman captain into great perplexity. He had not understood Paul's Hebrew address, and concluded from the general excitement that his prisoner must be guilty of some great crime. The loud demands of the people that Paul be delivered into their hands made the commander tremble. He ordered him to be immediately taken unto the barracks and examined by scourging, that he might be forced to confess his guilt. (LP 220.1)

The body of the apostle was stretched out, like that of a common malefactor, to receive the lashes. There was no friend to stand by him. He was in a Roman barrack, surrounded only by brutal soldiers. But, as on a former occasion at Philippi, he now rescued himself from this degradation, and gained advantage for the gospel, by appealing to his rights as a Roman citizen. (LP 220.2)

He quietly said to the centurion who had been appointed to superintend this examination, "Is it lawful for you to scourge a man that is a Roman, and uncondemned?" The centurion immediately went and told the chief captain, saying, "Take heed what thou doest; for this man is a Roman." (LP 220.3)

On hearing this, Lysias was alarmed for himself. A Roman might not be punished before he had been legally condemned, nor punished in this manner at all. The chief captain well knew how stringent were the laws protecting the rights of citizenship, and that if the statement were true he had, in his proceedings against Paul, violated these laws. (LP 220.4)

He immediately went in person to the prisoner, and questioned him concerning the truth of the centurion's report. Paul assured him that he was indeed a Roman citizen; and when the officer exclaimed, "With a great sum obtained I this freedom," Paul declared, "But I was free born." The preparation for torture went no farther, and those commissioned to conduct his examination left him. Paul was, however, still held in custody, as the nature of his offense had not yet been inquired into. (LP 221.1)

On the next day the chief captain summoned a meeting of the Jewish Sanhedrim, with the high priest, and brought Paul down from the castle, under the protection of a sufficient force to guard against any attempt upon his life. The apostle now stood in the presence of that council of which he himself had been a member,—that council by which Stephen had been condemned. The memory of that scene, and of his own efforts to secure the condemnation of the servant of Christ, came vividly before his mind. As he looked upon those who were to be his judges, he recognized many who had been his associates in the school of Gamaliel, and who had also united with him in persecuting the disciples of Jesus. They were now as eager to put Paul to death as they had been to destroy Stephen. (LP 221.2)

The apostle's bearing was calm and firm. The peace of Christ, ruling in his heart, was expressed upon his countenance. But his look of conscious innocence offended his accusers, and when he fearlessly addressed them, "Men and brethren, I have lived in all good conscience before God until this day," their hatred was kindled afresh, and the high priest ordered him to be smitten upon the mouth. At this inhuman command, Paul exclaimed, "God shall smite thee, thou whited wall, for sittest thou to judge me after the law, and commandest me to be smitten contrary to the law?" These words were not an outburst of passion. Under the influence of the Holy Spirit, Paul uttered a prophetic denunciation similar to that which Christ had uttered in rebuking the hypocrisy of the Jews. The judgment pronounced by the apostle was terribly fulfilled when the iniquitous and hypocritical high priest was murdered by assassins in the Jewish war. But the bystanders regarded the words of Paul as profane, and exclaimed with horror, "Revilest thou God's high priest?" Paul answered, with his usual courtesy, "I wist not, brethren, that he was the high priest; for it is written, Thou shalt not speak evil of the ruler of thy people." (LP 221.3)

Paul was convinced that he could not hope for a fair trial and just decision at this tribunal. And his natural penetration and shrewdness enabled him to take advantage of the circumstances. The Sanhedrim council was made up of Pharisees and Sadducees, who had long been at variance upon the doctrine of the resurrection. Knowing this, the apostle cried out, in clear, decided tones, "Brethren, I am a Pharisee, the son of a Pharisee; of the hope and resurrection of the dead I am called in question." (LP 222.1)

These words, appealing to the sympathies of those who agreed with him in regard to the resurrection, brought a change in the council. The two parties began to dispute among themselves, and thus the strength of their opposition against Paul was broken; for however well united they were in warring against the gospel, they were divided by an insurmountable barrier in other matters of religious faith. The Pharisees flattered themselves that they had found in Paul a champion against their powerful rivals; and their hatred against the Sadducees was even greater than their hatred against Christ and his apostles. With great vehemence they now began to vindicate Paul, using nearly the same language that Gamaliel had used many years before: "We find no evil in this man; but if a spirit or an angel hath spoken to him, let us not fight against God." (LP 222.2)

The sentence was hardly completed before the judgment hall

became a scene of the wildest confusion. The Sadducees were eagerly trying to get possession of the apostle, that they might put him to death, and the Pharisees were as eagerly trying to protect him. Again it seemed that he would be torn in pieces by the angry combatants. Lysias, being informed of what was taking place, immediately gave orders to his soldiers to bring the prisoner without delay back to the fortress. (LP 223.1)

Thus closed the scenes of this eventful day. Evening found Paul still in the Roman barrack, the rude soldiery his sole companions, their brutal jests and revolting blasphemy the only sounds that fell upon his ear. He was not now nerved up by the presence of his enemies, nor was he supported by the sympathy of his friends. The future seemed enveloped in darkness. He feared that his course might not have been pleasing to God. Could it be that he had made a mistake after all in this visit to Jerusalem? Had his great desire to be in union with his brethren led to this disastrous result? (LP 223.2)

The position which the Jews as God's professed people occupied before an unbelieving world, caused the apostle intense anguish of spirit. How would those heathen officers look upon their conduct,— claiming to be worshippers of Jehovah, and assuming sacred office, yet giving themselves up to the control of blind, unreasoning passion, seeking to destroy even their brethren who dared to differ from them in religious faith, and turning their most solemn deliberative council into a scene of strife and wild confusion such as Roman senators or magistrates would not stoop to engage in. The cause of his God had been reproached, his national religion brought into disrepute. (LP 224.1)

And now he was in prison, and his enemies, in their desperate malice, would resort to any means to put him to death. Could it be that his work for the churches was closed, and that ravening wolves were to enter in, not sparing the flock? The cause of Christ was near his heart, and with deep anxiety he contemplated the perils of the scattered churches, exposed to the persecutions of just such men as he had encountered in the Sanhedrim council. In distress and discouragement he wept and prayed. The Lord was not unmindful of his servant. He had guarded him from the murderous throng in the temple courts, he had been with him before the Sanhedrim council, he was with him in the fortress, and was pleased to reveal himself to his faithful witness. As on trying occasions several times before, Paul was now comforted and encouraged by a vision in the night season. Such as visitation had been granted him in the house of Aquila and Priscilla at Corinth, when he was contemplating leaving the city for a more safe and prosperous field. And now the Lord stood by him and said, "Be of good cheer, Paul; for as thou hast testified of me in Jerusalem, so must thou bear witness also at Rome." Paul had long looked forward to a visit to Rome; he greatly desired to witness for Christ there, but had felt that his purposes were frustrated by the enmity of the Jews. He little thought even now, that it would be as a prisoner of the Lord, that he would go to Rome. (LP 224.2)

In the peaceful hours of the night, while the Lord was visiting his discouraged servant, the enemies of Paul were eagerly plotting his destruction. "And when it was day, certain of the Jews banded together, and bound themselves under a curse, saying that they would neither eat nor drink till they had killed Paul. And they were more than forty which had made this conspiracy." Here was such a fast as the Lord through Isaiah had condemned many years before,—a fast "for strife and debate, and to smite with the fist of wickedness." The Jews thus sought to give to their diabolical plan the sanction of religion. Having fortified themselves by their dreadful oath, they came to the chief priests and members of the Sanhedrim, and made known their purpose. It was proposed to request that Paul be again brought before the court as if for a further investigation of his case, and that the assassins would lie in wait and murder him while on his way from the fortress. Such was the horrible crime masked under a show of religious zeal. Instead of rebuking the Satanic scheme, the priests and rulers eagerly acceded to it. Paul had spoken the truth when he compared Ananias to a whited sepulchre. (LP 225.1)

The next day the plot would have been carried into effect, had not God by his providence interposed to save the life of his servant. When Peter had been made a prisoner and condemned to death, the brethren had offered earnest prayer to God day and night for his deliverance. But no such interest was manifested in behalf of him who was looked upon as an apostate from Moses, a teacher of dangerous doctrines. It was not to the elders whose counsel had brought him into this dangerous position, but to the watchful sympathy of a relative, that Paul owed his escape from a violent death. (LP 226.1)

A nephew of the apostle, to whom he was strongly attached, heard of the murderous conspiracy, and without delay reported the matter to his uncle. Paul immediately called for one of the centurions, and requested him to take the young man to the commandant, saying that he had important information to give him. The youth was accordingly brought in before Claudius Lysias, who received him kindly, and taking him aside, inquired the nature of his message. The young man related the particulars of the conspiracy, and with deep feeling entreated the commandant not to grant the request which would be surely made, that Paul be again brought before the council. Lysias listened with close attention. He saw the difficulties of the situation, and instantly formed his plans. Choosing, however, not to reveal them, he dismissed the youth, with the single admonition: "See thou tell no man that thou hast showed these things to me." (LP 226.2)

When the young man had gone, the commandant "called unto him two centurions, saying, Make ready two hundred soldiers to go to Caesarea, and horsemen threescore and ten, and spearmen two hundred, at the third hour of the night; and provide them beasts, that they may set Paul on, and bring him safe unto Felix the governor." (LP 227.1)

Lysias gladly improved this opportunity to get Paul off his hands. He was the object of so great animosity, and his presence created so widespread an excitement, that a riot might occur among the people at any time, with consequences dangerous to the commandant himself. The Jews as a people were in a state of excitement and irritation, and tumults were of frequent occurrence. A short time previous, a Roman knight of far higher rank than Lysias himself, had been violently taken and dragged by the maddened Jews around the walls of Jerusalem, and finally beheaded, because he received a bribe from the Samaritans. Upon the suspicion of similar crimes, other high officials had been imprisoned and disgraced. Should Paul be murdered, the chief captain might be charged with having been bribed to connive at his death. There was now sufficient reason to send him away secretly, and thus get rid of an embarrassing responsibility. (LP 227.2)

It was important that no time be lost. At nine in the evening, the body of soldiers, with Paul in the midst, marched out of the fortress, and through the dark and silent streets of the city, and at a rapid pace pursued their journey toward Caesarea. At Antipatris, thirty-five miles from Jerusalem, the travellers halted. There was now little danger of attack, and in the morning the four hundred foot-soldiers were sent back to Jerusalem, while the horsemen continued their journey. (LP 227.3)

The distance from Antipatris to Caesarea was but twenty-five miles, and it was in the broad light of day that Paul, attended by "threescore and ten horsemen," entered the city. How unlike his present escort was the humble Christian company that had attended him on the journey from Caesarea but a few days before! Notwithstanding his changed surroundings, he was recognized by Philip and others of his Christian associates, whose hearts were shocked and saddened at the swift realization of their forebodings. (LP 228.1)

The centurion in charge of the detachment delivered his prisoner to Felix the governor, also presenting a letter with which he had been intrusted by the chief captain:— (LP 228.2)

"Claudius Lysias unto the most excellent governor Felix sendeth greeting. This man was taken of the Jews, and should have been killed of them; then came I with an army, and rescued him, having understood that he was a Roman. And when I would have known the cause wherefore they accused him, I brought him forth into their council; whom I perceived to be accused of questions of their law, but to have nothing laid to his charge worthy of death or of bonds. And when it was told me how that the Jews laid wait for the man, I sent straightway to thee, and gave commandment to his accusers also to say before thee what they had against him. Farewell." (LP 228.3)

After reading the communication, Felix inquired to what province the prisoner belonged, and being informed that he was of Cilicia, he ordered him to be kept in Herod's judgment hall, stating that he would hear the case when the accusers also should come from Jerusalem. (LP 228.4)

The case of Paul was not the first in which a servant of God had found among the heathen an asylum from the malice of the professed people of Jehovah. In their rage against Paul, the Jews had added another crime to the dark catalogue which marked the history of that people. They had still further hardened their hearts against the truth, and had rendered their doom more certain. (LP 229.1)

There are but few who perceive the full import of the words of Christ, when in the synagogue at Nazareth he announced himself as the Anointed One. He declared his mission to comfort, bless, and save the sorrowing and the sinful, and then, seeing that pride and unbelief controlled the hearts of his hearers, he reminded them how God had in time past turned away from his chosen people, because of their unbelief and rebellion, and had manifested himself to those in a heathen land who had not rejected the light from Heaven. The widow of Sarepta and Naaman the Syrian had lived up to all the light they had. Hence they were accounted more righteous than God's chosen people who had backslidden from him, and sacrificed principle to convenience and worldly honour. (LP 229.2)

It is impossible for the worldly and pleasure-loving to rightly value the messages of warning and reproof which God sends to correct the errors of his people. They cannot distinguish between the earnestness and zeal of the faithful servant, and the trifling, superficial spirit of him who is unfaithful. One declares that the sword is coming; the other puts far off the evil day. One faithfully reproves sin; the other excuses and palliates it. As the professed people of God depart from him and lose the simplicity of the faith, the words of his messengers seem to them unnecessarily harsh and severe. They cherish prejudice and unbelief, and finally place themselves fully on Satan's side. His suggestions seem pleasant and palatable; they are controlled, in spirit and opinion, by the arch-deceiver, and having permitted him to direct their thoughts, they soon permit him to direct their actions. (LP 229.3)

Christ presented before the assembly at Nazareth a fearful truth when he declared that with backsliding Israel there was no safety for the faithful messenger of God. They would not know his worth, or appreciate his labours. While they professed to have great zeal for the honour of God and the good of Israel, they were the worst enemies of both. They were by precept and example leading the people farther and farther from obedience to God and purity and simplicity of faith,—leading them where he could not reveal himself as their defence in the day of trouble. God sent Elijah to the widow of Sarepta, because he could not trust him with Israel. (LP 230.1)

These cutting reproofs, though presented by the Majesty of Heaven, the Jews of Nazareth refused to hear. They had but a moment before witnessed to the gracious words that proceeded from his lips; the Spirit of God was speaking to their hearts; but the instant a reflection was cast upon them,—at the first intimation that persons of other nations could be more worthy of the favour of God than they,—those proud, unbelieving Jews were frantic with rage. They would have taken the life of the Son of God, had not angels interposed for his deliverance. Those men of Nazareth manifested the same spirit toward Christ which their forefathers had manifested toward Elijah. Blinded by Satan, they could not perceive the divine character of the Son of God, or appreciate the truth and purity of his instructions. (LP 230.2)

The Saviour's words of reproof to the men of Nazareth apply in the case of Paul, not only to the unbelieving Jews, but to his own brethren in the faith. Had the leaders in the church fully surrendered their feelings of bitterness toward the apostle, and accepted him as one specially called of God to bear the gospel to the Gentiles, the Lord would have spared him to them to still labour for the salvation of souls. He who sees the end from the beginning, and who understands the hearts of all, saw what would be the result of the envy and jealousy cherished toward Paul. God had not in his providence ordained that Paul's labours should so soon end; but he did not work a miracle to counteract the train of circumstances to which their own course gave rise. (LP 231.1)

The same spirit is still leading to the same results. A neglect to appreciate and improve the provisions of divine grace, has deprived the church of many a blessing. How often would the Lord have prolonged the life of some faithful minister, had his labours been appreciated. But if the church permit the enemy of souls to pervert their understanding, so that they misrepresent and misinterpret the words and acts of the servant of Christ; if they allow themselves to stand in his way and hinder his usefulness, the Lord removes from them the blessing which he gave. (LP 231.2)

Satan is constantly working through his agents to dishearten and destroy those whom God has chosen to accomplish a great and good work. They may be ready to sacrifice even their own life for the advancement of the cause of Christ, yet the great deceiver will suggest doubts, distrust, jealousy, concerning them, that if entertained will undermine confidence in their integrity of character, and thus cripple their usefulness. Too often he succeeds in working through their own brethren, to bring upon them such sorrow and anguish of heart that God graciously interposes to give his persecuted servants rest. After the hands are folded upon the pulseless breast, after the voice of warning and encouragement is silent, then death may accomplish that which life has failed to do; then the obdurate may be aroused to see and prize the blessings they have cast from them. (LP 232.1)

The great work for us as Christians is not to criticise the character and motives of others, but to closely examine our own heart and life, to jealously guard ourselves against the suggestions of Satan. We should bear in mind that it is not the hearers of the law that are justified before God, but the doers of the law. If the principles of God's law rule in our hearts, we shall have the spirit of Christ; we shall manifest in our daily life that mercy which is better than sacrifice. Every Christian must be a learner in the school of Christ; and there is need of diligent and persevering effort to reach that standard of righteousness which God's word requires. Every one has a work to do to learn the lessons of justice, humility, patience, purity, and love. These traits of character are more precious in the sight of our Lord than offerings of gold or silver. They are more acceptable to him than the most costly sacrifice. (LP 232.2)

There is the same dislike of reproof and correction among the professed people of God today as in the days of our Saviour. There is the same disposition to lean toward the world and to follow its mocking shadows. The presence of ambitious, selfish, time-serving members is imperilling the church, whose greatest danger is from worldly conformity. Such members are constantly exerting an influence to unite the church more closely with the world. They are doing the work of Satan. When God sends his servants with words of warning or counsel, these traitors to their holy trust reject the Heaven-sent message, and thus not only slight the grace of Christ themselves, but lead others also to smother their convictions and lose the proffered blessing. (LP 233.1)

By resistance to the truth, the hearts of such are settling down into the fatal hardness of confirmed impenitence. They are deceiving themselves, and deceiving others. They are Christians by profession; they pay outward homage to Christ; they unite in the services of the sanctuary; and yet the heart, whose loyalty alone Jesus prizes, is estranged from him. They have a name to live, but are dead. They are left to the darkness they have chosen,—the blackness of eternal night. (LP 233.2)

It is a fearful thing for those who profess to be children of God, to cross the line of demarcation that should separate the church from the world. Such are Satan's most effective agents. He works through them with decision, zeal, and persistency, to devise and execute such enormities against those who are true to God, as the common sinner would seem incapable of. The very light they have slighted makes their darkness tenfold greater than it otherwise would be. When men refuse to accept the light which God in mercy sends them, they know not where they are going. They take only one step at a time away from the right path; but these successive steps lead directly to perdition. They place themselves on Satan's ground, and his spirit controls them. They cannot perceive the great change in themselves. None are transformed at once; but they enter Satan's school instead of the school of Christ, and the great deceiver educates them to do his work. (LP 233.3)

Trial at Caesarea

Five days after Paul's arrival at Caesarea, his accusers also came down from Jerusalem, accompanied by one Tertullus, an orator whom they had engaged as their counsel. The case was granted a speedy hearing. Paul was brought before the assembly, and Tertullus proceeded to specify the charges against him. This wily orator judged that flattery would have more influence upon the Roman governor than the simple statements of truth and justice. He therefore began his speech with praise of Felix: "Seeing that by thee we enjoy great quietness, and that very worthy deeds are done unto this nation by thy providence, we accept it always, and in all places, most noble Felix, with all thankfulness." (LP 234.1)

Tertullus here descended to bare-faced falsehood. The character of Felix was base and contemptible. It was said that he "practised all kinds of lust and cruelty with the power of a king and the temper of a slave." It is true that he had rendered some service to the nation by his vigilance in ridding the country of robbers, and he pursued and drove away the Egyptian rebel for whom Claudius Lysias had hastily mistaken Paul; but his acts of cruelty and oppression caused him to be universally hated. The treacherous cruelty of his character is shown by his brutal murder of the high priest Jonathan, to whom he was largely indebted for his own position. Jonathan, though really little better than Felix himself, had ventured to expostulate with him for some of his acts of violence, and for this, the procurator had caused him to be assassinated while employed in his official duties in the temple. (LP 235.1)

An example of the unbridled licentiousness that stained his character is seen in his alliance with Drusilla, which was consummated about this time. Through the deceptive arts of Simon Magus, a Cyprian sorcerer, Felix had induced this princess to leave her husband and to become his wife. Drusilla was young and beautiful, and, moreover, a Jewess. She was devotedly attached to her husband, who had made a great sacrifice to obtain her hand. There was little indeed to induce her to forego her strongest prejudices and to bring upon herself the abhorrence of her nation for the sake of forming an adulterous connection with a cruel and elderly profligate. Yet the Satanic devices of the conjurer and the betrayer succeeded, and Felix accomplished his purpose. (LP 235.2)

The Jews present at Paul's examination shared in the general feeling toward Felix; yet so great was their desire to gain his favour in order to secure the condemnation of Paul, that they assented to the flattering words of Tertullus. These men in holy office, robed in the sacerdotal garments, were very exact in the observance of customs and ceremonies, very scrupulous to avoid outward pollution, while the soul-temple was defiled with all manner of iniquity. The outward contact with anything deemed unclean was a great offense in their eyes, while the murder of Paul was considered a justifiable act. What an illustration of the blindness that can come upon the human mind! Here were the representatives of those who claimed to be God's covenant people. Like the barren fig-tree, they were clothed with pretentious leaves, but destitute of the fruits of holiness; "having a form of godliness, but denying the power thereof." Filled with malice toward a pure and good man, seeking by every means to take his life, and extolling a vindictive profligate! (LP 236.1)

There are many today who estimate character in the same manner. Prompted by the adversary of all righteousness, they call evil good, and truth falsehood. It is as the prophet has described,— "Truth is fallen in the street, and equity cannot enter." It is because such is the condition and spirit of the world that God calls upon his people to come out and be separate. Those who mingle with the world will come to view matters from the worldling's stand-point, instead of seeing as God sees. "What communion hath light with darkness? And what concord hath Christ with Belial? or what part hath he that believeth with an infidel? God's people will see as he sees. The pure and good will be honoured and loved by those who are good. (LP 236.2)

In his speech against Paul, Tertullus charged that he was a pestilent fellow, who created sedition among the Jews throughout the world, and who was consequently guilty of treason against the emperor; that he was a leader of the sect of Nazarenes, and chargeable with heresy against the laws of Moses; and that he had profaned the temple, virtually an offense not only against the Jewish but the Roman law, which protected the Jews in their religious worship. He then falsely stated that Lysias, the commandant of the garrison, had violently taken Paul from the Jews as they were about to judge him by their ecclesiastical law, and had thus improperly forced them to bring the matter before Felix. These lying statements were skilfully designed to induce the procurator to deliver Paul over to the Jewish court. All the charges were vehemently supported by the Jews present, who made no effort to conceal their hatred against the prisoner. (LP 237.1)

Felix had sufficient penetration to read the disposition and character of Paul's accusers. He perceived the motives of their flattery, and saw also that they had failed to substantiate their charges. Turning to the accused, he beckoned to him to answer for himself. Paul wasted no words in fulsome compliments, but simply stated that he could the more cheerfully defend himself before Felix, since the latter had been so long a procurator, and therefore had so good an understanding of the laws and customs of the Jews. Step by step he then refuted the charges brought against him. He declared that he had caused no disturbance in any part of Jerusalem, nor had he profaned the sanctuary: "They neither found me in the temple disputing with any man, neither raising up the people, neither in the synagogues, nor in the city; neither can they prove the things whereof they now accuse me." (LP 237.2)

While confessing that "after the way which they call heresy" he had worshipped the God of his fathers, he asserted that he had never swerved from his belief in the law and the prophets, and that in conformity with the Scriptures he held the faith of the resurrection of the dead; and he further declared that it was the ruling purpose of his life to "have always a conscience void of offense toward God and toward man." (LP 238.1)

In a candid, straightforward manner he then stated the object of his visit to Jerusalem, and the circumstances of his arrest and trial: "Now after many years I came to bring alms to my nation, and offerings. Whereupon certain Jews from Asia found me purified in the temple, neither with multitude nor with tumult. Who ought to have been here before thee, and object, if they had aught against me. Or else let these same here say, if they have found any evil doing in me, while I stood before the council, except it be for this one voice, that I cried standing among them, Touching the resurrection of the dead, I am called in question by you this day." (LP 238.2)

The apostle spoke with earnestness and evident sincerity, and his words carried with them a conviction of their truthfulness. Moreover, his statements were in harmony with the letter of Claudius Lysias. Felix himself had so long resided at Caesarea—where the Christian religion had been known for many years— that he had a better knowledge of that religion than the Jews supposed, and he was not deceived by their representations. The words of Paul made a deep impression upon his mind, and enabled him to understand still more clearly the motives of the Jews. He would not gratify them by unjustly condemning a Roman citizen, neither would he give him up to them to be put to death without a fair trial. Yet Felix knew no higher motive than self-interest, and his love of praise and desire for promotion controlled him. Fear of offending the Jews held him back from doing justice in the case, and releasing a man whom he knew to be innocent. He deferred all further action in the case until Lysias should be present, saying, "When Lysias the chief captain shall come down, I will know the uttermost of your matter." (LP 238.3)

Paul was again placed in charge of a centurion, but with orders that he should enjoy greater freedom than before his examination.

While it was necessary for him to be strictly guarded, as a protection from the plots of the Jews, and also because he was still a prisoner, his friends were to be allowed to visit him and minister to his comfort. (LP 239.1)

It was not long after this that Felix and his wife Drusilla summoned Paul to a private interview. Drusilla felt considerable interest in the apostle, having heard an account of him from her husband, and she was desirous of hearing the reasons for his belief in Christ. Thus Paul, as a prisoner of the Lord, had an opportunity to present the truths of the gospel to some souls whom he could not otherwise have approached. A cruel and licentious Roman governor and a profligate Jewish princess were to be his sole audience. They were now waiting to listen to truths which they had never listened to before, which they might never hear again, and which, if rejected, would prove a swift witness against them in the day of God. (LP 239.2)

Paul considered this God-given opportunity, and he improved it faithfully. He knew that the man and woman before him had the power to put him to death, or to preserve his life; yet he did not address them with praise or flattery. He knew that his words would be to them a savour of life or of death, and, forgetting all selfish considerations, he sought to arouse them to the peril of their souls. (LP 240.1)

The gospel message admits of no neutrality. It counts all men as decidedly for the truth or against it; if they do not receive and obey its teachings, they are its enemies. Yet it knows no respect of person, class, or condition. It is addressed to all mankind who feel their need of its gracious invitations. Said Christ: "I came not to call the righteous, but sinners to repentance." (LP 240.2)

The apostle felt that whoever might listen to his words, the gospel had a claim upon them; they would either stand among the pure and holy around the great white throne, or with those to whom Christ should say: "Depart from me, ye that work iniquity." He knew that he must meet every hearer before the tribunal of Heaven, and must there render an account, not only for all that he had said and done, but for the motive and spirit of his words and deeds. (LP 240.3)

So violent and cruel had been the course of Felix, that few had ever before dared even to intimate to him that his character and conduct were not faultless. But Paul had no such fears. With perfect respect for the position of his hearers, he plainly declared his faith in Christ, and the reasons for that faith, and was thus led to speak particularly of those virtues essential to Christian character, but of which the haughty pair before him were so strikingly destitute. (LP 241.1)

He presented before his hearers the character of God—his righteousness, justice, and equity —and the nature and obligation of his

146

law. He clearly showed man's duty to live a life of sobriety and temperance, keeping the passions under the control of reason, in conformity to God's law, and preserving the physical and mental powers in a healthful condition. A day of judgment would surely come, when all would be rewarded according to the deeds done in the body. Wealth, position, or honorary titles would be powerless to elevate man in the favour of God, or to ransom him from the slavery of sin. This life was his period of probation, in which he was to form a character for the future, immortal life. Should he neglect his present privileges and opportunities, it would prove an eternal loss; no new probation would be vouchsafed to him. All who should be found unholy in heart or defective in any respect when judged by the law of God, would suffer the punishment of their guilt. (LP 241.2)

Paul dwelt especially upon the far-reaching claims of God's law. He showed how it extends to the deep secrets of man's moral nature, and throws a flood of light upon that which has been concealed from the sight and knowledge of men. What the hands may do or the tongue may utter, —what the outer life can exhibit,—but imperfectly reveals man's moral character. The law extends to the thoughts, motives, and purposes of the heart. The dark passions that lie hidden from the sight of men, the jealousy, revenge, hatred, lust, and wild ambition, the evil deeds meditated upon in the dark recesses of the soul, yet never executed for want of opportunity,—of all these God's law makes a record. Men may imagine that they can safely cherish these secret sins; but it is these that sap the very foundation of character; for out of the heart "are the issues of life." (LP 241.3)

Paul then endeavoured to direct the minds of his hearers to the one great Sacrifice for sin. He pointed back to those sacrifices that were shadows of good things to come, and then presented Christ as the antitype of all those ceremonies, —the object to which they pointed as the one only source of life and hope for fallen man. Holy men of old were saved by faith in the blood of Christ. As they saw the dying agonies of the sacrificial victims, they looked across the gulf of ages to the Lamb of God that was to take away the sin of the world. (LP 242.1)

God justly claimed the love and obedience of all his creatures. He had given them in his law a perfect standard of right. But they forgot their Maker, and chose to follow their own way in opposition to his will. They had returned enmity for a love that was as high as Heaven and as broad as the universe. God could not bring down his law to meet the standard of wicked men, neither could man, fallen by sin, meet the demands of the law by a blameless character and life. But by faith in Christ the sinner could be cleansed from his guilt, and he enabled to render obedience to the law of his Maker. God did not bestow his grace to lessen the binding claims of the law, but to establish it. "Mercy and truth are met together; righteousness and peace have kissed each other." (LP 242.2)

Thus Paul the prisoner urged upon Jew and Gentile the claims of the divine law, and presented Jesus, the despised Nazarene, as the Son of God, the world's Redeemer. The Jewish princess well understood the sacred character of that law which she had so shamelessly transgressed; but her prejudice against the Man of Calvary steeled her heart against the word of life. But Felix, who had never before listened to the truth, was deeply agitated as the Spirit of God sent conviction to his soul. Conscience, now aroused, made her voice heard. He felt that Paul's words were true. Memory went back over the guilty past. With terrible distinctness came up before him the secrets of his early life of lust and bloodshed, and the black record of his later years,—licentious, cruel, rapacious, unjust, steeped with the blood of private murders and public massacres. Never before had the truth been thus brought home to his heart. Never before had his soul been thus filled with terror. The thought that all the secrets of his career of crime were open before the eye of God, and that he must be judged according to his deeds, caused him to tremble with guilty dread. (LP 243.1)

But instead of permitting his convictions to lead him to repentance, he eagerly sought to dismiss these disagreeable reflections. The interview with Paul was cut short. "Go thy way for this time," he said, "when I have a convenient season, I will call for thee." (LP 243.2)

How wide the contrast between the course of Felix and that of the jailer of Philippi! The servants of the Lord were brought in bonds to the jailer, as was Paul to Felix. The evidence they gave of being sustained by a divine power, their rejoicing under suffering and disgrace, their fearless calmness when the earth was reeling with the earthquake's shock, and their spirit of Christlike forgiveness, sent conviction to the jailer's heart. He did not, like Felix, banish these convictions, but with trembling and in deep humility inquired the way of salvation; and having learned the way, he walked in it, with all his house. Felix trembled, but did not repent; the jailer with trembling confessed his sins and found pardon. Felix bade the Spirit of God depart; the jailer joyfully welcomed it to his heart and to his house. The one cast his lot with the workers of iniquity; the other chose to become a child of God and an heir of Heaven. (LP 244.1)

For two years no further action was taken against Paul, yet he remained a prisoner. Felix several times visited him, and listened attentively to his words. But the real motive for this apparent friendliness was a desire for gain, and he intimated to Paul that by the payment of a large sum of money he might secure his release. The apostle, however, was of too noble a nature to free himself by a bribe. He was innocent of all crime, and he would not stoop to evade the law. Furthermore, he was himself too poor to pay such a ransom, had he been disposed to do so, and he would not, in his own behalf, appeal to the sympathy and generosity of his converts. He also felt that he was in the hands of God, and he would not interfere with the divine purposes respecting himself. (LP 244.2)

Toward the close of this time there arose a fearful strife among the population of Caesarea. There had been frequent disputes, which had become a settled feud, between the Jews and the Greeks, concerning their respective rights and privileges in the city. All the splendour of Caesarea, its temples, its palaces, and its amphitheatre, were due to the ambition of the first Herod. Even the harbour, to which Caesarea owed all its prosperity and importance, had been constructed by him at an immense outlay of money and labour. The Jewish inhabitants were numerous and wealthy, and they claimed the city as theirs, because their king had done so much for it. The Greeks, with equal persistency, maintained their right to the precedence. (LP 245.1)

Near the close of the two years, these dissensions led to a fierce combat in the market-place, resulting in the defeat of the Greeks. Felix, who sided with the Gentile faction, came with his troops and ordered the Jews to disperse. The command was not instantly obeyed by the victorious party, and he ordered his soldiers to fall upon them. Glad of an opportunity to indulge their hatred of the Jews, they executed the order in the most merciless manner, and many were put to death. As if this were not enough, Felix, whose animosity toward the Jews had increased every year, now gave his soldiers liberty to rob the houses of the wealthy. (LP 245.2)

These daring acts of injustice and cruelty could not pass unnoticed. The Jews made a formal complaint against Felix, and he was summoned to Rome to answer their charges. He well knew that his course of extortion and oppression had given them abundant ground for complaint, but he still hoped to conciliate them. Hence, though he had a sincere respect for Paul, he decided to gratify their malice by leaving him a prisoner. But all his efforts were in vain; though he escaped banishment or death, he was removed from office, and deprived of the greater part of his ill-gotten wealth. Drusilla, the partner of his guilt, afterward perished, with their only son, in the eruption of Vesuvius. His own days were ended in disgrace and obscurity. (LP 246.1)

A ray of light from Heaven had been permitted to shine upon this wicked man, when Paul reasoned with him concerning righteousness, temperance, and a judgment to come. That was his Heaven-sent opportunity to see and to forsake his sins. But he said to the Spirit of God, "Go thy way for this time; when I have a convenient season, I will call for thee." He had slighted his last offer of mercy. He was never to receive another call from God. (LP 246.2)

Paul Appeals to Caesar

The governor appointed in the place of Felix, was Porcius Festus, a far more honourable ruler. He had a higher sense of the responsibility of his position, and, refusing to accept bribes, he endeavoured to administer justice. Three days after his arrival at Caesarea, Festus went up to Jerusalem. Here he was speedily importuned by the Jews, who lost no time in presenting their accusations against Paul. The long imprisonment of Paul had not softened their malignant hatred, nor shaken their determination to take his life. They urged that he should be tried by the Sanhedrim, and requested that he be immediately sent to Jerusalem. Although this request was so plausible, it concealed a deep-laid plot. They were resolved not to leave him even to the decision of the Sanhedrim council, but to summarily dispose of the case by murdering him on the way. (LP 246.3)

At Caesarea, Festus had already met the popular clamour against Paul, but at Jerusalem the demand for his death was not merely the cry of the mob. A deputation of the most honourable personages of the city, headed by the high priest, formally presented the request concerning Paul, not doubting that this new and inexperienced official could be moulded at pleasure, and that to gain their favour he would readily grant all that they desired. (LP 247.1)

But Festus was not a man who would sacrifice justice to gain popularity. The Jews soon found that they were dealing with one who more resembled a Gallio than a Felix. With keen insight he penetrated the motive that prompted their request, and courteously declined to send for Paul. He stated, however, that he himself would soon return to Caesarea, and that he would there give them a fair opportunity to prefer their charges against him. (LP 247.2)

This was not what they wanted. Their former defeat was not forgotten. They well knew that in contrast with the calm bearing and forcible arguments of the apostle, their own malignant spirit and baseless accusations would appear in the worst possible light. Again they urged that Paul be brought to Jerusalem for trial. But Festus answered decidedly that whatever their practice might be, it was not the custom of the Romans to sacrifice any man's life merely to gratify his accusers, but to bring the accused face to face with his accusers before impartial witnesses, and to give him an opportunity to defend himself. God in his providence controlled the decision of Festus, that the life of the apostle might be preserved. (LP 247.3)

Finding their purposes defeated, the Jewish leaders at once organized a powerful deputation to present their accusations at the court of the procurator. After a stay of eight or ten days in Jerusalem, Festus returned to Caesarea, and the next day took his seat at the tribunal to hear the case. The Jews, on this occasion being without a lawyer, preferred their charges themselves. The trial was a scene of passionate, unreasoning clamour on the part of the accusers, while Paul with perfect calmness and candour clearly showed the falsity of their statements. (LP 248.1)

The Jews repeated their charges of heresy, treason, and sacrilege, but could bring no witnesses to sustain them. They endeavoured to intimidate Festus as they had once intimidated Pilate by their pretended zeal for the honour of Caesar. But Festus had too thorough an understanding of the Roman law to be deceived by their clamour. He saw that the real question in dispute related wholly to Jewish doctrines, and that, rightly understood, there was nothing in the charges against Paul, could they be proved, that would render him worthy of death, or even imprisonment. Yet he saw clearly the storm of rage that would be created if Paul were not to be condemned or delivered into their hands. (LP 248.2)

He looked with disgust upon the scene before him,—the Jewish priests and rulers, with scowling faces and gleaming eyes, forgetting the dignity of their office, eagerly reiterating their accusations, in tones that grew louder and louder until the tribunal rang with their cries of rage. Heartily desiring to end it all, he turned to Paul, who stood calm and self-possessed before his adversaries, and asked if he was willing to go to Jerusalem under his protection, to be tried by the Sanhedrim. (LP 249.1)

This would virtually transfer the matter from Roman to Jewish jurisdiction. Paul knew that he could not look for justice from that people who were by their crimes bringing down upon themselves the wrath of God. Like the prophet Elijah, he would be safer among the heathen than with those who had rejected the light from Heaven, and hardened their hearts against the truth. When his life had been imperilled by the wrath of his enemies, it was heathen magistrates that had been his deliverers. Gallio, Lysias, and even Felix, had not hesitated to proclaim his innocence, while every Jewish tribunal had condemned him, without proving his guilt. (LP 249.2)

Paul was weary of strife, weary of the fierce reiteration of charges, again and again refuted, and as often renewed. His active spirit could ill endure the repeated delays and wearing suspense of his trial and imprisonment. How repulsive to him had been the daily contact with the coarse, idle, unprincipled soldiery, the frequent sounds of contention, and the rumours of strife and bloodshed between Jew and Gentile. He had nothing more to hope for from Jewish priests or rulers; but as a Roman citizen he had one special privilege, he could appeal to Caesar, and for a time, at least, his enemies would be kept at bay. (LP 249.3)

To the governor's question, Paul made answer, I stand at Caesar's tribunal. Here, and not before the Sanhedrim, I ought to be judged. Turning to the procurator, he appealed to him directly: Even you, Festus, are convinced that no charges have been sustained against me. I have never in any respect wronged the Jews. If I have committed any crime, it is not against them, but against the emperor; and if found guilty, I do not refuse to die. But if the accusations they bring against me cannot be proved, no one can give me into their power as a favour. I appeal unto Caesar. (LP 250.1)

Festus knew nothing of the conspiracies of the Jews to murder Paul, and he was surprised at this appeal to Caesar. It was not flattering to the pride of the Roman procurator, that the first case brought before him should be thus referred to higher authority. However, the words of the apostle put a stop to the proceedings of the court. Felix held a brief consultation with his counsel, and all agreeing that the appeal was legally admissible, he said to the prisoner: "Hast thou appealed unto Caesar? unto Caesar shalt thou go." This was said in a tone and manner which seemed to imply that Paul little knew what an appeal to Caesar meant. (LP 250.2)

Once more the hatred born of Jewish bigotry and self-righteousness had driven the servant of God to turn for protection to a heathen ruler. It was the same hatred that forced the prophet Elijah to flee for succour to the widow of Sarepta; that constrained the heralds of the gospel to proclaim their message to the Gentiles. It is the same spirit that the people of God in this age have yet to meet. In the great crisis through which they are soon to pass, they will become better acquainted with the experience of Paul. Among the professed followers of Christ, there is the same pride, formalism, vainglory, selfishness, and oppression, that existed in the Jewish nation. Before the warfare shall be ended and the victory won, we as a people are to experience trials similar to those of Paul. We shall encounter the same hardness of heart, the same cruel determination, the same unyielding hatred. (LP 250.3)

Men professing to be representatives of Christ will take a course similar to that taken by priests and rulers in their treatment of Paul. All who would fearlessly serve God according to the dictates of their own conscience, will need moral courage, firmness, and a knowledge of God and his word, to stand in that evil day. Persecution will again be kindled against those who are true to God; their motives will be impugned, their best efforts misinterpreted, their names cast out as evil. Then will it come to pass, as foretold by Christ, that whoever shall seek to destroy the faithful, will think that he is doing God service.

Then Satan will work with all his fascinating power, to influence the heart and becloud the understanding, to make evil appear good, and good evil. Then it is that he is through his agents to "show great signs and wonders, insomuch that, if it were possible, they shall deceive the very elect." (LP 251.1)

God would have his people prepared for the soon-coming crisis. Prepared or unprepared, we must all meet it. Only those whose characters are thoroughly disciplined to meet the divine standard will be able to stand firm in that testing time. But when enemies shall be on every side, watching them for evil, the God of Heaven will be watching his precious jewels for good. When secular rulers unite with the ministers of religion to come between God and our conscience, then those who cherish the fear of God will be revealed. When the darkness is deepest, then the light of a noble, Godlike character will shine the brightest. When every other trust fails, then it will be seen who have an abiding trust in God. (LP 252.1)

The stronger and purer the faith of God's people, and the firmer their determination to obey him, the more will Satan stir up the rage of those who claim to be righteous, while they trample upon the law of God. In that coming emergency, rulers and magistrates will not interpose in behalf of God's people. There will be a corrupt harmony with all who have not been obedient to the law of God. In that day, all time-servers, all who have not the genuine work of grace in the heart, will be found wanting. It will require the firmest trust, the most heroic purpose, to hold fast the faith once delivered to the saints. (LP 252.2)

Address before Agrippa

As Paul had appealed to Caesar, it was the duty of Festus to see that he was sent to Rome. Some time passed, however, before a suitable ship could be provided, and as other prisoners were to be sent with Paul, the consideration of their cases also occasioned some delay. This delay gave Paul an opportunity to present the reasons of his faith before the principal men of Caesarea, both Jews and Gentiles, and also before the last of the Herods who bore the title of Jewish kings. (LP 252.3)

"After certain days King Agrippa and Bernice came unto Caesarea, to salute Festus." Knowing that Agrippa was well versed in the laws and customs of the Jews, Festus during this visit called his attention to the case of Paul, as a prisoner left in bonds by Felix. Agrippa's interest was aroused by the account which Festus gave of the case, and he expressed a desire to see and hear Paul for himself. Accordingly the next day was fixed upon as the time for such an interview. Paul was not now to defend himself before a new tribunal, but merely to gratify the curiosity of a private audience; to furnish an hour's entertainment for the procurator's distinguished guests, and for an invited company representing the wealth and nobility of Caesarea. The chief officers of the army were to be present, and also the leading citizens of the town, and Festus determined to make it an occasion of the most imposing display, in honour of his visitors. (LP 253.1)

In all the pomp and splendour of royalty, Agrippa and Bernice went to the audience-room, attended by a train of followers in the costly apparel of Eastern display. Proudly the haughty ruler with his beautiful sister swept through the assembly, and seated himself by the procurator's side. At his command, Paul, still manacled as a prisoner, was led in, and the king gazed with cold curiosity upon him, now bowed and pale from sickness, long imprisonment, and continual anxiety. (LP 253.2)

What a contrast was there presented! Agrippa and Bernice were destitute of the traits of character which God esteems. They were transgressors of his law, corrupt in heart and in life. God and angels abhorred their course of sin. But because they possessed, in a limited degree, power and position, they were the favourites of the world. That aged prisoner, standing chained to his soldier guard, presented nothing imposing or attractive in his dress or appearance, that the world should pay him homage. Yet this man, apparently without friends or wealth or position, had an escort that worldlings could not see. Angels of Heaven were his attendants. Had the glory of one of those shining messengers flashed forth, the pomp and pride of royalty would have paled before it; king and courtiers would have been stricken to the earth, as were the Roman guards at the sepulchre of Christ. All Heaven was interested in this one man, now held a prisoner for his faith in the Son of God. Says the beloved John: "The world knoweth us not, because it knew Him not." The world knows not Christ, neither will it know those who exemplify Christ. They are sons of God, children of the royal family; yet their princely claims are not perceived by the world. They may excite their curiosity, but they are not appreciated or understood. They are to them uninteresting and unenvied. (LP 254.1)

Festus himself presented Paul to the assembly, in these words: "King Agrippa, and all men which are here present with us, ye see this man, about whom all the multitude of the Jews have dealt with me, both at Jerusalem and also here, crying that he ought not to live any longer. But when I found that he had committed nothing worthy of death, and that he himself hath appealed to Augustus, I have determined to send him. Of whom I have no certain thing to write unto my lord. Wherefore I have brought him forth before you, and specially before thee, O King Agrippa, that, after examination had, I might have somewhat to write. For it seemeth to me unreasonable to send a prisoner, and not withal to signify the crimes laid against him." (LP 254.2)

King Agrippa now gave Paul liberty to speak for himself. The apostle knew of how little worth are the outward circumstances of worldly wealth and position, and he was not disconcerted by the brilliant display or the high rank of that titled audience. The imposing dress of the procurator and his guests, the swords of the soldiers, and the gleaming armour of their commanders, could not for a moment daunt his courage or disturb his self-control. Stretching forth his manacled right hand, he said: "I think myself happy, King Agrippa, because I shall answer for myself this day before thee touching all the things whereof I am accused of the Jews. Especially because I know thee to be expert in all customs and questions which are among the Jews; wherefore I beseech thee to hear me patiently." (LP 255.1)

Did the mind of Agrippa at these words revert to the past history of his family, and their fruitless efforts against Him whom Paul was preaching? Did he think of his great-grandfather Herod, and the massacre of the innocent children of Bethlehem? of his great-uncle Antipas, and the murder of John the Baptist? of his own father, Agrippa I., and the martyrdom of the apostle James? Did he see in the disasters which speedily befell these kings an evidence of the displeasure of God in consequence of their crimes against his servants? Did the pomp and display of that day remind Agrippa of the time when his own father, a monarch more powerful than he, stood in that same city, attired in glittering robes, while the people shouted that he was a god? Had he forgotten how, even before the admiring shouts had died away, vengeance, swift and terrible, had befallen the vainglorious king? Something of all this flitted across Agrippa's memory; but his vanity was flattered by the brilliant scene before him, and pride and self-importance banished all nobler thoughts. (LP 255.2)

Paul again related the familiar story of his conversion from the stubborn unbelief of a rigid and bigoted Pharisee to faith in Jesus of Nazareth as the world's Redeemer. He described the heavenly vision that filled him with unspeakable terror, though afterward it proved to be a source of the greatest consolation,—a revelation of divine glory, in the midst of which sat enthroned Him whom he had despised and hated, whose followers he was even then seeking to destroy. Transforming mercy had made Paul a new man from that hour, a sincere penitent and a fervent believer in Jesus. It was then that he was called to be an apostle of Christ, "by the will of God." (LP 256.1)

Paul had never seen Christ while he dwelt upon the earth. He had indeed heard of him and his works, but he could not believe that the promised Messiah, the Creator of all worlds, the Giver of all blessings, would appear upon earth as a mere man. He had looked for him to come in robes of majesty, attended with royal pomp, and proclaimed by the angelic host as king of the Jews. But he found that he had not read the Scriptures aright; Christ came as prophecy foretold, a humble man, preaching the word of life in meekness and humility. He came to awaken the noblest impulses of the soul, to satisfy its longings, and to crown the work and warfare of life with infinite reward. (LP 256.2)

Paul had vainly looked for a Messiah to deliver the nation from the bondage of foreign kings, but he had found in Christ a Saviour from the bondage of sin. Life had been to him a blind and baffling conflict, an unequal battle, a fever of unsatisfied desires, until he had seen Christ. Then his longings were satisfied, his fears banished, his burdens lightened. He had found Him of whom Moses and the prophets had written, —Jesus of Nazareth, the Saviour of the world. (LP 257.1)

Why, he asked, should it appear incredible that Christ should rise from the dead? It had once been so to himself; but how could he disbelieve what he had himself seen and heard in that noonday vision? He could bear witness to the resurrection of the dead; for he had looked upon the crucified and risen Christ,—the same who walked the streets of Jerusalem, who died on Calvary, who broke the bands of death, and ascended to Heaven from Olivet. He had seen him and had talked with him as verily as had Cephas, James, John, or any other of the disciples. And how could he be disobedient when the Voice from Heaven sent him forth to open the eyes of Jews and Gentiles, that they might turn from darkness to light, and from the power of Satan unto God, that they might receive forgiveness of sins, and an inheritance among them that are sanctified? In Damascus, in Jerusalem, and throughout all Judea, and to the Gentiles, he had preached repentance toward God, faith in Christ, and a life consistent therewith. (LP 257.2)

This, and this only, was what led the Jews to seize him in the temple, and seek to put him to death; but the Lord had delivered him from this and every other danger. The testimony which he bore concerning Jesus of Nazareth was no blasphemy, no heresy, no apostasy, but a truth in perfect harmony with all the teachings of Moses and the prophets. (LP 258.1)

The apostle was dwelling upon his favourite theme, in that solemn, earnest, impassioned manner which had been so powerful an agent in his mission. In the all-absorbing interest of his subject, he lost sight of kings and governors and chief captains, of wealth, rank, and titles. He was bearing the testimony which was the object of his life, and he could speak with the assurance of long familiarity and the fire of intense conviction. None who heard him could doubt his sincerity. But in the full tide of his eloquence he was suddenly stopped short. The facts related were new to Festus, as to nearly all present. The whole audience had listened spell-bound to Paul's account of wonderful experiences and visions, of revelations and ancient prophecies, and of a Jewish prophet who had been rejected and crucified, yet who had risen from the dead and ascended to Heaven; and who only could forgive sins and lighten the darkness of Jews and Gentiles. The last remark was too much for Festus to credit. He suddenly cried out in an excited manner: "Paul, thou art beside thyself! much learning doth make thee mad." (LP 258.2)

The apostle replied calmly and courteously: "I am not mad, most noble Festus, but speak forth the words of truth and soberness. For the king knoweth of these things, before whom also I speak freely; for I am persuaded that none of these things are hidden from him, for this thing was not done in a corner." Then, turning to Agrippa, he addressed him directly: "King Agrippa, believest thou the prophets? I know that thou believest." (LP 259.1)

The Jewish king had been instructed in the law and the prophets, and he had learned from credible witnesses some of the facts of which Paul had spoken. Hence, the arguments which were so new and strange to Festus, were clear and convincing to Agrippa. And he could but be affected by that burning zeal which neither stripes nor imprisonment could quench. For a time he forgot the dignity of his position, lost sight of his surroundings, and, conscious only of the truths which he had heard, seeing only the humble prisoner standing as God's ambassador, he answered involuntarily, "Almost thou persuadest me to be a Christian." (LP 259.2)

With solemn earnestness, the apostle made answer: "I would to God that not only thou, but also all that hear me this day, were both almost and altogether such as I am," adding, as he raised his fettered hands, "except these bonds." All who heard him were convinced that Paul was no common prisoner. One who could speak as he had spoken, and present the arguments that he had presented, who was so filled with the exaltation of an inspiring faith, so enriched by the grace of Christ, so calm in the consciousness of peace with God and man; one who could wish that all those princely and distinguished people might have the same hope and confidence and faith that sustained him, but who, without the least desire for revenge, could pray that they might be spared the conflicts, sorrows, and afflictions which he had experienced,—such a man could not be an impostor. (LP 259.3)

Festus, Agrippa, and Bernice were the criminals who should in justice have worn the fetters placed upon the apostle. All were guilty of grievous crimes. These offenders had that day heard the offer of salvation through the name of Christ. One, at least, had been almost persuaded to accept of grace and pardon. But to be almost persuaded, means to put aside the proffered mercy, to be convinced of the right way, but to refuse to accept the cross of a crucified Redeemer. (LP 260.1)

King Agrippa's curiosity was satisfied, and rising from his seat, he signified that the interview was at an end. As the assembly dispersed, the case of Paul was freely discussed, and all agreed that, while he might be an enthusiast or a fanatic, he could not in any sense be regarded as a legal criminal; he had done nothing worthy of death or imprisonment. (LP 260.2)

Though Agrippa was a Jew, he did not share the bigoted zeal and blind prejudice of the Pharisees. He had no desire to see freedom of thought suppressed by violence. "This man," he said, "might have been set at liberty, if he had not appealed unto Caesar." But now that the case had been referred to that higher tribunal, it was beyond the jurisdiction of Festus or Agrippa. Yet, two years afterward, the result of that day's proceedings saved the life so precious to the cause of God. Festus, finding that his own judgment of the case, on grounds of Roman justice, was sustained from a Jewish stand-point by the protector of the temple, sent a letter to the emperor, stating that no legal charge could be found against the prisoner. And Nero, cruel and unscrupulous as he was, dared not put to death a man whom Lysias, Felix, Festus, and Agrippa pronounced guiltless, and whom even the Sanhedrim could not condemn. (LP 260.3)

The Voyage and Shipwreck

"And when it was determined that we should sail into Italy, they delivered Paul and certain other prisoners unto one named Julius, a centurion of Augustus' band. And entering into a ship of Adramyttium, we launched, meaning to sail by the coasts of Asia; one Aristarchus, a Macedonian of Thessalonica, being with us." (LP 261.1)

Adramyttium was situated upon the west coast of the province of Asia; therefore the travellers could perform but a part of their journey in a ship bound for that city. But in some of the larger ports at which the vessel touched, they would be likely to find a ship in which they could embark for Rome. (LP 261.2)

In the first century of the Christian era, travelling by sea as well as by land was attended with far greater difficulty than at the present time. The arts of ship-building and navigation were not then matured as now. Mariners directed their course by the sun and stars; and when these did not appear, and there were indications of storm, they were fearful of trusting their vessels to the open sea. (LP 261.3)

The season of safe navigation was already far advanced, before the apostle's ship left Caesarea, and the time was fast approaching when travel by sea would be closed for the year. Every day's delay increased the peril of the voyage. But the journey which would be difficult and dangerous to the ordinary traveller, would be doubly trying to the apostle as a prisoner. Roman soldiers were held responsible with their own lives for the security of their prisoners, and this had led to the custom of chaining prisoners by the right wrist to the left wrist of soldiers, who relieved each other in turn. Thus not only could the apostle have no movement free, but he was placed in close and constant connection with men of the most uncongenial and absolutely repulsive character; men who were not only uneducated and unrefined, but who, from the demoralizing influence of their surroundings, had become brutal and degraded. This custom, however, was less rigidly observed on shipboard than when prisoners were ashore. One circumstance greatly lightened the hardships of his lot. He was permitted to enjoy the companionship of his brethren, Luke and Aristarchus. In his letter to the Colossians, he speaks of the latter as his "fellow-prisoner." But it was as an act of choice, because of his affection for Paul, that Aristarchus shared his bondage, and ministered to him in his afflictions. (LP 262.1)

The voyage began prosperously, and the day after they started, they cast anchor in the harbour of Sidon. Here Julius, the centurion who had listened to the apostle's address before Agrippa, and had thus been favourably disposed toward him, "courteously entreated Paul," and being informed that there were Christians in the place, he "gave him liberty to go unto his friends to refresh himself." The favour was highly appreciated by the apostle, who was in feeble health, and but scantily provided with comforts for the long journey. His brief stay in Sidon was like an oasis in his barren and dreary path, and proved a comfort and encouragement to him during the anxious, storm-tossed weeks upon the sea. (LP 263.1)

Upon leaving Sidon, the ship encountered contrary winds; and being driven from a direct course, its progress was very slow. At Myra, in the province of Lycia, the centurion found a large Alexandrian ship, bound for the coast of Italy, and to this he immediately transferred his prisoners. But the winds were still contrary, and the ship's progress slow and difficult. Says Luke, "When we had sailed slowly many days, and scarce were come over against Cnidus, the wind not suffering us, we sailed under Crete, over against Salmone; and, hardly passing it, came unto a place which is called the Fair Havens." (LP 263.2)

At Fair Havens they were compelled to remain for some time, waiting for favourings winds. During this time the Jewish season of navigation ended. Gentiles considered it safe to travel until a later date; but there was no hope of completing the voyage. The only question now to be decided was, whether to stay where they were or attempt to reach a more favourable place to spend the winter. (LP 263.3)

The matter was earnestly discussed, and was finally referred by the centurion to Paul, who had won the respect of both sailors and soldiers. The apostle unhesitatingly advised that they remain where they were. Said he, "Sirs, I perceive that this voyage will be with hurt and much damage, not only of the lading and ship, but also of our lives." But the owner of the ship, who was on board, and the majority of passengers and crew, were unwilling to accept this counsel. They urged that the harbour of Fair Havens was but imperfectly protected from the wintry winds, and that the neighbouring town, being so small, would afford little occupation for three hundred sailors and passengers during a stay of several months. Port Phenice, but thirty-four miles distant, had a well-sheltered harbour, and was in all other respects a far more desirable place in which to winter. (LP 264.1)

The centurion decided to follow the judgment of the majority. Accordingly, "when the south wind blew softly," they set sail from Fair Havens, with the flattering prospect that a few hours would bring them to the desired harbour. All were now rejoicing that they had not followed the advice of Paul: but their hopes were destined to be speedily disappointed. They had not proceeded far, when a tempestuous wind, such as in that latitude often succeeds the blowing of the south wind, burst upon them with merciless fury. From the first moment that the wind struck the vessel, its condition was hopeless. So sudden was the blow, that the sailors had not a moment in which to prepare, and they could only leave the ship to the mercy of the tempest. (LP 264.2)

After a time they neared the small island of Clauda, and while under its shelter they did all in their power to make ready for the worst. The boat would be their only means of escape, in case the ship should founder; but while in tow it was every moment likely to be dashed to pieces. The first work was to hoist it on board the ship. This was no easy task; for it was with the utmost difficulty that the seamen could perform the simplest duty. All possible precaution was taken to render the ship firm and secure, and then there was nothing left to do but to drift at the mercy of wind and wave. There was no place into which they could run for shelter, the wind was driving them, and even the poor protection afforded by the little island would not avail them long. Such was the disastrous ending of the day which had begun with soft breezes and high hopes. (LP 265.1)

All night the tempest raged, and the ship leaked. The next day, all on board—soldiers, sailors, passengers, and prisoners—united in throwing overboard everything that could be spared. Night came again, but the wind did not abate. The storm-beaten ship, with its shattered mast and rent sails, was tossed hither and thither by the fury of the gale. Every moment it seemed that the groaning timbers must give way as the vessel reeled and quivered under the tempest's shock. The leak rapidly increased, and passengers and crew worked constantly at the pumps. There was not a moment's rest for one on board. "The third day," says Luke, "we cast out with our own hands the tackling of the ship; and when neither sun nor stars in many days appeared, and no small tempest lay on us, all hope that we should be saved was then taken away." A gloomy apathy settled upon those three hundred souls, as for fourteen days they drifted, helpless and hopeless, under a sunless and starless heaven. They had no means of cooking; no fire could be lighted, the utensils had been washed overboard, and most of the provisions were water-soaked and spoiled. In fact while their good ship was wrestling with the tempest, and the waves talked with death, no one desired food. (LP 265.2)

In the midst of that terrible scene, the apostle retained his calmness and courage. Notwithstanding he was physically the greatest sufferer of them all, he had words of hope for the darkest hour, a helping hand in every emergency. In this time of trial, he grasped by faith the arm of infinite power, his heart was stayed upon God, and amid the surrounding gloom his courage and nobility of soul shone forth with the brightest lustre. While all around were looking only for swift destruction, this man of God, in the serenity of a blameless

161

conscience, was pouring forth his earnest supplications in their behalf. (LP 266.1)

Paul had no fears for himself; he felt assured that he would not be swallowed up by the hungry waters. God would preserve his life, that he might witness for the truth at Rome. But his human heart yearned with pity for the poor souls around him. Sinful and degraded as they were, they were unprepared to die, and he earnestly pleaded with God to spare their lives. It was revealed to him that his prayer was granted. When there was a lull in the tempest, so that his voice could be heard, he stood forth on the deck and said:— (LP 266.2)

"Sirs, ye should have hearkened unto me, and not have loosed from Crete, and to have gained this harm and loss. And now I exhort you to be of good cheer; for there shall be no loss of any man's life among you, but of the ship. For there stood by me this night the angel of God, whose I am, and whom I serve, saying, Fear not, Paul; thou must be brought before Caesar; and, lo, God hath given thee all them that sail with thee. Wherefore, sirs, be of good cheer; for I believe God, that it shall be even as it was told me. Howbeit we must be cast upon a certain island." (LP 266.3)

At these words hope revived. Passengers and crew roused from their apathy, and put forth all possible exertion to save their lives. There was much yet to be done. Every effort within their power must be put forth to avert destruction; for God helps those only who help themselves. (LP 267.1)

It was the fourteenth night that they had been tossed up and down on the black, heaving billows, when, amid the sound of the storm, the sailors distinguished the roar of breakers, and reported that they were near some land. They "sounded, and found it twenty fathoms; and when they had gone a little further, they sounded again, and found it fifteen fathoms." They were now threatened by a new danger, of having their ship driven upon some rock-bound coast. They immediately cast out four anchors, which was the only thing that could be done. All through the remaining hours of that night they waited, knowing that any moment might be their last. The leak was constantly increasing, and the ship might sink at any time, even if the anchors held. (LP 267.2)

At last through rain and tempest the grey light fell upon their haggard and ghastly faces. The outlines of the stormy coast could be dimly seen, but not a single familiar landmark was visible. The selfish heathen sailors determined to abandon the ship and crew, and save themselves in the boat which they had with so much difficulty hoisted on board. Pretending that they could do something more to secure the safety of the ship, they unloosed the boat, and began to lower it into the sea. Had they succeeded, they would have been dashed in pieces upon the rocks, while all on board would have perished from their inability to handle the sinking vessel. (LP 267.3)

At this moment, Paul perceived the base design, and averted the danger. With his usual prompt energy and courage he said to the centurion and soldiers, "Except these abide in the ship, ye cannot be saved." The apostle's faith in God did not waver; he had no doubt concerning his own preservation, but the promise of safety to the crew had been conditional upon their performance of duty. The soldiers, on hearing Paul's words, immediately cut off the ropes of the boat, letting her fall off into the sea. (LP 268.1)

The most critical hour was still before them, when the skill, courage, and presence of mind of all on board would be tested. Again the apostle spoke words of encouragement, and entreated all, both sailors and passengers, to take some food, saying, "This day is the fourteenth day that ye have tarried and continued fasting, having taken nothing. Wherefore, I pray you to take some meat; for this is for your health; for there shall not an hair fall from the head of any of you." (LP 268.2)

Paul himself set the example. "When he had thus spoken, he took bread, and gave thanks to God in presence of them all; and when he had broken it, he began to eat. Then were they all of good cheer, and they also took some meat." That worn, drenched, discouraged throng of two hundred and seventy-six souls, who but for Paul would have become despairing and desperate, now took fresh courage, and joined with the apostle in their first meal for fourteen days. After this, knowing that it would be impossible to save their cargo, they righted up the ship by throwing overboard the wheat with which she was laden. (LP 268.3)

Daylight had now fully come, but they could see no landmarks by which to determine their whereabouts. However, "they discovered a certain creek with a shore, into the which they were minded, if it were possible, to thrust in the ship. And when they had taken up the anchors, they committed themselves unto the sea, and loosed the rudder bands, and hoisted up the mainsail to the wind, and made toward shore. And falling into a place where two seas met, they ran the ship aground; and the forepart stuck fast, and remained unmovable, but the hinder part was broken with the violence of the waves." (LP 269.1)

Paul and the other prisoners were now threatened by a fate more terrible than shipwreck. The soldiers saw that in this crisis it would be impossible for them to keep charge of their prisoners. Every man would have all that he could do to save himself. Yet if any of the prisoners were missing, the lives of those who had them in charge would be forfeited. Hence the soldiers desired to put all the prisoners to death.

The Roman law sanctioned this cruel policy, and the proposal would have been executed at once, but for him to whom soldiers and prisoners alike owed their preservation. Julius the centurion knew that Paul had been instrumental in saving the lives of all on board, and he felt that it would be the basest ingratitude to allow him to be put to death; and more, he felt convinced that the Lord was with Paul, and he feared to do him harm. He therefore gave orders to spare the lives of the prisoners, and directed that all who could swim should cast themselves into the sea and get to land. The rest seized hold of planks and other fragments of the wreck, and were carried landward by the waves. (LP 269.2)

When the roll was called, not one was missing. Nearly three hundred souls, sailors, soldiers, passengers, and prisoners, stood that stormy November morning upon the shore of the island of Melita. And there were some that joined with Paul and his brethren in giving thanks to God who had preserved their lives, and brought them safe to land through the perils of the great deep. (LP 270.1)

The shipwrecked crew were kindly received by the barbarous people of Melita. A rain having come on, the whole company were drenched and shivering, and the islanders kindled an immense fire of brushwood, and welcomed them all to its grateful warmth. Paul was among the most active in collecting fuel. As he was placing a bundle of sticks upon the fire, a viper that had been suddenly revived from its torpor by the heat, darted from the fagots and fastened upon his hand. The bystanders were horror-struck, and seeing by his chain that Paul was a prisoner, they said to one another, "No doubt this man is a murderer, whom, though he hath escaped the sea, yet vengeance suffereth not to live." But Paul shook off the creature into the fire, and suffered no harm. Knowing its venomous nature, they watched him closely for some time, expecting every moment to see him fall down, writhing in terrible agony. But as no unpleasant results followed, they changed their minds, and, like the people of Lystra, said that he was a god. By this circumstance Paul gained a strong influence over the islanders, and he sought faithfully to employ it in leading them to accept the truths of the gospel. (LP 270.2)

For three months the ship's company remained at Melita. During this time Paul and his fellow-labourers improved every opportunity to preach the gospel. The Lord wrought through them in a remarkable manner, and for Paul's sake the entire company were treated with great kindness; all their wants were supplied, and upon leaving they were liberally provided with everything needful for their voyage. The chief incidents of their stay are thus briefly related by Luke:— (LP 271.1)

"In the same quarters were possessions of the chief man of the island, whose name was Publius; who received us, and lodged us three days courteously. And it came to pass, that the father of Publius lay sick of a fever and of a bloody flux; to whom Paul entered in, and prayed, and laid his hands on him, and healed him. So when this was done, others also, which had diseases in the island, came, and were healed; who also honoured us with many honours; and when we departed, they laded us with such things as were necessary." (LP 271.2)

Arrival at Rome

With the opening of navigation, the centurion and his prisoners again set out on their journey. An Alexandrian ship, the Castor and Pollux, had wintered at Melita, on her way to Rome, and in this the travellers embarked. Though somewhat delayed by contrary winds, the voyage was safely accomplished, and the ship cast anchor in the beautiful harbour of Puteoli, on the coast of Italy. (LP 272.1)

There were a few Christians in this place, who entreated the apostle to remain with them seven days, and the privilege was kindly granted by the centurion. Since receiving Paul's Epistle to the Romans, the Christians of Italy had eagerly looked forward to a visit from the apostle. They had little expected to see him in chains as a prisoner, but his sufferings only endeared him to them the more. The distance from Puteoli to Rome being but a hundred and forty miles, and the seaport being in constant communication with the metropolis, the Roman Christians were informed of Paul's approach, and some of them started to meet and welcome him. (LP 272.2)

On the eighth day after landing, the centurion and his prisoners set out for Rome. Julius willingly granted the apostle every favour which it was in his power to bestow; but he could not change his condition as a prisoner, or release him from the chain that bound him to his soldier guard. It was with a heavy heart that Paul went forward to his long-expected visit to the world's metropolis. How different the circumstances from what he had anticipated! How was he, fettered and stigmatized as a criminal, to proclaim the gospel? His hopes of winning many souls to the truth at Rome, seemed destined to be disappointed. (LP 272.3)

The travellers reach Appii Forum, forty miles from Rome. As they make their way through the crowds that throng the great thoroughfare, the grey-haired old man, chained with a group of hardened-looking criminals, receives many a glance of scorn, and is made the subject of many a rude, mocking jest. Not one of all he meets bestows upon him a look of pity or sympathy. He meekly wears his chain, and silently, slowly pursues his way. (LP 273.1)

Suddenly a cry of joy is heard, and a man springs out from the passing throng and falls upon the prisoner's neck, embracing him with tears and rejoicing, as a son would welcome a long-absent father. Again and again is the scene repeated. With eyes made keen by loving expectation, many discern in the chained captive the one who spoke to them the words of life at Corinth, at Philippi, or at Ephesus. (LP 273.2)

The whole company is brought to a stand-still, as warm-hearted disciples eagerly flock around their father in the gospel. The soldiers are impatient of delay, yet they have not the heart to interrupt this happy meeting; for they too have learned to respect and esteem their prisoner. In that worn, pain-stricken face, the disciples see the image of Christ reflected. They assure Paul that they have not forgotten him or ceased to love him; that they are indebted to him for the joyful hope which animates their lives, and gives them peace toward God. In the ardour of their love they would bear him upon their shoulders the whole way to the city, could they but have the privilege. (LP 273.3)

Few realize the significance of those words of Luke, that when Paul saw his brethren, "he thanked God, and took courage." The apostle praised God aloud in the midst of that weeping, sympathizing throng, who were not ashamed of his bonds. The cloud of sadness that had rested upon his spirit had been swept away. He felt that his labours had not been in vain. Although his Christian life had been a succession of trials, sufferings, and disappointments, he felt in that hour abundantly repaid. He rejoiced that he had been permitted to preach Christ, to bring the light of eternal life and peace to so many souls who had been in the grossest darkness, without hope, and without God in the world. His step is firm, his heart joyful in hope. He will not complain of the past, or fear for the future. He knows that bonds and afflictions await him; but he knows too that it has been his life-work to deliver souls from a bondage infinitely more terrible, and he rejoices in his sufferings for Christ's sake. (LP 274.1)

At Rome the charge of the centurion Julius ended. Here he delivered up his prisoners to the captain of the emperor's guard. The good account which he gave of Paul, however, together with the letter of Festus, the procurator of Judea, caused the apostle to be favourably regarded by the chief captain, and instead of being thrown into prison, he was permitted to live in his own hired house. The trial of having constantly to be chained to a soldier was continued; but he was at liberty to receive his friends, and to labour for the advancement of the cause of Christ. (LP 274.2)

The Jews who had been banished from Rome some years previous, had been tacitly permitted to return, so that large numbers were now to be found there. To these, first of all, Paul determined to present the facts concerning himself and his work, before his enemies should have opportunity to embitter them against him. Three days after his arrival at Rome, therefore, he called together their leading men, and in a simple, direct manner stated the reasons why he had come to Rome as a prisoner. (LP 275.1)

"Men and brethren," he said, "though I have committed nothing against the people, or customs of our fathers, yet was I delivered prisoner from Jerusalem into the hands of the Romans, who, when they had examined me, would have let me go, because there was no cause of death in me. But when the Jews spake against it, I was constrained to appeal unto Caesar; not that I had aught to accuse my nation of. For this cause therefore have I called for you, to see you and to speak with you; because that for the hope of Israel I am bound with this chain." (LP 275.2)

He said nothing of the abuse which he had suffered at the hands of the Jews, or of their repeated plots to assassinate him. His words were marked with caution and kindness. He was not seeking to win personal attention or sympathy, but to defend the truth and to maintain the honour of the gospel. (LP 275.3)

In reply, his hearers stated that they had received no charges against him by letters public or private, and that none of the Jews who had come to Rome had accused him of any crime. They also expressed a strong desire to hear for themselves the reasons of his faith in Christ. "For as concerning this sect," they said, "we know that everywhere it is spoken against." It was supplanting the religion of their fathers, and causing disputations and dissensions which they considered injurious to the people. (LP 275.4)

Since they themselves desired it, Paul bade them set a day when he could present to them the truths of the gospel. At the time appointed, many came together, "to whom he expounded and testified the kingdom of God, persuading them concerning Jesus, both out of the law of Moses, and out of the prophets, from morning till evening." He related his own experience, and presented arguments from the Old-Testament scriptures with simplicity, sincerity, and power. Upon some minds, at least, his words made an impression which would never be effaced. All who were honestly seeking for truth were convinced, as Paul spoke of what he knew, and testified of what he had seen. (LP 276.1)

He showed that religion does not consist in rites and ceremonies, creeds and theories. If it did, the natural man could understand it by investigation, as he understands worldly things. Paul taught that religion is a practical, saving energy, a principle wholly from God, a personal experience of God's renewing power upon the soul. (LP 276.2)

He showed how Moses had pointed Israel forward to Christ as that Prophet whom they were to hear; how all the prophets had testified of him as God's great remedy for sin, the guiltless One who was to bear the sins of the guilty. He did not find fault with their observance of forms and ceremonies, but showed that while they maintained the ritual service with great exactness, they were rejecting Him who was the antitype of all that system. (LP 276.3)

He declared that in his unconverted state he had known Christ after the flesh, not by personal acquaintance, but by the conceptions which he, in common with others, cherished concerning his character and work. He had rejected Jesus of Nazareth as an impostor because he did not fulfil these expectations. But since Paul's conversion, his views of Christ and his mission were far more spiritual and exalted than the Jewish conception of the long-promised Messiah. He asserted that he did not present to them Christ after the flesh. Herod had seen Christ in the days of his humanity; Annas had seen him; Pilate and the chief priests and rulers had seen him; the Roman soldiers had seen him. But these had not seen him with an eye of faith, and discerned him spiritually as the glorified Redeemer. To apprehend Christ by faith, to have a spiritual knowledge of him, was more to be desired than a personal acquaintance with him as he appeared on earth. The communion with Christ which Paul now enjoyed, was more intimate and more enduring than a mere earthly and human companionship. (LP 277.1)

Some of Paul's hearers eagerly received the truth, but others stubbornly refused to be convinced. The testimony of the Scriptures was presented before them by one who was their equal in learning and their superior in mental power, and who had the special illumination of the Holy Spirit. They could not refute his arguments, but refused to accept his conclusions. The prophecies which the rabbis themselves applied to Christ were a great annoyance to these opposing Jews; for the apostle showed that the fulfilment of these very prophecies required them to accept of Christ. His humble entry into Jerusalem, his rejection by his own people, the treachery of Judas, the paltry sum paid for his betrayal, his death as a malefactor, even the bitter, stupefying draughts offered him in his dying agony, the lots cast upon his garments, his victory over death and the grave by the resurrection on the third day, his final exaltation on the right hand of God,—all these were in direct fulfilment of the words of the prophets. But the more conclusive the arguments presented, the more determined were the Jews in their opposition. Frenzied with malice, they reiterated their assertions that Jesus of Nazareth was a deceiver. (LP 277.2)

Further argument was useless. Paul closed with a solemn address, in which he applied to them the words of Isaiah, before quoted by Christ himself: "Well spake the Holy Ghost by Esaias the prophet unto our fathers, saying, Go unto this people and say, Hearing ye shall hear, and shall not understand; and seeing ye shall see, and not perceive; for the heart of this people is waxed gross, and their ears are dull of hearing, and their eyes have they closed; lest they should see with their eyes, and hear with their ears, and understand with their heart, and should be converted, and I should heal them." (LP 278.1)

Paul's words had not been in vain. Some fully accepted Jesus as the world's Redeemer, and, despite the opposition of their former brethren, became earnest advocates of the truth. (LP 278.2)

The people of God living near the close of time should learn a lesson from this experience of Paul's. We should not be disheartened because those who have no love for truth refuse to be convinced by the clearest evidence. We need not flatter ourselves that the formal and world-loving churches of this age are more ready to receive the teachings of God's word than were those of ages past. Paul's worst enemies were among the Jews, who made the highest claims to godliness. It was to this class that Christ said, "Ye know not the Scriptures, neither the power of God." The most bitter opposers of truth today are found among those who profess to be its defenders. (LP 278.3)

God has made his people the depositories of his law. They must uphold the claims of that down-trodden law against the opposition of ministers of the gospel, against men of learning, position, and authority. The evidence of its binding claims cannot be overthrown; yet its enemies will come again and again to the battle, urging the same arguments, every time refuted, and as often renewed. (LP 279.1)

Paul was led and taught by the Holy Spirit; but, notwithstanding this, those who were not thus taught were filled with jealousy and malice when they saw him advocating truths which they had not sanctioned. They were determined that he should move no faster than they. Had they, like the noble Bereans, searched the Scriptures with a humble, teachable spirit, they would have learned the truth as Paul preached it; but they studied only to find something to sustain themselves and condemn him. (LP 279.2)

The truth always involves a cross. Those who will not believe, oppose and deride those who do believe. The fact that its presentation creates a storm of opposition, is no evidence against the truth. The prophets and apostles imperilled their lives because they would conscientiously obey God. And our Saviour declares that "all that will live godly in Christ Jesus shall suffer persecution." This is the Christian's legacy. (LP 279.3)

Sojourn at Rome

According to Roman law, the trial of Paul could not take place until his accusers should be present in person to state their charges against him. They had not yet come from Palestine, nor was it known at Rome whether they had even started on the long journey. Therefore the trial might be postponed indefinitely. Little regard was shown for the rights of those supposed to have violated the law. It was often the case that an accused person was kept in prison a long time, by the delay of the prosecutors to prefer their charges; or his trial might be deferred by the caprice of those in power. A corrupt judge could hold a prisoner in custody for years, as did Felix in the case of Paul, to gratify popular prejudice, or in hope of securing a bribe. These judges were, however, amenable to a higher tribunal, and this would in some measure serve as a restraint upon them. But the emperor was subjected to no such restraint. His authority was virtually unlimited, and he often permitted caprice, malice, or even indolence, to hinder or prevent the administration of justice. (LP 280.1)

The Jews of Jerusalem were in no haste to present their accusations against Paul. They had been repeatedly thwarted in their designs, and had no desire to risk another defeat. Lysias, Felix, Festus, and Agrippa had all declared their belief in his innocence. His enemies could hope for success only in seeking by intrigue to influence the emperor in their favour. Delay would further their object, as it would afford them time to perfect and execute their plans. (LP 280.2)

In the providence of God, all this delay resulted in the furtherance of the gospel. Paul was not condemned to a life of inactivity. He was allowed free intercourse with his friends, and was permitted to dwell in a commodious house, where he daily presented the truth to those who flocked to listen to his words. Thus for two years he continued, "preaching the kingdom of God, and teaching those things which concern the Lord Jesus Christ, with all confidence, no man forbidding him." And his labours were not confined to the preaching of the gospel. The "care of all the churches" still rested upon him. He deeply felt the danger that threatened those for whom he had laboured so earnestly, and he sought as far as possible to supply by written communications the place of his personal instruction. He also sent out authorized delegates to labour among the churches he had raised up, and also in fields which he had not visited. These messengers rendered him faithful service, and being in communication with them, he was informed concerning the condition and dangers of the churches, and was enabled to exercise a constant supervision over them. (LP 281.1)

Thus while apparently cut off from active labour, Paul exerted a wider and more lasting influence than he could have exerted had he been free to travel among the churches as in former years. As a prisoner of the Lord, he had a firmer hold upon the affections of his brethren in the faith, and his words commanded even greater attention and respect than when he was personally with them. When they first learned that their beloved teacher had been made a prisoner, they mourned and would not be comforted. Not until he was removed from them, did they realize how heavy were the burdens which he had borne in their behalf. Heretofore they had largely excused themselves from responsibility and burden-bearing because they lacked his wisdom, tact, and indomitable energy; and now, left in their inexperience to learn the lessons they had shunned, and feeling that they were never more to be benefited by the apostle's labours, they prized the warning, counsel, and instruction which he sent them, as they had never before prized his teachings. And as they learned of his courage, faith, and meekness in his long imprisonment, they also were stimulated to greater fidelity and zeal in the cause of Christ. (LP 281.2)

Among the assistants of Paul in his labours were many of his former companions and fellow-workers. Luke, "the beloved physician," who had attended him in the journey to Jerusalem, through the two years' imprisonment at Caesarea, and upon his last perilous voyage, was with him still. Timothy also ministered to his comfort. Tychicus was his mail-bearer, taking his messages to the different churches which they had visited together. Demas and Mark also were with him. (LP 282.1)

Mark had once been refused by Paul as unworthy to accompany him, because, when his help was much needed, he had left the apostle and returned to his home. He saw that, as Paul's companion, his life must be one of constant toil, anxiety, and self-denial; and he desired an easier path. This led the apostle to feel that he could not be trusted, and that decision caused the unhappy dissension between Paul and Barnabas. (LP 282.2)

Mark had since learned the lesson which all must learn, that God's claims are above every other. He saw that there is no release in the Christian warfare. He had obtained a closer and more perfect view of his Pattern, and had seen upon his hands the scars of his conflict to save the lost and perishing. He was willing to follow his Master's example of earnestness and self-sacrifice, that he might win souls to Jesus and the blessedness of Heaven. And now, while sharing the lot of Paul the prisoner, Mark understood better than ever before, that it is infinite gain to win Christ at whatever cost, and infinite loss to win the world and lose the soul for whose redemption the blood of Christ was shed. Mark was now a useful and beloved helper of the apostle, and he continued faithful even unto the end. In writing from Rome just prior to his martyrdom, Paul bade Timothy, "Take Mark, and bring him with thee; for he is profitable to me for the ministry." (LP 282.3)

Demas was now a faithful helper of the apostle. A few years afterward, however, in the same letter to Timothy which commends Mark's fidelity, Paul writes, "Demas hath forsaken me, having loved this present world." For worldly gain, Demas bartered every higher and nobler consideration. How short-sighted, how unwise the exchange! Those who possess only worldly wealth or honour are poor indeed, however much they may proudly call their own. Those who choose to suffer for Christ's sake, will win eternal riches; they will be heirs of God, and joint-heirs with his Son. They may not have on earth a place to lay their heads; but in Heaven the Saviour whom they love is preparing mansions for them. Many, in their pride and ignorance, forget that lowly things are mighty. In order to be happy, we must learn self-denial at the foot of the cross. We want no earthly hope so firmly rooted that we cannot transplant it to paradise. (LP 283.1)

Paul was not alone in the trials which he endured from the love of ease and desire for worldly gain in his professed brethren. His experience is still shared by the faithful servants of Christ. Many, even of those who profess to believe the solemn truths for this time, feel but little moral responsibility. When they see that the path of duty is beset with perplexities and trials, they choose a way for themselves, where there is less effort needed; where there are fewer risks to run, fewer dangers to meet. By selfishly shunning responsibilities, they increase the burdens of the faithful workers, and at the same time separate themselves from God, and forfeit the reward they might have won. All who will work earnestly and disinterestedly, in his love and fear, God will make co-labourers with himself. Christ has hired them at the price of his own blood, the pledge of an eternal weight of glory. Of every one of his followers he requires efforts that shall in some degree correspond with the price paid and the infinite reward offered. (LP 284.1)

Among the disciples who ministered to Paul at Rome was Onesimus, a fugitive slave from the city of Colosse. He belonged to a Christian named Philemon, a member of the Colossian church. But he had robbed his master and fled to Rome. Here this pagan slave, profligate and unprincipled, was reached by the truths of the gospel. He had seen and heard Paul at Ephesus, and now, in the providence of God, he met him again in Rome. In the kindness of his heart, the apostle sought to relieve the poverty and distress of the wretched fugitive, and then endeavoured to shed the light of truth into his darkened mind. Onesimus listened attentively to the words of life which he had once despised, and was converted to the faith of Christ. He now confessed his sin against his master, and gratefully accepted the counsel of the apostle. (LP 284.2)

He had endeared himself to Paul by his piety, meekness, and sincerity, no less than by his tender care for the apostle's comfort and his zeal to promote the work of the gospel. Paul saw in him traits of character that would render him a useful helper in missionary labour, and he would gladly have kept him at Rome. But he would not do this without the full consent of Philemon. He therefore decided that Onesimus should at once return to his master, and promised to hold himself responsible for the sum of which Philemon had been robbed. Being about to despatch Tychicus with letters to various churches of Asia Minor, he sent Onesimus in his company and under his care. It was a severe test for this servant to thus deliver himself up to the master he had wronged; but he had been truly converted, and, painful as it was, he did not shrink from this duty. (LP 285.1)

Paul made Onesimus the bearer of a letter to Philemon, in which he with great delicacy and kindness pleaded the cause of the repentant slave, and intimated his own wishes concerning him. The letter began with an affectionate greeting to Philemon as a friend and fellow-labourer:— (LP 285.2)

"Grace to you, and peace, from God our Father and the Lord Jesus Christ. I thank my God, making mention of thee always in my prayers, hearing of thy love and faith, which thou hast toward the Lord Jesus, and toward all saints; that the communication of thy faith may become effectual by the acknowledging of every good thing which is in you in Christ Jesus." The apostle sought gently to remind Philemon that every good purpose and trait of character which he possessed must be accredited to the grace of Christ; for this alone caused him to differ from the perverse and sinful. The same grace could make the debased criminal a child of God and a useful labourer in the gospel. (LP 285.3)

Though Paul might with authority have urged upon Philemon his duty as a Christian, yet because of his love for him he would not command, but chose rather the language of entreaty: "As Paul the aged, and now also a prisoner of Jesus Christ, I beseech thee for my son Onesimus, whom I have begotten in my bonds, which in time past was to thee unprofitable, but now profitable to thee and to me." (LP 286.1)

He requests Philemon to receive him as his own child. He says that it was his desire to retain Onesimus, that he might act the same part in ministering to him in his bonds as Philemon would have done. But he did not desire his services unless Philemon should voluntarily set him free; for it might be in the providence of God that Onesimus had left his master for a season in so improper a manner, that, being converted, he might on his return be forgiven and received with such affection that he would choose to dwell with him ever after, "not now as a servant, but above a servant, a brother beloved." (LP 286.2)

The apostle added: "If thou count me therefore a partner, receive him as myself. If he hath wronged thee, or oweth thee aught, put that on mine account. I Paul have written it with mine own hand, I will repay it; albeit I do not say to thee how thou owest unto me even thine own self besides." (LP 286.3)

Paul voluntarily proposes to assume the debt of another; he will make reparation for a crime committed by another, that the guilty one may be spared the disgrace of punishment, and may again enjoy the privileges which he has forfeited. The apostle well knew the severity which masters exercised towards their slaves, and that Philemon was much incensed at the conduct of his servant. He therefore approached him in a manner to arouse his deepest and tenderest feelings as a Christian. The conversion of Onesimus has made him a brother in the faith, and any punishment inflicted on this new convert from pagan darkness would be regarded by Paul as though inflicted on himself. (LP 287.1)

How fitting an illustration of the love of Christ toward the repenting sinner! As the servant who had defrauded his master had nothing with which to make restitution, so the sinner who has robbed God of years of service has no means of cancelling the debt; Jesus interposes between the sinner and the just wrath of God, and says, I will pay the debt. Let the sinner be spared the punishment of his guilt. I will suffer in his stead. (LP 287.2)

After offering to assume the debt of Onesimus, Paul gently reminded Philemon how greatly he himself was indebted to the apostle; he owed to him his own self in a special sense, since God had made Paul the instrument of his conversion. He then, in a most tender, earnest appeal, besought Philemon that as he had by his liberalities refreshed the saints, so he would refresh the spirit of the apostle by granting him this cause of rejoicing. "Having confidence in thy obedience," he added, "I wrote unto thee, knowing that thou wilt also do more than I say." (LP 287.3)

This epistle is of great value as a practical illustration of the influence of the gospel upon the relation of master and servant. Slave-holding was an established institution throughout the Roman empire, and both masters and slaves were found in most of the churches for which Paul laboured. In the cities, where slaves many times outnumbered the free population, laws of the most terrible severity were considered necessary to keep them in subjection. A wealthy Roman owned hundreds of slaves, of every rank, of every nation, and of every accomplishment. The master had full control of the souls and bodies of these helpless beings. He could inflict upon them any suffering he chose; but if one of them in retaliation or self-defence ventured to raise a hand against his owner, the whole family of the offender would be inhumanly sacrificed, however innocent they might be. Even the slightest mistake, accident, or carelessness was punished without mercy. (LP 288.1)

Some masters, more humane than others, were more indulgent toward their servants; but the vast majority of the wealthy and noble gave themselves up without restraint, to the indulgence of lust, passion, and appetite, and they made their slaves the wretched victims of caprice and tyranny. The tendency of the whole system was hopelessly degrading. (LP 288.2)

It was not the apostle's work to violently overturn the established order of society. Had he attempted this, he would have prevented the success of the gospel. But he taught principles that struck at the very foundation of slavery, and that, carried into effect, would surely undermine the whole system. "Where the Spirit of the Lord is, there is liberty." The religion of Christ has a transforming power upon the receiver. The converted slave became a member of the body of Christ, and as such was to be loved and treated as a brother, a fellow-heir with his master of the blessings of God and the privileges of the gospel. In the same spirit were servants to perform their duties; "not with eye-service, as men-pleasers, but as the servants of Christ, doing the will of God from the heart." Christianity makes a strong bond of union between master and slave, king and subject, the gospel minister and the most degraded sinner who has found in Christ relief from his burden of crime. They have been washed in the same blood, quickened by the same Spirit; they are made one in Christ Jesus. (LP 288.3)

Caesar's Household

The gospel has ever achieved its greatest success among the humbler classes. "Not many wise men after the flesh, not many mighty, not many noble, are called." It could not be expected that Paul, a poor and friendless prisoner, would be able to gain the attention of the wealthy and titled classes of Roman citizens. Their whole life — physical, mental, and moral—was on a different plane from his. To them vice presented all its glittering allurements, and held them willing captives. But from the toil-worn, want-stricken victims of their oppression, even from the poor slaves, ignorant and degraded as they were, many gladly listened to the words of Paul, and found in the faith of Christ a hope and peace which cheered them under the hardships of their lot. (LP 289.1)

Yet while the apostle's work began with the humble and lowly, its influence extended, until it reached the very palace of the emperor. Rome was at this time the metropolis of the world. The haughty Caesars were giving laws to nearly every nation upon the earth. King and courtier were either wholly ignorant of the humble Nazarene, or they regarded him with hatred and derision. And yet in less than two years the gospel found its way from the prisoner's lowly home into the imperial halls. Paul is in bonds as an evil-doer; but "the word of God is not bound." (LP 290.1)

Among the saints who send greetings to the Philippian church, the apostle mentions chiefly them that are of Caesar's household. Nowhere could there exist an atmosphere more uncongenial to Christianity than in the Roman court under such a monster of wickedness as then stood at its head. Nero seemed to have obliterated from his soul the last trace of the Divine, and even of the human, and to bear only the impress of the Satanic. His attendants and courtiers were in general of the same character as himself, fierce, debased, and corrupt. To all appearance it would be impossible for Christianity to gain a foot-hold in the court and palace of Nero. (LP 290.2)

Yet in this case, as in so many others, was proved the truth of Paul's assertion, that the weapons of his warfare were "mighty through God to the pulling down of strong holds." Trophies of the cross were won, even in Nero's household. From the vile attendants of a viler king were gained converts who became sons of God. These were not Christians secretly, but openly. They were not ashamed of their faith. They felt the warmest affection for those who were older in Christian faith and experience, and they were not afraid or ashamed to acknowledge them as brethren. (LP 290.3)

And by what means was an entrance achieved and a firm footing gained for Christianity where even its admission seemed impossible? In former years the apostle had publicly proclaimed the faith of Christ with winning power; and by signs and miracles he had given unmistakable evidence of its divine character. With noble firmness he rose up before the sages of Greece, and by his knowledge and eloquence put to silence the arguments of proud philosophy. With undaunted courage he had stood before kings and governors, and reasoned of righteousness, temperance, and judgment to come, until the haughty rulers trembled as though already beholding the terrors of the day of God. (LP 291.1)

But no such opportunities were now granted the apostle, confined as he was to his own dwelling, and able to proclaim the truth only to those who sought him there. He had not, like Moses and Aaron, a divine command to go before the profligate king with the rod of God, and demand his attention, and in the name of the great I AM rebuke his cruelty and oppression. Yet it was at this very time, when its chief advocate was apparently cut off from public labour, that this great victory was won for the truth, and members were gained to the church from the very household of the king. (LP 291.2)

In his Epistle to the Philippians, Paul ascribes to his own imprisonment his success in bringing converts to the faith from Nero's household. He expresses himself as fearful lest the Philippians have thought that his afflictions have impeded the progress of the gospel. He assures them that the contrary effect has been produced: "I would ye should understand, brethren, that the things which happened unto me have fallen out rather unto the furtherance of the gospel; so that my bonds in Christ are manifest in all the palace, and in all other places." (LP 292.1)

It was not by the sermons of Paul, but by his bonds, that the attention of the court had been attracted to Christianity. It was as a captive that he had conquered rulers. It was with his chain that he had broken from so many souls the bonds that held them in the slavery of sin. Nor was this all. He declares: "And many of the brethren in the Lord, waxing confident by my bonds, are much more bold to speak the word without fear." (LP 292.2)

The patience and meekness with which he submitted to a long and unjust imprisonment drew the attention of the public, and forced the conviction upon many minds that where there was such a willingness to suffer, there must be an unwavering faith in the doctrines advocated. His cheerfulness under affliction and imprisonment was so unlike the spirit of the unfortunate and afflicted of the world, that they could but see that a power higher than any earthly influence was ever abiding with him. His courage and faith were a continual sermon. And by his example, other Christians were nerved to greater energy. They felt that they would not be losers in becoming the advocates of truth and pushing forward the work from which Paul was temporarily withdrawn. In these ways were the apostle's bonds influential, so that when to all appearance he could do the least, when his power and usefulness seemed cut off, then it was that he was gathering sheaves for Christ, in fields from which he seemed wholly excluded. (LP 292.3)

When a servant of God is withdrawn from active duty, when his voice is no longer heard in encouragement and reproof, we, in our short-sighted judgment, often conclude that his usefulness is at an end. But the Lord does not so regard it. The mysterious providences over which we so often lament, are designed of God to accomplish a work which otherwise might never have been done. (LP 293.1)

The Christian who manifests patience and cheerfulness under bereavement and suffering, who meets death with the peace and calmness of an unwavering faith, may accomplish far more toward overcoming the opposition of the enemies of the gospel than he could have effected had he laboured with his utmost energy day and night to bring them to repentance. (LP 293.2)

When the servants of Christ move actively through the land to contend against prevailing errors and superstitions, they are doing the work which the Lord has given them, standing in defence of the gospel. But when through Satan's malice, they are persecuted, their active labour hindered, and they cast into prison, as was Paul, and finally dragged to the scaffold or the stake, it is then that truth gains a greater triumph. Those who before doubted, are convinced of their sincerity, as they thus seal their faith with their blood. From the martyr's ashes springs an abundant harvest for the garner of God. (LP 293.3)

Let no one feel that because he is no longer able to labour openly and actively for God and his truth, he has no service to render, no reward to secure. A true Christian is never laid aside. God will use him effectually in health and in sickness, in life and in death. It is in the darkness of affliction, bereavement, trial, and persecution, that the light of Christian faith shines brightest, and the Lord's promises are found most precious. And when the grave receives the child of God, he being dead yet speaketh. His works do follow him. The memory of his words of admonition and encouragement, of his steadfast adherence to the truth under all circumstances, speaks more powerfully than even his living example. (LP 294.1)

Patience as well as courage has its victories. Converts may be made by meekness in trial, no less than by boldness in enterprise. If Christians would be reconciled to the apparent suspension of their usefulness, and would cheerfully rest from the strife, and lay off the burden of labour, they would learn sweet lessons at the feet of Jesus, and would see that their Master is using them as effectively when they seem to be withdrawn from employment, as when in more active labour. (LP 294.2)

When the Christian churches first learned that Paul contemplated a visit to Rome, they looked forward to a signal triumph of the gospel. Paul had borne the truth to many lands; he had proclaimed it in great cities. Might not this champion of the faith succeed in winning souls to Christ, even in the court of Nero? But their anticipations were crushed by the tidings that Paul had gone to Rome as a prisoner. They had confidently hoped to see the gospel, once established at this great centre, extend rapidly to all nations, until it should become a prevailing power in the earth. How great their disappointment! Human calculations had failed, but not the purpose of God. Paul could not labour as he had hoped, yet before the close of that two years' imprisonment he was able to say, "My bonds in Christ are manifest in all the palace, and in all other places;" and among those who send greetings to the Philippians, he mentions chiefly them that are of Caesar's household. (LP 294.3)

The zeal and fidelity of Paul and his fellow-workers, no less than the faith and obedience of those converts to Christianity, under circumstances so forbidding, should be a rebuke to slothfulness and unbelief in the followers of Christ. Never let us, by our human, short-sighted judgment, limit the plans and work of God. Never let us excuse ourselves from efforts to win souls to Christ, even in the most unpromising fields. The apostle and his subordinate ministers might have argued that the servants of Nero were subjected to the fiercest temptations, surrounded by the most formidable hindrances, exposed to the most bitter opposition, and that under such circumstances it would be in vain to call them to repentance and to faith in Christ. Should they be convinced of the truth, how could they render obedience? But the gospel was presented to those souls, and there were some among them who decided to obey it at any cost. Notwithstanding the obstacles and dangers, they would walk in the light, trusting in God for opportunity to let their light shine forth to others. (LP 295.1)

Who is placed in circumstances more unfavourable to a religious life, or required to make greater sacrifices, to encounter greater dangers, or to bring upon himself fiercer opposition, than would follow the exchange of heathenism for Christianity by those who were in office in the court of Caesar? No man can be so situated that he cannot obey God. There is too little faith with Christians of today. They are willing to work for Christ and his cause only when they themselves can see a prospect of favourable results. Divine grace will aid the efforts of every true believer. That grace is sufficient for us under all circumstances.

The Spirit of Christ will exert its renewing, perfecting power upon the character of all who will be obedient and faithful. (LP 296.1)

God is the great I AM, the source of being, the centre of authority and power. Whatever the condition or situation of his creatures, they can have no sufficient excuse for refusing to answer the claims of God. The Lord holds us responsible for the light shining upon our pathway. We may be surrounded by difficulties that appear formidable to us, and because of these we may excuse ourselves for not obeying the truth as it is in Jesus; but there can be no excuse that will bear investigation. Could there be an excuse for disobedience, it would prove our heavenly Father unjust, in that he had given us conditions of salvation with which we could not comply. (LP 296.2)

Servants employed in an irreligious family are placed in circumstances somewhat similar to those of the members of Caesar's household. Such are deserving of sympathy; for if they seek to live a religious life, their situation is often one of great trial. A bad example is constantly before them,—an example of Sabbath-breaking and of neglect of religion. Few religious privileges are granted them; and should they manifest an interest in religion, they might lose the favour of their employer, and bring upon themselves the ridicule of their companions. He who is thus situated has more than a common battle to fight, if he stands forth as a witness for Christ, a candidate for Heaven. But there can be nothing in his surroundings to excuse him for neglecting the claims of God. Whatever the difficulties in his path, they will be powerless to hinder him if he is determined to seek first the kingdom of God and his righteousness. (LP 297.1)

The Christian should not array before his imagination all the trials which may occur before the end of the race. He has but to begin to serve God, and each day live and labour for the glory of God that day, and obstacles which appeared insurmountable will gradually grow less and less; or, should he encounter all that he has feared, the grace of Christ will be imparted to him according to his need. Strength increases with the difficulties met and overcome. (LP 297.2)

Daniel, the Hebrew captive, the prime minister of a royal realm, encountered great obstacles to a life of fidelity to God. But at the very beginning of his career, he determined that whatever might oppose, he would make the law of God his rule of action. As he maintained his steadfastness amid the lesser trials which he daily met in the court of a heathen king, his faith, courage, and firmness grew stronger; and when the royal decree went forth forbidding him to offer supplication to his God, he was able, with the den of lions open before him, to stand true to principle and to God. (LP 297.3)

He whose heart is fixed to serve God, will find opportunity to serve him. He will pray, he will read the word of God, he will seek virtue and forsake vice. He can brave contempt and derision while looking unto Jesus, the author and finisher of our faith, who endured the contradiction of sinners against himself. Help and grace are promised by Him whose words are truth. God will not fail to fulfill his promise to all who trust in him. (LP 298.1)

Are any tempted to make their circumstances an excuse for neglecting the religion of Christ? Let them remember that Satan can frame one difficulty after another to bar the way of those who will permit themselves to be thus hindered. Let them consider the situation of the disciples in Caesar's household, the fierce depravity of the emperor, the profligacy of the court. It was like rushing into the fire to accept of Christ under such circumstances. If those Christian converts could maintain their fidelity amid all the difficulties and dangers of such surroundings, no one can offer a sufficient reason for neglecting the claims of duty. There is no such thing as an impossibility to obey God. (LP 298.2)

There is another fact concerning those disciples which is worthy of our attention. Not only were converts won to the truth in Caesar's household, but they remained in that household after their conversion. They did not feel at liberty to abandon their post of duty. The truth had found them where they were, and there they would remain, and by their life and character testify of its transforming power. The example of those Christians has great weight, from the fact that they had direct intercourse with Paul, and therefore enjoyed the benefit of his instruction and counsel. It teaches that believers are not always to withdraw from positions of difficulty and trial, and place themselves where there would be less temptation or opposition. (LP 298.3)

Let us ever bear in mind that our Saviour left the heavenly courts, and came to a world polluted by sin. By his own life he has shown his followers how they can be in the world, and yet not be of the world. He came not to partake of its delusive pleasures, to be swayed by its customs, or to follow its practices, but to seek and to save the lost. With this object, and this only, can the Christian consent to remain in the company of the ungodly. (LP 299.1)

No one who is seeking to save his soul should without good reason place himself in an uncongenial atmosphere, or where he will be surrounded by hindrances to a religious life; but if in such a position he has received the truth, he should diligently inquire if God has not there a work for him to do for the saving of other souls. That one Christian in the midst of unbelievers, may, in the providence of God, be like the piece of leaven "hid in three measures of meal," that is to do its work until the whole mass is leavened. A consistent Christian life will accomplish more good than could be accomplished by many sermons. Whatever the Christian's station, be it exalted or humble, he will manifest the power of true religion by the faithful performance of the duties of that station. (LP 299.2)

It is not the absence of temptation or trial that is most favourable for the development of Christian character. Where there are fewest difficulties to meet, the Christian is in the greatest danger of spiritual slothfulness. The God of all grace has promised that his people shall not be tempted above that which they are able to bear, but that with the temptation he will make a way of escape. Constant exposure to rebuffs and opposition, will lead the Christian to greater watchfulness and more earnest prayer to the mighty Helper. Extraordinary trials, endured through the grace of God, will give him a deeper experience and greater spiritual strength, as vigilance, patience, and fortitude are called into exercise. (LP 300.1)

The followers of Christ should expect to be regarded by the world with no more favour than was their Master. But he who has God for his friend and helper can afford to spend a long winter of chilling neglect, abuse, and persecution. By the grace which Christ imparts, he can maintain his faith and trust in God under the sorest trials. He recalls the Saviour's example, and he feels that he can endure affliction and persecution if he may thus gain simplicity of character, lowliness of heart, and an abiding trust in Jesus. The triumph of Christian faith is to suffer, and be strong; to submit, and thus conquer; to be killed all the day long, and yet to live; to bear the cross, and thus win the crown of immortal glory. (LP 300.2)

Paul at Liberty

While Paul's labours were blessed to the conversion of many souls and the strengthening and encouragement of the believers, clouds were gathering that threatened his own safety as well as the prosperity of the church. When, on his arrival at Rome, he was placed in charge of the captain of the imperial guards, the office was filled by a man of justice and integrity, by whose clemency he was left comparatively free to pursue the work of the gospel. But before the close of the two years' imprisonment, this man was replaced by an official whose vice and tyranny rendered his name infamous. The apostle could expect no favour from this slave of lust and cruelty. (LP 301.1)

The Jews were now more active than ever before in their efforts against Paul. They had found an able helper in the profligate woman whom Nero had made his second wife, and who, being a Jewish proselyte, would lend all her influence to second their murderous designs against the Christian champion. (LP 301.2)

Paul had little reason to hope for justice from the Caesar to whom he had appealed. Nero was more debased in morals, more frivolous in character, and at the same time capable of more atrocious cruelty, than any ruler who had preceded him. The reins of government could not have been intrusted to a more inhuman despot. The first year of his reign had been marked by the poisoning of his young step-brother, who was the rightful heir to the throne. He had steadily descended from one depth of vice and crime to another, until he had murdered his own mother, and then his wife. There was no atrocity which he would not perpetrate, no vile act to which he would not stoop. In every noble mind he inspired abhorrence and contempt. (LP 301.3)

The details of iniquity practised in the court of this prodigy of vice are too degrading, too horrible, for description. His abandoned wickedness created disgust and loathing, even in many who were forced to share his crimes. They were in constant fear as to what enormities he would suggest next. Yet even such crimes as Nero's did not shake the allegiance of his subjects. He was acknowledged as the absolute ruler of the whole civilized world. And more than this, he was made the recipient of divine honours, and worshipped as a god. (LP 302.1)

From the stand-point of human judgment, Paul's condemnation before such a judge was certain. But the apostle felt that he had nothing to fear, so long as he preserved his loyalty and his love to God. His life was not in the hands of Nero, and if his work was not yet done, the Roman emperor would be powerless to destroy him. He who had hitherto been his protector could shield him still from the malice of the Jews, and from the power of Caesar. (LP 302.2)

And God did shield his servant. At Paul's examination the charges against him were not sustained, and, contrary to the general expectation,— with a regard for justice wholly at variance with his character,—Nero declared the prisoner guiltless. Paul's fetters were struck off, and he was again a free man. (LP 302.3)

Had his trial been longer deferred, or had he from any cause been detained in Rome during the following year, he would have perished in the dreadful persecution which then took place. The converts to Christianity had become so numerous during Paul's imprisonment as to attract the attention and arouse the enmity of the authorities. The ire of the emperor was especially excited by the conversion of members of his own household; he still thirsted for blood, and soon found a pretext to make the Christians the objects of his merciless cruelty. A terrible fire about this time occurred in Rome, by which nearly one-half the city was consumed. Nero himself caused the flames to be kindled, and then, to avert suspicion, he made a pretence of great generosity in assisting the homeless and destitute. He was, however, accused of the crime. The people were excited and enraged, and Nero determined to clear himself, and also to rid the city of a class whom he feared and hated, by charging the act upon the Christians. (LP 302.4)

The Satanic device succeeded. Thousands of the followers of Christ—men, women, and children—were put to death in the most cruel manner. Some were crucified, some covered with the skins of wild beasts, and torn in pieces by dogs, others were clothed in garments of inflammable material, and set on fire at night to illuminate the circus of the Vatican and the pleasure gardens of Nero. Thus this monster in human form amused the public by exhibiting his victims in their dying agonies, while he himself stood by, taking the keenest delight in their misery. Degraded and hardened as were the Romans, and bitter as was their prejudice against the Christians, the constant repetition of these horrible, heart-sickening scenes excited even their compassion. (LP 303.1)

From this terrible ordeal, Paul was spared, having left Rome soon after his release. This last precious interval of freedom was earnestly improved in labouring among the churches. He sought to establish a firmer union between the Greek and Eastern churches which he had raised up, and to guard them against the subtle heresies that were creeping in to corrupt the faith. The trials and anxieties which he had endured, had preyed upon his physical and mental energies. The infirmities of age were upon him. He felt that his work was nearly accomplished. (LP 304.1)

At Jerusalem and at Antioch he had defended Christianity against the narrow restrictions of Judaism. He had preached the gospel to the pagans of Lycaonia, to the fanatics of Galatia, to the colonists of Macedonia, to the frivolous art-worshippers of Athens, to the pleasure-loving merchants of Corinth, to the half-barbarous nations of Dalmatia, to the islanders of Crete, and to slaves, soldiers, and men of rank and station, in the multitudes at Rome. Now he was doing his last work. (LP 304.2)

The Final Arrest

Though Paul's labours were chiefly among the churches, he could not escape the observation of his enemies. Since Nero's persecution, Christians were everywhere the objects of hatred and suspicion. Any evil-disposed person could easily secure the arrest and imprisonment of one of the proscribed sect. And now the Jews conceived the idea of seeking to fasten upon Paul the crime of instigating the burning of Rome. Not one of them for a moment believed him guilty; but they knew that such a charge, made with the faintest show of plausibility, would seal his doom. An opportunity soon offered to execute their plans. At the house of a disciple in the city of Troas, Paul was again seized, and from this place he was hurried away to his final imprisonment. (LP 304.3)

The arrest was affected by the efforts of Alexander the coppersmith, who had so unsuccessfully opposed the apostle's work at Ephesus, and who now seized the opportunity to be revenged on one whom he could not defeat. Paul in his second Epistle to Timothy afterward referred to the machinations of this enemy of the faith: "Alexander the coppersmith did me much evil. The Lord reward him according to his works." In his first epistle he spoke in a similar manner of Hymeneus and Alexander as among those who "concerning faith have made shipwreck;" "whom," he says, "I have delivered unto Satan, that they may learn not to blaspheme." These men had departed from the faith of the gospel, and furthermore had done despite to the Spirit of grace by attributing to the power of Satan the wonderful revelations made to Paul. Having rejected the truth, they were filled with hatred against it, and sought to destroy its faithful advocate. (LP 305.1)

Reformatory action is always attended with loss, sacrifice, and peril. It always rebukes love of ease, selfish interests, and lustful ambition. Hence, whoever initiates or prosecutes such action must encounter opposition, calumny, and hatred from those who are unwilling to submit to the conditions of reform. It is no easy matter to overcome sinful habits and practices. The work can be accomplished only with the help of divine grace; but many neglect to seek such help, and endeavour to bring down the standard to meet their deficiencies, instead of bringing themselves up to meet the standard of God. Such was the effort of these men who were so severely dealt with for their sins. They were endangering the purity of the believers, and it was necessary that a firm, decided course be pursued to meet the wrong and hurl it from the church. Paul had faithfully reproved their sin, —the vice of licentiousness so prevalent in that age,—but they had refused to be corrected. He had proceeded according to the instructions of Christ regarding such cases, but the offenders had given no token of repentance, and he had therefore excommunicated them. They had then openly apostatized from the faith, and united with its most bitter opponents. When they rejected the words of Paul, and set themselves to hinder his labours, they were warring against Christ; and it was by the inspiration of the Spirit of God, and not as an expression of personal feeling, that Paul pronounced against them that solemn denunciation. (LP 305.2)

On his second voyage to Rome, Paul was accompanied by several of his former companions; others earnestly desired to share his lot, but he refused to permit them thus to imperil their lives. The prospect before him was far less favourable than at the time of his former imprisonment. The persecution under Nero had greatly lessened the number of Christians in Rome. Thousands had been martyred for their faith, many had left the city, and those who remained were greatly depressed and intimidated. At Paul's first arrival, the Jews of Rome had been willing to listen to his arguments; but through the influence of emissaries from Jerusalem, and also because of the received charges against the Christians, they had become his bitter enemies. (LP 306.1)

No warm-hearted disciples now met Paul and his companions at Appii Forum and Three Taverns as before, when he was constrained to thank God and take courage. There was now no one like the courteous and kindly Julius, to say a word in his favour, no statement from Festus or Agrippa to attest his innocence. The change which had taken place in the city and its inhabitants—the city still scarred and blackened from the terrible conflagration, and the people, by tens of thousands, reduced to the most squalid poverty—seemed to harmonize with the change in his own condition and prospects. Through the surging crowds that still thronged the streets of Rome, and that looked upon him and his fellow-Christians as the authors of all their misery, Paul passed, not now to his own hired house, but to a gloomy dungeon, there to remain, chained night and day, until he should finish his course. (LP 307.1)

To visit Paul now was not, as during his first imprisonment, to visit a man against whom no charge had been sustained, and who had won favourable opinions from princes and rulers. It was to visit one who was the object of universal hatred, who was accused of instigating the basest and most terrible crime against the city and the nation. Whoever ventured to show him the slightest attention, thereby made himself the object of suspicion, and endangered his own life. Rome was now filled with spies, who stood ready to bring an accusation against any one on the slightest occasion. None but a Christian would visit a Christian; for no other would incur the odium of a faith which even intelligent men regarded as not merely contemptible, but treasonable. (LP 307.2)

One by one, Paul saw his friends leaving him. The first to depart were Phygellus and Hermogenes. Then Demas, dismayed at the thickening clouds of difficulty and danger, forsook the persecuted apostle to seek for ease and security in a worldly life. Crescens was sent on a mission to the churches of Galatia, Titus to Dalmatia, Tychicus to Ephesus. Luke, the beloved physician and faithful friend, was still with him. This was a great comfort to Paul, who had never needed the companionship and ministration of his brethren more than now, enfeebled as he was by age, toil, and infirmities, and confined in the damp, dark vaults of a Roman prison. And, as he was dependent upon the aid of an amanuensis, the services of Luke were of great value, enabling him still to communicate with his brethren and the world without. (LP 308.1)

An unexpected encouragement was granted the apostle at this time, by the visit of Onesiphorus, an Ephesian Christian who came to Rome not long after Paul's arrival. He knew that Paul was somewhere in that city as a prisoner, and he determined to find him. This was no easy matter in a city crowded with prisoners, where suspicion was everywhere, and had only to fasten upon an unfortunate victim to consign him to prison and perhaps to death. But notwithstanding the difficulties, Onesiphorus searched for Paul until he found him. Not satisfied with one visit, he went again and again to his dungeon, and did all in his power to lighten the burden of his imprisonment. The fear of scorn, reproach, or persecution, was powerless to terrify this true-hearted Ephesian, when he knew that his beloved teacher was in bonds for the truth's sake, while he himself, in every respect far less worthy, walked free. (LP 308.2)

The visit of Onesiphorus, testifying to his loving fidelity at a time of loneliness and desertion, was a bright spot in Paul's prison experience. In the last letter ever written by him, he thus speaks of this faithful disciple: "The Lord give mercy unto the house of Onesiphorus; for he oft refreshed me, and was not ashamed of my chain. But when he was in Rome, he sought me out very diligently, and found me. The Lord grant unto him that he may find mercy of the Lord in that day." (LP 309.1)

The desire for love and sympathy was implanted in the heart by God himself. Christ in his hour of agony in Gethsemane, while bearing the guilt of sinful men, longed for the sympathy of his disciples. And Paul, though almost indifferent to hardship and suffering, yearned for sympathy and companionship. God would have his people cherish love and sympathy for one another. Humanity, elevated, ennobled, and rendered Godlike, is worthy of respect and esteem. The sons and daughters of God will be tender-hearted, pitiful, courteous, to all men, "especially unto them who are of the household of faith." But Paul was bound to his fellow-disciples by a stronger tie than even that of Christian brotherhood. The Lord had revealed himself to Paul in a special manner, and had made him instrumental in the salvation of many souls. Many churches might in truth regard him as their father in the gospel. Such a man, who had sacrificed every earthly consideration in the service of God, had a special claim upon the love and sympathy of his converts and fellow-labourers. (LP 309.2)

Paul before Nero

When Paul was summoned to appear before the emperor for his trial, it was with the near prospect of certain death. The aggravated nature of the crime charged against him, and the prevailing animosity toward the Christians, left little ground for hope of a favourable issue. (LP 310.1)

It was the practice among the Greeks and Romans to allow an accused person an advocate to present his case in a court of justice, and to plead in his behalf. By force of argument, by his impassioned eloquence, or by entreaties, prayers, and tears, such an advocate would often secure a decision in favour of the prisoner, or failing in this, would mitigate the severity of his sentence. But no man ventured to act as Paul's counsel or advocate; no friend was at hand, even to preserve a record of the charges brought against him by his accusers, or of the arguments which he urged in his own defence. Among the Christians at Rome, there was not one who came forward to stand by him in that trying hour. (LP 310.2)

The only record of the occasion is given in the words of Paul himself, in the second letter to Timothy: "At my first answer no man stood with me, but all men forsook me; I pray God that it may not be laid to their charge. Notwithstanding, the Lord stood with me, and strengthened me; that by me the preaching might be fully known, and that all the Gentiles might hear; and I was delivered out of the mouth of the lion." (LP 311.1)

Paul before Nero—how striking the contrast! The very height of earthly power, authority, and wealth, as well as the lowest depths of crime and iniquity, had been reached by the haughty monarch before whom the man of God answered for his faith. In his power and greatness, Nero stood unrivalled, unapproached. There were none to question his authority, none to resist his will. The kings of the earth laid their crowns at his feet. The most powerful armies marched at his command. The ensigns of his navies upon the seas betokened victory. His statue was set up in the halls of justice, and the decrees of senators and the decisions of judges were but the echo of his will. Millions of subjects bowed in obedience to his mandates. The name of Nero made the world tremble. To incur his displeasure was to lose property, liberty, and life. His frown was more to be dreaded than the pestilence. Yet while surrounded by all the outward semblance of earthly pomp and greatness, adored and reverenced as a god in human form, he possessed the heart of a demon. (LP 311.2)

191

Paul the aged prisoner, without money, without friends, without counsel, had been brought forth from a loathsome dungeon to be tried for his life. He had lived a life of poverty, self-denial, and suffering. With a sensitive nature that thirsted for love and sympathy, he had braved misrepresentation, reproach, hatred, and abuse; shrinking with nervous dread from pain and peril, he had fearlessly endured both. He had been, like his Master, a homeless wanderer upon the earth; he had lived and suffered for the truth's sake, seeking to relieve the burdens of humanity, and to exemplify in his life the life of Christ. How could the capricious, passionate, licentious tyrant, who had no conception of the value of a self-denying, virtuous, noble life, be expected to understand or appreciate the character and motives of this son of God? (LP 311.3)

Paul and Nero face to face!—the youthful monarch bearing upon his sin-stamped countenance the shameful record of the passions that reigned within; the aged prisoner's calm and benignant face telling of a heart at peace with God and man. The results of opposite systems of training and education stood that day contrasted,—the life of unbounded self-indulgence and the life of utter self-sacrifice. Here were the representatives of two religions,—Christianity and paganism; the representatives of two theories of life,—the simplicity of self-denying endurance, ready to give up life itself, if need be, for the good of others, and the luxury of all-absorbing selfishness, that counts nothing too valuable to sacrifice for a momentary gratification; the representatives of two spiritual powers,—the ambassador of Christ and the slave of Satan. Their relative position showed to what extent the course of this world was under the rule of the prince of darkness. The wretch whose soul was stained with incest and matricide, was robed in purple, and seated upon the throne, while the purest and noblest of men stood before the judgment-seat, despised, hated, and fettered. (LP 312.1)

The vast hall which was the place of trial was thronged by an eager, restless crowd that surged and pressed to the front to see and hear all that should take place. Among those gathered there were the high and the low, the rich and the poor, the learned and the ignorant, the proud and the humble. Yet all alike were destitute of the true knowledge of the way of life and salvation. (LP 313.1)

Again the Jews urge against the prisoner the old charges of sedition and heresy, while both Jews and Romans accuse him of instigating the burning of the city. While his enemies were vehemently urging their accusations, Paul preserved a quiet dignity; no shade of fear or anger disturbed the peaceful serenity that rested upon his countenance. The people and even the judges beheld him with surprise. They had been present at many trials, and had looked upon many a criminal; but never had they seen a man wear such a look of holy calmness as did the prisoner before them. The keen eyes of the judges, accustomed as they were to read the countenances of their prisoners, searched the face of Paul for some hidden trace of crime, but in vain. When he was permitted to speak in his own behalf, all listened with eager interest to his words. (LP 313.2)

Once more Paul had an opportunity to raise aloft before a wondering multitude the banner of the cross of Christ. With more than human eloquence and power, he that day urged home upon their hearts the truths of the gospel. The wisdom of God was revealed through his servant. As Paul stands before the emperor of the world, his words strike a chord which vibrates in the hearts of even the most hardened, and which thrills in unison with the mission of angels. Truth, clear and convincing, overthrows error and refutes falsehood. Never before had that company listened to words like these. Light was shining into darkened minds that would gladly follow the guidance of its precious rays. The truths spoken on that occasion would never die. Though the utterance of a feeble and aged prisoner, they were destined to shake the nations. They were endowed with a power that would live through all time, influencing the hearts of men when the lips that uttered them should be silent in a martyr's grave. (LP 313.3)

As Paul gazed upon the throng before him,—Jews, Greeks, Romans, with strangers from many lands,—his soul was stirred with an intense desire for their salvation. He lost sight of the occasion, of the perils which surrounded him, of the terrible fate which seemed so near. He looked above all this, to Jesus, the Divine Intercessor, the Advocate pleading before the throne of God in behalf of sinful men. Earnestly he pointed his hearers to the great Sacrifice made in behalf of the fallen race, and presented before them man in his true dignity and value. An infinite price had been paid for man's redemption; provision had been made that he might be exalted to share the throne of God and to become the heir of immortal riches. By angel messengers, earth was connected with Heaven, and all the deeds of man, good or evil, were open before the eye of Infinite Justice. (LP 314.1)

Thus pleads the advocate of truth; faithful among the faithless, loyal and true among the disloyal and disobedient, he stands as God's representative, and his words are as a voice from Heaven. There is no trace of fear, sadness, or discouragement in countenance or manner. Strong in his conscious innocence, clothed with the panoply of truth, he rejoices that he is a son of God. His words are like a shout of victory above the roar of the battle. The cause of truth to which he has devoted his life, he makes appear as the only cause that can never fail. Though he may perish for the truth's sake, the gospel will not perish. God lives, and the truth will triumph. (LP 314.2)

His countenance glows with the light of Heaven, as though

reflecting the rays of the sun. Many who looked upon him in that hall of judgment "saw his face as it had been the face of an angel." Tears dimmed many eyes that had never before been seen to weep. The gospel message found its way to the minds and hearts of many who would never have listened to it but for the imprisonment of Paul. (LP 315.1)

Never had Nero heard the truth as he heard it upon that occasion. Never had the enormous guilt of his own life been revealed to him as it was revealed that day. The light of Heaven had pierced the sin-polluted chambers of his soul. He quaked with terror at the thought of a tribunal before which he, the ruler of the world, should be arraigned, and where his deeds should meet a just reward. He was afraid of the apostle's God, and he dared not pass sentence upon Paul, against whom no accusation had been sustained. A sense of awe for a time restrained his bloodthirsty spirit. (LP 315.2)

For a moment, Heaven had been opened before him by the words of Paul, and its peace and purity had appeared desirable. That moment the invitation of mercy was extended even to the guilty and hardened Nero. But only for a moment. The command was issued for Paul to be taken back to his dungeon; and as the door closed upon the messenger of God, so the door of repentance was forever closed against the emperor of Rome. Not another ray of light was ever to penetrate the dense darkness that enveloped him. There needed only this crowning act of rejection of divine mercy to call down upon him the retributive justice of God. (LP 316.1)

It was not long after this that Nero sailed on his expedition to Greece, where he disgraced himself and his kingdom by the most contemptible and debasing frivolity. He returned to Rome with great pomp, and in his golden palace, surrounded by the most infamous of his courtiers, he engaged in scenes of revolting debauchery. In the midst of their revelry, a voice as of a tumult in the streets was heard, and a messenger was despatched to learn the cause. He hastily returned with the appalling news that Galba, at the head of an avenging army, was marching rapidly upon Rome, that insurrection had already broken out in the city, and the streets were filled with an enraged mob threatening death to the emperor and all his supporters, and rapidly urging their way toward the palace. (LP 316.2)

The wretched tyrant, as cowardly as he was cruel, was completely unmanned. He sprang from the table at which he had been feasting and drinking, overturning it in his blind terror, and dashing the most costly wares to fragments. Like one beside himself, he rushed hither and thither, beating his forehead, and crying, "I am lost! I am lost!" He had not, like the faithful Paul, a powerful, compassionate God to rely upon in his hour of peril. He knew that if taken prisoner he would be subjected to insult and torture, and he considered how he might end his miserable life with as little pain as possible. He called for poison, but when it was brought, he dared not take it; he called for a sword, but after examining its sharp edge, he laid it also aside. Then, disguised in woman's clothing, he rushed from his palace, and fled through the dark, narrow streets to the Tiber; but as he looked into its murky depths, his courage again failed. One of the few companions who had followed him, suggested that he escape to a country-seat a few miles distant, where he might find safety. Concealing his face, he leaped upon a horse, and succeeded in making his escape. (LP 316.3)

While the emperor was thus ingloriously fleeing for his life, the Roman senate, emboldened by the insurrection and the approach of Galba, passed a decree declaring Nero to be the enemy of his country, and condemning him to death. The news of this decision being brought to Nero by one of his companions, the monarch inquired what manner of death he was to suffer, and was told that he was to be stripped naked, to be fastened by his head in the pillory, and to be scourged to death. The monster who had delighted to inflict upon Christians the most inhuman torture, shrank with horror at the mere thought of enduring like torture himself. He seized a dagger, and again endeavoured to nerve himself to plunge it into his heart; but the prick of the instrument was all that he could endure. As he threw it aside with a groan of despair, horsemen were heard approaching. His retreat was discovered; a few moments, and he would be in the power of his enemies. Terrified alike at the thought of torture and suicide, he still hesitated, and was compelled at last to let a slave help his trembling hand force a dagger into his throat. Thus perished the tyrant Nero, at the early age of thirty-two. (LP 317.1)

God in his infinite mercy bears long with the transgressors of his law. In the days of Abraham he declared that the idolatrous Amorites should still be spared until the fourth generation; for their iniquity was not yet full, and he could not give command for their destruction. For more than four hundred years he spared them, but when, instead of turning to repentance, they hardened their hearts in iniquity, and made war upon his people, their day of probation closed, and the mandate went forth for their utter extinction. With unerring accuracy, the Infinite One keeps a record of the impiety of nations and individuals. Long is his mercy tendered to them, with calls to repentance; but when their guilt reaches a certain limit, which he has fixed, then mercy ceases her pleadings, and the ministration of wrath begins. (LP 318.1)

Paul's Last Letter

From the judgment-hall of Caesar, Paul returned to his prison-house, knowing that he had gained for himself only a brief respite; his enemies would not rest until they had secured his death. Yet he knew that truth had triumphed for the time, and that to have proclaimed a crucified and risen Saviour before the vast throng who had listened to his words, was in itself a victory. A work had that day begun which would increase and prosper, and which the emperor of Rome, with all his pomp and power, would seek in vain to destroy or hinder. (LP 318.2)

The apostle's speech had gained him many friends, and he was visited by some persons of rank, who accounted his blessing of greater value than the favour of the emperor of the world. But there was one friend for whose sympathy and companionship he longed in those last trying days. That friend was Timothy, to whom he had committed the care of the church at Ephesus, and who had therefore been left behind when he made his last voyage to Rome. The affection between this youthful labourer and the apostle began with Timothy's conversion through the labours of Paul; and the tie had strengthened as they had shared together the hopes and perils and toils of missionary life, until they seemed to be as one. The disparity in their age and the difference in their character made their interest and love for each other more earnest and sacred. The ardent, zealous, indomitable spirit of Paul found repose and comfort in the mild, yielding, retiring character of Timothy. The faithful ministration and tender love of this tried companion had brightened many a dark hour of the apostle's life. All that Melancthon was to Luther, all that a son could be to a loved and honoured father, that was the youthful Timothy to the tried and lonely Paul. (LP 319.1)

And now, sitting day after day in his gloomy cell, knowing that at a word or nod from the tyrant Nero his life may be sacrificed, Paul thinks of Timothy, and determines to send for him. Under the most favourable circumstances, several months must elapse before Timothy can reach Rome from Asia Minor. Paul knows that his own life, for even a single day, is uncertain, and he fears that Timothy may arrive too late, or may hesitate through fear of the dangers to be encountered. He has important counsel and instruction for the young man to whom so great responsibility is intrusted, and while urging him to come without delay, he dictates the dying testimony which he may not be spared to utter. His soul is filled with loving solicitude for his son in the gospel, and for the church under his care, and he earnestly seeks to impress upon him the importance of fidelity to his sacred trust. (LP 320.1)

The words of Paul to Timothy apply with equal force to all the ministers of Christ, to the close of time: "I charge thee therefore before God, and the Lord Jesus Christ, who shall judge the quick and the dead at his appearing and his kingdom: Preach the word; be instant in season, out of season; reprove, rebuke, exhort with all long-suffering and doctrine." (LP 320.2)

This solemn charge to one so zealous and faithful as was Timothy, is an emphatic testimony to the great importance and responsibility of the gospel ministry. The apostle summons Timothy, as it were, before the bar of infinite justice, and in the most impressive manner charges him to preach the word; not the customs or sayings of men, but the word of God; to preach it as one in earnest,—"instant in season, out of season,"— whenever an opportunity was presented; at stated times and occasionally; to large congregations, to private circles; by the way, at the fireside; before friends and enemies; to one as well as to many; whether he could speak with safety or would be exposed to hardship and peril, reproach and loss. (LP 320.3)

Timothy suffered from physical infirmities, and the apostle, tender and compassionate as he was, felt it necessary to warn him to neglect no duty on this account. And fearing that his mild, yielding disposition might lead him to shun an essential part of his work, Paul exhorts him to be faithful in reproving sin, and even to rebuke with sharpness those who were guilty of gross evils. Yet he is to do this "with all long-suffering and doctrine;" he must manifest the patience and love of Christ, and must explain and enforce his reproofs and exhortations by the word of God. (LP 321.1)

To hate and reprove sin, and at the same time to manifest pity and tenderness for the sinner, is a difficult attainment. The more earnest our own efforts to attain to holiness of heart and life, the more acute will be our perception of sin, and the more decided our disapproval of any deviation from right. We must guard against undue severity toward the wrong-doer. But while we should seek to encourage him in every effort to correct his errors, we must be careful not to lose sight of the exceeding sinfulness of sin. While there is need of Christlike patience and love toward the erring, there is constant danger of manifesting so great toleration for his error that he will consider himself undeserving of reproof, and will reject it as uncalled-for and unjust. (LP 321.2)

Ministers of the gospel whose characters are otherwise almost faultless, frequently do great harm by allowing their forbearance toward the erring to degenerate into toleration of their sins, and even participation with them. In this easygoing way they excuse and palliate

197

that which the word of God condemns; and after a time they become so blinded as even to commend the very ones whom God commands them to reprove. The only safe-guard against these dangers is to add to patience godliness,—to reverence God, his character and his law, and to keep his fear ever before the mind. By communion with God, through prayer and the reading of his word, we should cultivate such a sense of the holiness of his character that we shall regard sin as he regards it. (LP 322.1)

Godliness leads to brotherly kindness; and those who do not cherish the one, will surely lack the other. He who has blunted his moral perceptions by sinful leniency toward those whom God condemns, will erelong commit a greater sin by severity and harshness toward those whom God approves. Viewed through the perverted medium of an unconsecrated spirit, the very integrity and faithfulness of the true-hearted Christian will appear censurable. (LP 322.2)

By the pride of human wisdom, by contempt for the influence of the Holy Spirit, and disrelish for the humbling truths of God's word, many who profess to be Christians, and who feel competent to teach others, will be led to turn away from the requirements of God. Paul declared to Timothy: "The time will come when they will not endure sound doctrine; but after their own lusts shall they heap to themselves teachers, having itching ears; and they shall turn away their ears from the truth, and shall be turned unto fables." (LP 322.3)

The apostle does not here refer to the openly irreligious, but to professed Christians who have indulged inclination until they are enslaved by their own ungoverned passions,—"led away with divers lusts." Such desire to hear doctrines that will not interfere with their sinful course, or condemn their pleasure-loving propensities. Hence they are offended by the plain words of the faithful servants of Christ, and choose those teachers who will praise and flatter them instead of rebuking their sins. These teachers "they heap to themselves" as special favourites. Even among the professed ministers of Christ, there are many who do not preach the word, but the opinions of men. They have turned away their ears from truth. The Lord has spoken to them in his word; but they do not care to hear his voice, because it condemns their practices. (LP 323.1)

In his ten holy precepts, God has given a rule for man's life, a law which Christ declares is not to abate one jot of its claims upon men through all their generations, to the close of time. That law is still the believer's rule of life, the sinner's condemnation. That law Christ came to magnify and make honourable. He showed that it is based upon the broad foundation of love to God and men, and that obedience to its precepts comprises the whole duty of man. In his own life he gave men a perfect example of obedience to the law of God. In his sermon on the mount he showed how its requirements extend beyond the outward acts, and take cognizance of the thoughts and intents of the heart. That law, obeyed, will lead men to deny ungodliness and worldly lusts, and to live "soberly, righteously, and godly, in this present world." (LP 323.2)

But the enemy of all righteousness has taken the world captive, and has led them to make void the law of God. As Paul foresaw, the people have turned away from the plain, searching truths of God's word, and, having itching ears, they have heaped to themselves teachers who present to them the fables that they desire. These teachers trample under their feet the fourth commandment, and instead of the day which God has blessed and sanctified, they honour a day which he has not commanded, and upon which he did not rest. The first day of the week, whose sacredness rests wholly on the authority of the papacy, "the man of sin," is observed as a holy day by Catholics and Protestants alike, instead of the day which God has set apart, and upon which he has placed his blessing. Thus the Creator of the world is insulted, and Satan laughs in triumph at the success of his devices. (LP 324.1)

With the growing contempt for God's holy law, there is an increasing distaste for religion, an increase of pride, love of pleasure, disobedience to parents, and self-indulgence; and thoughtful minds everywhere anxiously inquire, What can be done to correct these alarming evils? The answer is found in Paul's exhortation to Timothy: "Preach the word." In that word are the only safe principles of action. It is a transcript of the will of God, an expression of divine wisdom. It opens to man's understanding the great problem of life. It will prove a guide to all who heed it, so that their lives will not be wasted in misdirected efforts. God has declared his will, and it is absolute madness for men to change or even question that which has gone out of his lips. After Infinite Wisdom has spoken, there can be no doubtful questions for man to settle, no wavering probabilities for him to adjust. All the interests of time and of eternity are involved in a frank, earnest concurrence of the mind and will of men with the expressed will of God. Obedience is the highest dictate of reason as well as of conscience. Those who choose to listen to other voices and to follow other guides, will be turned unto fables, and, trusting to these, they will in the day of God meet with infinite loss. (LP 324.2)

Paul continues his charge: "Watch thou in all things, endure afflictions, do the work of an evangelist, make full proof of thy ministry." Now that Paul is called to finish his course, he would have Timothy supply his place, and guard the churches from the fables and heresies with which Satan and his agents would in various ways endeavour to seduce them from the simplicity of the truth. He therefore admonishes him to shun all temporal pursuits and entanglements which would prevent him from giving himself wholly to this work; to endure with cheerfulness the opposition, reproach, and persecution to which his faithfulness would expose him; to "make full proof of his ministry," by employing to the uttermost every means of doing good to the souls of men for whom Christ died. (LP 325.1)

Paul had never been afraid or ashamed to confess Christ before men. He had stood in no doubtful position, but under all circumstances had unhesitatingly committed himself upon the side of justice and righteousness. His own life was a living illustration of the truths he taught; and herein lay his power with the people. The voice of duty was to him the voice of God. Cherishing in his own soul the principles of truth, he never shrank from maintaining them in full view of the world. His soul was ever pervaded with a deep and abiding sense of his responsibility before God; and he lived in close and constant communion with Him who is the fountain of justice, mercy, and truth. He clung to the cross of Christ as the only guarantee of success. The love of Christ was the omnipotent, undying motive which upheld him in his conflicts with self and the power of Satan, in his struggles with spiritual wickedness in high places, in his life-long labours, as he pressed forward against the unfriendliness of the world and the burden of his own infirmities. (LP 325.2)

What the church needs in these days of peril is an army of workers, who, like Paul, have educated themselves for usefulness, who have a deep experience in the things of God, and who are inspired with earnestness and zeal in his service. Cultivated, refined, sanctified, self-sacrificing men are needed; men who will not shun trial and responsibility, but who will lift the burdens wherever they may find them; men who are brave, who are true; men who have Christ formed within them, and who, with lips touched with holy fire, "will preach the word" amid the thousands who are preaching fables. For the want of such workers, the cause of God, languishes, and fatal errors, like a deadly poison, taint the morals and blight the hopes of a large part of the human race. (LP 326.1)

As the faithful, toil-worn standard-bearers are offering up their lives for the truth's sake, who will come forward to take their places? Will our young men accept the holy trust at the hand of their fathers? Are they now preparing to fill the vacancies made by the death of the faithful? Will the apostle's charge be heeded, the call to duty be heard, amid the incitements to selfishness and ambition which allure the youth? (LP 326.2)

Paul concludes his letter with various personal messages, and again and again repeats the urgent request that Timothy use all diligence to come to him soon, and if possible to come before winter. He describes his loneliness from the desertion of some friends and the necessary absence of others, and lest Timothy should still hesitate, fearing that the church at Ephesus demanded his labours, he states that he has already despatched Tychicus to fill the place of Timothy in his absence. And then he adds the touching request, "The cloke that I left at Troas, with Carpus, when thou comest, bring with thee, and the books, but especially the parchments." At his second arrest, Paul was seized and hurried away so suddenly that he had no opportunity to gather up his few "books and parchments," or even to take with him his cloak. And now winter was coming on, and he knew that he would suffer with cold in his damp prison-cell. He had no money to buy another garment, he knew that his end might come at any moment, and with his usual self-forgetfulness and fear to burden the church, he desired that no expense should be incurred on his account. (LP 327.1)

After describing the scenes of the trial already past, the desertion of his brethren, and the sustaining grace of a covenant-keeping God, and sending greeting to faithful fellow-labourers, Paul closes by commending his beloved Timothy to the guardianship of the Chief Shepherd, who, though the under-shepherds might be stricken down, would still care for his servants and his flock. (LP 327.2)

Martyrdom of Paul and Peter

The apostles Paul and Peter were for many years widely separated in their labours, it being the work of Paul to carry the gospel to the Gentiles, while Peter laboured especially for the Jews. But in the providence of God, both were to bear witness for Christ in the world's metropolis, and upon its soil both were to shed their blood as the seed of a vast harvest of saints and martyrs. (LP 328.1)

About the time of Paul's second arrest, Peter also was apprehended and thrust into prison. He had made himself especially obnoxious to the authorities by his zeal and success in exposing the deceptions and defeating the plots of Simon Magus the sorcerer, who had followed him to Rome to oppose and hinder the work of the gospel. Nero was a believer in magic, and had patronized Simon. He was therefore greatly incensed against the apostle, and was thus prompted to order his arrest. (LP 328.2)

The emperor's malice against Paul was heightened by the fact that members of the imperial household, and also other persons of distinction, had been converted to Christianity during his first imprisonment. For this reason he made the second imprisonment much more severe than the first, granting him little opportunity to preach the gospel; and he determined to cut short his life as soon as a plausible pretext could be found for so doing. Nero's mind was so impressed with the force of the apostle's words at his last trial that he deferred the decision of the case, neither acquitting nor condemning him. But the sentence was only deferred. It was not long before the decision was pronounced which consigned Paul to a martyr's grave. Being a Roman citizen, he could not be subjected to torture, and was therefore sentenced to be beheaded. (LP 328.3)

Peter, as a Jew and a foreigner, was condemned to be scourged and crucified. In prospect of this fearful death, the apostle remembered his great sin in denying Jesus in the hour of trial, and his only thought was, that he was unworthy of so great an honour as to die in the same manner as did his Master. Peter had sincerely repented of that sin, and had been forgiven by Christ, as is shown by the high commission given him to feed the sheep and lambs of the flock. But he could never forgive himself. Not even the thought of the agonies of the last terrible scene could lessen the bitterness of his sorrow and repentance. As a last favour he entreated his executioners that he might be nailed to the cross with his head downward. The request was granted, and in this manner died the great apostle Peter. (LP 329.1)

Paul was led in a private manner to the place of execution. His persecutors, alarmed at the extent of his influence, feared that converts might be won to Christianity, even by the scenes of his death. Hence few spectators were allowed to be present. But the hardened soldiers appointed to attend him, listened to his words, and with amazement saw him cheerful and even joyous in prospect of such a death. His spirit of forgiveness toward his murderers, and his unwavering confidence in Christ to the very last, proved a savour of life unto life to some who witnessed his martyrdom. More than one erelong accepted the Saviour whom Paul preached, and fearlessly sealed their faith with their blood. (LP 329.2)

The life of Paul, to its very latest hour, testified to the truth of his words in the second Epistle to the Corinthians: "For God, who commanded the light to shine out of darkness, hath shined in our hearts, to give the light of the knowledge of the glory of God in the face of Jesus Christ. But we have this treasure in earthen vessels, that the excellency of the power may be of God, and not of us. We are troubled on every side, yet not distressed; we are perplexed, but not in despair; persecuted, but not forsaken; cast down, but not destroyed; always bearing about in the body the dying of the Lord Jesus, that the life also of Jesus might be made manifest in our body." His sufficiency was not in himself, but in the presence and agency of the divine Spirit that filled his soul, and brought every thought into subjection to the will of Christ. The fact that his own life exemplified the truth he proclaimed, gave convincing power to both his preaching and his deportment. Says the prophet, "Thou wilt keep him in perfect peace, whose mind is stayed on Thee; because he trusteth in Thee." It was this Heaven-born peace, expressed upon the countenance, that won many a soul to the gospel. (LP 330.1)

The apostle was looking into the great beyond, not with uncertainty or in dread, but with joyful hope and longing expectation. As he stood at the place of martyrdom, he saw not the gleaming sword of the executioner, or the green earth so soon to receive his blood; he looked up through the calm blue heaven of that summer's day to the throne of the Eternal. His language was, O Lord, thou art my comfort and my portion. When shall I embrace thee? when shall I behold thee for myself, without a dimming veil between? (LP 330.2)

Paul carried with him through his life on earth the very atmosphere of Heaven. All who associated with him felt the influence of his connection with Christ and companionship with angels. Here lies the power of the truth. The unstudied, unconscious influence of a holy life is the most convincing sermon that can be given in favour of Christianity. Argument, even when unanswerable, may provoke only opposition; but a godly example has a power which it is impossible wholly to resist. (LP 331.1)

While the apostle lost sight of his own near sufferings, he felt a deep solicitude for the disciples whom he was about to leave to cope with prejudice, hatred, and persecution. He endeavoured to strengthen and encourage the few Christians who accompanied him to the place of execution, by repeating the exceeding precious promises given for those who are persecuted for righteousness' sake. He assures them that nothing shall fail of all that the Lord hath spoken concerning his tried and faithful ones. They shall arise and shine; for the light of the Lord shall arise upon them. They shall put on their beautiful garments when the glory of the Lord shall be revealed. For a little season they may be in heaviness through manifold temptations, they may be destitute of earthly comfort; but they must encourage their hearts by saying, I know in whom I have believed. He is able to keep that which I have committed to his trust. His rebuke will come to an end, and the glad morning of peace and perfect day will come. (LP 331.2)

Paul declared to his brethren, It did not appear to our fathers what great and good things should be given to those who believe in Jesus. They desired to see the things which we see, and to hear the things which we hear, but they died without the sight or the knowledge. The greater light which we have received is shed upon us by the gospel of Christ. Holy men of old were acknowledged and honoured of God because they were faithful over a few things; and it is only those that improve with the same fidelity their greater trust, who will with them be counted profitable servants, and be crowned with glory, honour, and immortality. (LP 332.1)

This man of faith beholds the ladder presented in Jacob's vision,—the ladder which rested upon the earth and reached to the highest heavens, and upon which angels of God were ascending and descending. He knows that this ladder represents Christ, who has connected earth with Heaven, and finite man with the infinite God. He hears angels and archangels magnifying that glorious name. His faith is strengthened as he calls to mind that patriarchs and prophets relied upon the same Saviour who is his support and consolation, and for whom he is giving his life. Those holy men who from century to century sent down their testimony for the truth, and the apostles, who to preach the gospel of Christ went out to meet religious bigotry and heathen superstition, who counted not their lives dear unto themselves if they might bear aloft the light of the cross amid the dark mazes of infidelity,—all these he hears witnessing to Jesus as the Son of the Most High, the Saviour of the world. The martyr's shout of triumph, the fearless testimony for the faith, falls upon his ear from the rack, the stake, the dungeon, from the dens and caves of the earth, from steadfast souls who are destitute, afflicted, tormented, yet of whom the world is not worthy. With a continually strengthening assurance they declare, "I know whom I have believed." And as they yield up their lives as witnesses for the faith, they bear a solemn, condemning testimony to the world, declaring that He in whom they trusted has proved himself able to save to the uttermost. (LP 332.2)

The Captain of our salvation has prepared his servant for the last great conflict. Ransomed by the sacrifice of Christ, washed from sin in his blood, and clothed in his righteousness, Paul has the witness in himself that his soul is precious in the sight of his Redeemer. His life is hid with Christ in God, and he is persuaded that He who has conquered death is able to keep that which is committed to his trust. His mind grasps the Saviour's promise, "I will raise him up at the last day." His thoughts and hopes are centred in the second advent of his Lord. And as the sword of the executioner descends, and the shadows of death gather about the martyr's soul, his latest thought springs forward, as will his earliest thought in the great awakening, to meet the Lifegiver who shall welcome him to the joy of the blest. (LP 333.1)

Well-nigh a score of centuries have passed since Paul the aged poured out his blood as a witness for the word of God and for the testimony of Christ. No faithful hand recorded for the generations to come, the last scenes in the life of this holy man; but inspiration has preserved for us his dying testimony. Like a trumpet peal has his voice rung out through all the ages, nerving with his own courage thousands of witnesses for Christ, and wakening in thousands of sorrow-stricken hearts the echo of his own triumphant joy: "I am now ready to be offered, and the time of my departure is at hand. I have fought a good fight, I have finished my course, I have kept the faith. Henceforth there is laid up for me a crown of righteousness, which the Lord, the righteous Judge, shall give me at that day; and not to me only, but unto all them also that love his appearing." (LP 334.1)

www.ingramcontent.com/pod-product-compliance
Lightning Source LLC
La Vergne TN
LVHW091217080426
835509LV00009B/1032